Mass Salem

The first centenary of the North church and society

Mass Salem

The first centenary of the North church and society

ISBN/EAN: 9783337262204

Printed in Europe, USA, Canada, Australia, Japan

Cover: Foto ©Lupo / pixelio.de

More available books at **www.hansebooks.com**

THE FIRST CENTENARY

OF THE

NORTH CHURCH AND SOCIETY,

IN

SALEM, MASSACHUSETTS.

Commemorated July 19, 1872.

SALEM.
Printed for the Society.
1873.

PRINTED AT
THE SALEM PRESS,
F. W. PUTNAM & CO.,
Proprietors.

TO

THE MEMORY

OF

THOMAS BARNARD, D.D.

AND HIS ASSOCIATES

IN THE

ORGANIZATION OF THIS CHURCH AND SOCIETY,

THIS VOLUME

IS REVERENTLY DEDICATED.

CONTENTS.

Introduction,	1
Exercises at the Church,	5
Memorial Sermon,	9
Exercises at Normal Hall,	63
Address from G. B. Loring,	66
Rhymed Reminiscences, by C. T. Brooks,	69
Address by Joseph Allen, of Northborough,	81
Address by E. R. Hoar, of Concord,	83
Address by W. G. Eliot, of St. Louis, Mo.,	85
Address by Thomas T. Stone, of Bolton, Mass.,	87
Address by C. H. Brigham, of Ann Arbor, Mich.,	89
Address by Wm. Mountford, of Boston,	91
Address by John W. Chadwick, of Brooklyn, N. Y.,	103
Address by George L. Chaney, of Boston,	106
Address by William O. White, of Keene, N. H.,	111
Letter from Charles Lowe,	114
Letter from Henry W. Foote,	116
Letter from James W. Thompson,	118
Letter from Edwin M. Stone,	119
Letter from S. E. Peabody,	121
Address by R. M. Hodges, of Cambridge,	121
Address by D. B. Hagar,	125
Address by Caleb Foote,	126
Note from O. B. Frothingham,	127
Some Memoranda of the Choir, by Henry K. Oliver,	131

CONTENTS.

THE CHURCH,	153
Covenant,	155
Early Members,	157
Officers,	163
Minister's Library,	164
The Sunday School,	165
Extracts from the Records and Notes,	166
MINISTERS,	170
Thomas Barnard,	171
John Emery Abbot,	173
John Brazer,	175
Octavius Brooks Frothingham,	177
Charles Lowe,	179
Edmund Burke Willson,	181
THE FIRST MEETING HOUSE,	183
THE SECOND MEETING HOUSE,	190
PROPRIETORS AND OCCUPANTS OF PEWS IN THE FIRST HOUSE,	197

ILLUSTRATIONS.

Portrait of Rev. T. Barnard (Frontispiece).
Pickman House. 154
Portrait of Rev. J. E. Abbot. 173
Portrait of Rev. J. Brazer. 175
Portrait of Rev. O. B. Frothingham. 177
Portrait of Rev. C. Lowe. 179
Portrait of Rev. E. B. Willson. 181
First Meeting House. 183
Second Meeting House. 190

INTRODUCTION.

EARLY in the month of April, 1872, the Standing Committee of the Proprietors of the North Meeting-house voted that the one hundredth anniversary of the founding of the North Church and Society should be commemorated by appropriate public services, and called a general meeting of the worshippers, to be held on the 16th of that month, at the vestry, to take the matter into consideration. At that meeting the action of the Committee was unanimously ratified, and the necessary Committees were chosen to carry the proposed observance into effect.

The first meeting of the Proprietors for organization had been held on the 3d of March, 1772. The first meeting of the members of the church, and their gathering into church order and fellowship, and the adoption of a covenant, had taken place on the 19th of July, 1772. It was voted that the latter should be the day commemorated.

The writer of the historical discourse herein contained takes this opportunity to express his obligations and his thanks to those who have kindly aided him in his search for the materials embodied in it, especially to the President of the Essex Institute, Dr. HENRY WHEATLAND, who opened to his use the valuable stores of the library of that institution, besides directing him to many important sources of information.

He has not thought it necessary to cite often the authority on which his statements rest. In addition to the usual authorities for such facts, viz :— the records of the church, and of the proprietors of the North Meeting-house, funeral and other discourses, biographical memoirs, published sermons of the clergymen of whom notices are given, newspapers of the period, the recollections of living witnesses, and current traditions, he has had access to a very helpful collection of miscellaneous papers, mostly in manuscript, containing lists of names, accounts, etc., left by Ichabod Tucker, Esq., nearly all of which are now in possession of the Essex Institute; while he has often had recourse to Felt's Annals and Curwen's Journal and Letters, with the biographical sketches appended by its editor, GEORGE A. WARD, Esq.

MEMORIAL SERVICES.

Exercises at the Church.

I.

VOLUNTARY (FROM THE ORGAN).

II.

SCRIPTURE SENTENCES.

BY REV. CHARLES T. BROOKS, OF NEWPORT, RHODE ISLAND.

ONE generation passeth away, and another generation cometh.

The fathers, where are they? and the prophets, do they live forever?

We are strangers before thee, and sojourners, as were all our fathers; our days on earth are as a shadow, and there is none abiding.

Lord, Thou hast been our dwelling-place in all generations.

One generation shall praise Thy works to another, and shall declare Thy mighty acts. . . . . . They shall abundantly utter the memory of Thy great goodness, and shall sing of Thy righteousness.

Oh, that men would praise the Lord for His goodness, and for His wonderful works to the children of men!

I have considered the days of old, the years of ancient times. . . . . I will remember the years of the right hand of the Most High. . . . . I will remember the works of the Lord; surely I will remember Thy wonders of old. . . . . . which we have heard and known, and our fathers have told us. . . . . . That the generation to come might know them, even the children which should be born; who should arise and declare them unto their children; that they might set their hope in God and not forget the work of the Lord, but keep His commandment.

O Lord God of our fathers, keep this forever in the imagination of the thoughts of the heart of Thy people, and prepare their heart to Thee!

In Judah is God known. . . . . . In Salem is His tabernacle.

I was glad when they said unto me, Let us go into the house of the Lord! . . . . . Our feet shall stand within Thy gates, O Jerusalem!

If I forget thee, O Jerusalem! may my right hand forget her cunning; yea, let my tongue cleave to the roof of my mouth, if I prefer not Jerusalem above my chief joy!

Pray for the peace of Jerusalem! they shall prosper that love thee. Peace be within thy walls and prosperity within thy palaces. For my brethren and companions' sakes I will now say, Peace be within thee!

III.

CENTENNIAL HYMN AND MUSIC.

BY GEORGE PEABODY.

Six verses and the Invocation sung.

God, Almighty and Eternal,
  From Thy throne, in realms sublime,
Hear our earnest supplications,
  Bless our offerings at this time.

Gathered round our cherished altar,
  May we now renew the Flame
Which our Fathers long since kindled
  To the glory of Thy name.

Here they bowed in adoration;
  Here invoked, and not in vain,
Blessings, which by Thy great mercy,
  With their children still remain.

Countless blessings still descending
  Both on us and on our land,
May we not forget the Giver,
  In the bounties of his hand.

God, we thank Thee, that so many
  Of the wise and good have found
Joy and comfort in Thy worship,
  On this consecrated ground.

Man beheld in Thy Creation,
  Governed by unerring Laws,
Proof that ofttimes gave assurance
  Of a self-existent cause.

But the glorious Confirmation
  In Thy written word we find,—
Book of books!— the guide, instructor,
  Hope, and solace of mankind.

There alone we read the record
  Of Thy blessed Son on earth,
By whose Life and Resurrection
  Man has gained a nobler birth.

Unrevealed are those deep mysteries
  That his cross and death attend,
But his pure and holy precepts
  None can fail to comprehend.

Naught by ancient sages spoken
  Can dispel our doubts and fears,
Comfort bring to sin and suffering,
  Or restrain the mourner's tears.

May we, urged by their example,
  Follow in the path they trod,
Keeping Christ's plain rule before us,
  Love to man and faith in God.

Veiled art Thou, our Heavenly Father,
  And to mortal sight unknown,
Yet in every age and nation
  Thy parental care is shown.

In the days of heathen darkness,
  Ere Thy chosen Prophet came,
Mid the thunders of Mount Sinai,
  Thy commandments to proclaim,

In the brightness of *his* Being
  All Earth's shadows pass away,
And the human heart rejoices
  In the light of endless day.

May that Light spread through the nations
  Shine wherever man is found,
And Thy Praise in songs of triumph
  Throughout Heaven and earth resound.

INVOCATION.

Gracious God! continue with us,
  Aid us to deserve Thy love,
And through Christ at last admit us
  To his promised Rest above.

IV.
PRAYER.

BY REV. JONATHAN COLE OF NEWBURYPORT.

V.
HYMN (FOR THE OCCASION).

BY REV. CHARLES T. BROOKS.

Sung by the Congregation to the Tune of Duke Street.

O God! whose wisdom, power and love
  No age can waste, no shadow dim,
To Thee, in cloudless light above,
  We raise the grateful, reverent hymn.

God of our Sires! to Thee, their Guide,
  Their Guard through life's uncertain way,
To Thee in whom their souls abide,
  Unending thanks their sons shall pay.

Amid the war-cloud's gathering storm,
  Our fathers built their altar here;
They leaned on Thy almighty arm,
  Beheld Thy face and felt no fear.

To-day in peace their children come
  To muse upon the years gone by;
To sing their grateful harvest-home,
  And wave the votive sheaves on high.

The house our fathers built to Thee,
  'Mid human works no longer stands,
Their nobler shrine by faith we see—
  That house in heaven not made with hands.

Thanks for the memory of the Sires,
  Their lofty zeal, their strenuous life;—
Our hearts with hope that memory fires,
  And nerves our souls for Christian strife.

While ages roll and worlds decay,
  Grant us, by faith and hope and love,
Bright visions of unchanging day,
  Fair mansions in the realm above!

VI.

DISCOURSE.

BY REV. EDMUND B. WILLSON, MINISTER OF THE SOCIETY.

VII.

HYMN (FOR THE OCCASION).

BY REV. CHARLES T. BROOKS.

Sung by the Congregation to the Tune of Telemann's Chant.

Thou whose word to being woke
  Earth and heaven, this beauteous frame,
Father! we to-day invoke
  Blessings in Thy hallowed name!

On this ancient Church of Thine,
  Thou who makest all things new,
O Eternal Beauty, shine!
  Spirit, shed Thy freshening dew!

May the calm of reverend age
  Blending with the glow of youth
Mark her for Thy heritage,
  God of Wisdom, Grace and Truth!

Tender memories o'er this hour
  Mingling lights and shadows cast;
Songs of trust and words of power
  Cheer us from the living past.

Many a sweet and saintly name
  Breathes a fragrance on the air,
Kindles here devotion's flame,
  Stirs the soul to praise and prayer.

Perfect gifts, O God, are Thine;
  May they lift our souls above,
Fill us with Thy life Divine,
  Endless life and boundless love!

VIII.

BENEDICTION.

BY REV. JAMES T. HEWES, MINISTER OF THE FIRST CHURCH IN SALEM.

MEMORIAL SERMON.

WALK ABOUT ZION, AND GO ROUND ABOUT HER; TELL THE TOWERS THEREOF; MARK YE WELL HER BULWARKS; CONSIDER HER PALACES; THAT YE MAY TELL IT TO THE GENERATION FOLLOWING. FOR THIS GOD IS OUR GOD FOREVER AND EVER; HE WILL BE OUR GUIDE EVEN UNTO DEATH. — *Ps. xlviii*: 12, 13, 14.

WE can understand to-day, in some degree, the emotions with which the psalmist wrote, as he looked upon the sacred places which war had spared, dear and still safe, beautiful as transfigured in the light of religious associations, wherein the altar of a past worship yet stood with its fire unquenched.

Our altar still stands. Its fire is burning yet, after a hundred years. War has passed over its worshippers. Time has dismissed, one by one, its earlier congregations, and brought, one by one, new generations to stand in their places. We think of those who are to follow us, and hope that our children, and their children, may worship where we do now.

There are times when, enamored with the promises and expectations of the future, the past is not unlikely to seem all a dead past, profitless, may be, even as a study for living men who hope to hold and fill the present hour worthily.

Believing progress, however, to be possible only by charting its way along by landmarks that are fixed, and voyaging always from certainties found, to other certainties sought, I am sure that the study of the past can be vindicated equally well, whether at the bar of utility or of ideality. If it were otherwise, there is a debt which the present—which is the future of the past—owes to that past, and which it will pay, if it is an honest present, to its successor.

He, indeed, who turns his back on the past, on the plea that he must live in and work for the future, recognizes in his very aspiration the lineage between the foregoing and the aftergoing; the continuity of flow that makes the past and future, morning and evening of the same day. There is no dead past, any more than there is lifelessness in those visions and imaginings, which are the ideals wherefrom we construct the future. All the dying we know in the universe is a dying on—into life.

But to-day I scarcely aspire even to make a study of the past. A simple recital of some of the leading events, and just an outlining touch here and there of some of the leading characters belonging to the earliest periods of this church's history, seems to me the fittest, in truth the only possible, memorial that I can offer to-day. To do this, *and more*, there is not time. To do other than this, and leave this unattempted, would be, I am persuaded, to mistake the wishes and the just expectations of most of those who have assembled here.

To name one hundred years of human history, especially the last one hundred years, is to start the recollective imagination on an excursion from which, if let go unchecked, it would scarcely return in a summer's day. What history written and unwritten have these years made! Not to stray from our own shores, the longest day of summer would not suffice to tell how this America has enlarged and changed— from a dozen and one thinly peopled colonies, dependencies of a distant kingdom, lying along the borders of our Eastern Sea, with no apparent tendency to integration, come to be a powerful nation of thirty-seven states, of continental width, with population four times doubled, notwithstanding a war which has no parallel in modern times for its havoc of life, unless the late European war has matched its numbers. How should the hours be enough to relate the story of our two civil wars alone, one of which made of the scattered dozen and one provinces a consolidated republic in the beginning of the century, and the other, at its end, removed by bloodiest surgery, but needful, that seed of death, of which the nation must rid itself or perish!

How should all the summer days be enough to show the steps of that vast unfolding civilization which has bridged the seas, calls pupils from Japan to American schools and colleges, gathers to a June festival singers and musicians by tens of thousands, speaking half a dozen languages, from the old world and the new, and brings the students of every science and art and philosophy, and form of knowledge, and type of religion, into one school of fellow-learners, where each fresh thought, and new discovery, and latest certified fact, becomes the immediate possession of all, giving earnest that the early christian vision may yet come true, and *mankind* extend its broader title over all the narrower terms of race and place, making all the nations that dwell on all the face of the earth, to be of one blood and of the family of the Everlasting Father!

A history of a hundred years, though it be but local history and deal with a communion of a few hundred souls only, has the same elements of interest that belong to the larger story of mankind. It touches human life at all points.

With many, such an occasion as this speaks first to sentiment and feeling. If I ask you to spend the hour with me among facts mostly, and to indulge me with a pretty liberal sprinkling of dates besides, it will not be because I despise sentiment; but because first in order comes the gathering of the material for it, the narrative; the reconstruction of this material into a pictured past, fresh with life, not to say the gathering of various wisdom from it, must be left very much to you.

It is not because of the great age of this religious society that we keep this day of memorial. Ours is not an old church, as oldness is accounted in this community. The Mother church of us all, the First Church in Salem, had observed her own one hundredth anniversary more than forty years before this society was formed. We take rank as the fourth in the order of time, of the *congregational* churches within the present territorial limits of Salem; the eighth, if all the churches formed from the First Church are taken into the account, disregarding territorial limits. This last number includes a church in what is now Beverly, early known as Bass River; one in Marblehead; one in Danvers, then known as Salem Village; and one in Peabody, then the "Middle District" of Salem.

Of the religious societies now existing in Salem, of all denominations, this is the sixth in age; the First, formed in 1629; the Friends' Meeting, in 1658; the East, or church of the Eastern District, as it was then designated, in 1718; St. Peter's (Episcopal), in 1733; the Third Congregational in 1735 (which is either the South or the Tabernacle Church, according as a question of identity in dispute between them is decided, a question on which this is not the occasion to pass judgment).

The causes which led to the gathering of this church, and the circumstances attending it, were somewhat peculiar.

The First Church had for its minister, in the year 1770, Rev. Thomas Barnard, a man of about fifty-four years of age, an able preacher and a pastor much beloved by his people. In the spring of that year he was stricken by paralysis, and his work was to pass into other hands. He had a son, Thomas Barnard, junior, educated for his own profession, and who, though but twenty-two years old, had been four years out of college and had completed his preparatory professional studies. He was employed to supply his father's pulpit till the next annual meeting of the parish, a term of some five or six months. This he did so acceptably to a considerable part of the people, that a strong desire was felt by them to make him a colleague pastor with his father. In this, however, there was not unanimity. So, when the question came up, as it did from time to time in church and parish, between the first of December, 1770, and the middle of the following summer, whether other candidates should be heard, or Mr. Barnard the younger should be settled, the vote was very evenly balanced on several occasions. Once, in the church, the vote was just equal; at another time, *for* hearing others, nine; for *not* hearing more, seven; and neuter, four (male members only voting). After a time the question took the form of a choice between

Mr. Barnard and Mr. Asa Dunbar, who, meantime, had become deservedly a favorite candidate in the church, and was afterwards settled.

On the 10th of June, 1771, a vote was taken with the result: *for* Mr. Dunbar, thirteen: *against*, eleven. And yet there was delay. The parish was divided, like the church, just about equally. A meeting of the society was held on the 26th of June, at which a *property* vote was taken, which gave a majority for concurring in the choice of Mr. Dunbar, of "$4/1$" (four shillings and one penny).

A property vote is defined in the records as one in which the "votes were accounted according to the several interests of the voters in proportion to their several taxes:" pew, or church taxes it is presumed. By such a vote it was finally decided, Nov. 25, 1771 (£97–13–8½ to £81–9–9½) that the proprietors would concur with the church in the choice of Mr. Dunbar.*

No wonder that there should have been reluctance on the part of the majority to push matters to a decision, when decision threatened to be division. The minority was nearly half the people. It embraced many highly esteemed for their intelligence and moral worth: one who had held the office of Ruling Elder in the church thirty-five years: one of the deacons, nearly twenty years in office and much respected: three out of five of the Standing Committee of the Proprietors for the year just preceding: the gentlemen chosen Clerk and Treasurer this same year of 1771; and not a few

---

* At one time a proposition was made and voted affirmatively, to lay aside both these candidates; and a later attempt to repeal this vote failed. But, of course, at this stage of the contest it made no difference. Each party clung to its favorite with greater determination.

lending the weight of social importance and large wealth to their opposition.*

Meantime, also, a tender regard for the presumed preference of the sick elder pastor, however scrupulously he might refrain from giving it expression, had its influence, without doubt, to confirm the minority in their choice, and to induce hesitation in the majority.

The controversy could have but one event. The delay wrought no change of purpose or feeling on either side, and when towards the end of the year it became apparent that neither could yield, propositions began to be made and considered for a friendly separation, which was, soon and without serious difficulty, effected. Those who stood by the church, settling Mr. Dunbar, handsomely agreed to buy the pews of those who desired to leave, at such prices "as three or more indifferent men might value them at." And a like amicable arrangement was made with regard to the church property. The departing members asked, with a confiding assurance that their proposal would be met in a generous spirit, that they might be dismissed "with a just and equitable part of the temporalities" of the church. And their confidence was not misplaced. Five-twelfths of all that belonged wholly to the church was divided to them; and they express no discontent with the apportionment.

It is nothing unusual for a church to owe its origin to a dissension among friends and members of the same church. I suppose this perhaps to be the rule, other causes the exceptions, in the history of church "origins."

---

*I can count the names of nearly thirty pew holders of the First Church in 1771, which appear in the first list of pew purchasers in the new North Church; which number I suppose, did not include the names of all the families which were *occupants* of pews, and which left the First Church to become worshippers at the North.

But in this case was no rancorous quarrel running into harsh aspersions, no charge of bad motive, no schismatic bitterness over unstatable differences of doctrine. The genuine regrets of parting friends have left their frequent traces on the pages of the records we have searched. They will not suffer themselves to forget what is due to christian courtesy and an ancient and honorable fellowship. They do not indulge in those criminations, which many times make the church strife so much more reckless and disreputable than ordinary worldly contentions.

There was soreness and lamentation; if possibly a drop of anger on either side, at what was deemed an unyielding obstinacy on the other, it came to no angry utterance and its complaint sounded more like a sorrow. The brethren and sisters asking a dismission from the church, allude to the divisions which have arisen, say they have desired and sought to prevent a separation, "and that we might still continue (as through the goodness of God for many years past we have done) in perfect peace and unity." But as "for diverse reasons we cannot consent to the calling and settling Mr. Dunbar . . . with so small a majority (if any) of the church," there seems "no way left for us but separation." They hope they may still have "occasional communion" with those they are leaving. "And now, brethren," they say, "not doubting of your complying with our reasonable desire, it shall not cease to be our ardent wish and prayer that we may so conduct our parting as shall cast no reflection on our holy religion or on ourselves; and that, although we may hereafter worship in separate assemblies, our hearts may be united, and, by our christian deportment to each other, we may . . . meet in that blessed assembly whose peace, unity and charity will never fail, and where discord will find no place."

Every kind word was reciprocated by the church. Every reasonable expectation was met. True, the brethren of the church expressed almost pathetically their "great concern and uneasiness at so unhappy a breach and separation;" declared that they had used their utmost endeavors to prevent it; that they were sensible how much the interest of religion and peace and the tranquillity of the people depend on their being united. They "even now wish that those brethren would consider the matter and not urge a dismission, as we [they] know of no just reasons why any should object to the choice of Mr. Dunbar," whom they consider "admirably qualified for a gospel preacher, and as we [they] think, full as likely to promote the true interest of religion as any other whatever." They conclude: "But if God in his holy providence has so ordered it as that this small church must be divided and split in pieces, and these brethren will separate from us, we herein join with them in the wish (as it shall be in our endeavor) that a spirit of love and Christian fellowship may continue between us notwithstanding our separation."

I am impressed with the honor and fairness which characterized these proceedings. It is rarely that a church falling into division hopeless of cure, and coming to be cut in very halves, still bears itself with a patience and generosity such as were here exhibited; or that a seceding body carries its difficult purpose through with so little record of passion and acrimony, so much of honorable feeling.

This general maintenance of a spirit of good-will was no doubt aided much by the relationship existing between two of the three men about whom these movements and interests principally centred: the crippled father, pastor of the First Church, fully possessing the love and respect of both sides, and his son, the warm-hearted young man, minister-elect of the church that was to be, who had so gained the affection of those who adhered to him, that they were willing to encounter the costs and risks of founding a new church (and that, be it remembered, when the times were troubled and the future uncertain) as well as to take the pangs of breaking old bonds, numerous, close and sacred, rather than forego the ministrations of the man they had chosen.

As a proof of the interest taken by the senior pastor of the First Church in the new enterprise that made his son the shepherd of half the flock he had himself lately tended, and as showing how the joint possession, as it were, of the father, by the two churches, and their common love and veneration for him, would tend to bridge the chasm naturally widening between them, it may be mentioned that Rev. Mr. Barnard, senior, invalid as he was, copied the entire body of the records of the First Church into the volume which was to contain the records of the North Church; so that we have the records of the First Church complete, as introductory to our own, written out fairly and legibly by the elder Barnard's own hand, making one hundred and sixty-seven closely written foolscap pages.

I shall find no better place than this, though a little in anticipation of the natural progress of my narrative, to tell how well justified was the judgment of either party in the matter at issue, and how fully the ancient communion was before long restored between them, and how faithfully it was maintained afterwards.

Mr. Dunbar proved himself the well-furnished and com-

petent minister that his supporters took him to be; while
the long and useful pastorate of Thomas Barnard, junior, in
the North Church, showed that the devotion with which he
had inspired his early friends was no ephemeral enthusiasm;
it became a steady and life-long esteem founded upon the
substantial qualities of personal worth.

When Mr. Barnard (of the North Church) gave the Hand
of Fellowship to Mr. Dunbar's successor, Mr. John Prince,
in 1779, the act was made more than usually graceful and
cordial by his reference to the man who had been the preferred and successful candidate for the place, which it had
once been hoped that he might himself fill. He mentions
him as the "pastor uncommonly dear" to his people, and
adds: "I feel peculiarly happy this day, when I consider
that this event unites our churches together, which were
originally of the same body, in every christian office of love
and friendship." And he went home to record upon the
church book: "Every lover of peace rejoiced heartily on
this occasion, for it settled a long difference which had subsisted between them, and united them in the bonds of
friendship."

The ministers of these two churches, Thomas Barnard
and John Prince, were from that day fast friends. Their
friendship endured unbroken for a period of thirty-five
years, till the minister of the First Church came to comfort
the people of the North, suddenly bereaved, by death, of
their beloved minister; when he betrayed, in word and
manner, that his own sense of loss was scarcely less, if less,
than that of the most attached parishioners of his friend.
They two had been of one mind and one heart. Both liberal,
practical, valuing personal character and honest devotion to

truth above the formulated doctrines of church creeds, they had been sincere fellow-laborers in the christian church, giving and receiving sympathy in severe personal trials, which had come to each in turn. The friend-ship which found expression in the sermon preached by Dr. Prince, after the death of Dr. Barnard, tender in feeling, and warm with discriminating praise, was a fit and beautiful ripening into expression of that fraternal spirit which had at no time been fatally ruptured between the First and North Churches, and was now cemented more closely than ever.*

On the 14th of February, 1772, a piece of land on the corner of North and Lynde streets, where the dwelling house of the Hon. Otis P. Lord now stands, was bought for a meeting house lot, in anticipation of the wants of the future society.† There were forty-two associates in the purchase, and John Nutting, who sold the land, made the forty-third proprietor. On the 3d of March following, the proprietors of this land met at the Town Hall, in obedience to a warrant issued by Peter Frye, Esq., a Justice of the Peace, and served by Clark Gayton Pickman, one of the proprietors, and proceeded to an organization. This was, in fact, the legal institution of the society known as *The Proprietors of the North Meeting House*, by popular designation "the North Society," although the major part

---

* In a note, Dr. Prince records the following interesting particulars: — "It is a singular concurrence in our walks of life, and one that has some effect upon the social feelings, that we were educated at the same university, and after we graduated kept the same schools in the same town; studied divinity with the same clergyman; settled in the ministry in the same town; the same person preached our ordination sermons; and we received honorary degrees from the same university."

† On the western line, I am told by one of our most indefatigable and trustworthy antiquarians, Wm. P. Upham, Esq., of what was early known as Sharpe's Training Field.

of those who constituted its membership were still members of the First Church or Parish.

The first vote after organization was "that the land aforesaid be improved by erecting thereon a meeting house for the public worshipping of God, for the use of the proprietors." The second: "That William Browne, Edward Augustus Holyoke, Joseph Blaney and Samuel Curwen, Esqs., and Messrs. John Felt, and Richard Ward, and Clark Gayton Pickman, be a committee for the building of said meeting house," and "the question being put whether the proprietors would give any particular directions to the committee about the building said house—it passed in the negative:" an instance of rare and commendable abstinence from the exercise of that careful scrutiny so natural to the New England mind, which trusts nothing to official agents, loves to see to everything for itself, not neglecting to inspect, supervise and advise concerning every minute detail, however unfamiliar, of which the pages of early records, both ecclesiastical and municipal, bear such ample testimony.

On the 11th of May the laying of the foundation for the new meeting house was begun. It was first opened for public worship on Sunday, Aug. 23, 1772, though not yet nearly completed. After occupying it three Sundays the proprietors determined to add side-galleries, which had not been originally contemplated in the plan of the building committee, and which added thirty-eight pews to the one hundred and one which took up the space upon the lower floor.

Early in October, the bell, which had been ordered from London, arrived. On the 19th of October the spire was raised. It was not till the early part of the following year, however, that the house was considered finished, and that the pews were sold; nearly five months after the society began to meet in it.

This was called "the large new meeting house" in the papers of that time. From the frequency with which it was asked for for civic celebrations on the 4th of July, and for other public days, it is inferred that it must have been — and indeed it is well remembered by many of you to have been — one of the most spacious and commodious churches of the town. Its precise dimensions we do not find; we should probably have had them among the records, to the size of every joist, if the proprietors had not given everything in such a trusting manner to that Building Committee. Its one hundred and one pews on the lower floor were square and roomy, and four broad aisles ran lengthwise, north and south, giving eight tiers of pews in width. Its tower end, the front, was upon Lynde street, the tower itself rising from the ground, and containing the vestibule to the church on the first floor, and the entrance to the organ and singing gallery on the second floor. Originally, it was surmounted by a spire; but this being regarded as insecure some twenty years after, and requiring frequent and costly repairs, it was taken down in 1796, and replaced by a simple cupola, or dome, covering the belfry, the form in which it is remembered by those who look back thirty-eight years. The outside entrances were five; three into the tower on its north, east and west sides, and two on the southern end of the main building, near the corners. One broad entrance led from the porch in the tower to the interior of the house. There was no side entrance to the body of the building. The pulpit was on the southern end. A carriage-way passed around on the eastern and southern sides, the sides not lying on the broader streets. That first meeting house continued to be used as a house of worship till this house was built, in 1836. It was afterwards appropriated to manufacturing and other purposes for a while, and after some years was taken down.*

The corner-stone of *this* church building was laid May 16, 1835 (sixty-three years, almost to a day, from the laying of the foundation of the first building). It was dedicated June 22, 1836. Its interior, at first finished very plain and without ornament, was renewed and brought into its present tasteful form, under the cultivated eye and experienced direction of that lover of the beautiful, the late Francis Peabody, Esq., in 1847. The plat of ground on which it stands is bounded on its eastern side by land which was once in possession of Roger Williams; his homestead.

In the earlier periods of New England Congregationalism, the church as distinct from the assembly of worshippers — or the parish, or town, as the case might be — took the lead in all matters pertaining to public worship, the call and settlement of pastors, the determination of the conditions of communion, the use of ordinances, and, indeed, pretty much everything but the raising and appropriation of money.

The parish, for the most part, limited itself in quiet times to concurrence in the doings of the church, in all matters in which they had a common interest; though the concurrence

---

* No picture of it has been preserved; but a recent attempt to present a view of its front has been made, and is generally regarded by those who remember its appearance, as a faithful likeness. The drawing of which the cut in the appendix is a copy, now in possession of the Essex Institute, was executed by Dr. George A. Perkins, partly from memory and partly from a sketch made when the church was standing.

was no mere form, as repeated instances of refusal to concur in church action on the part of parishes sufficiently attest. It was a voluntary thing; this surrender of precedence. Usage alone gave it authority. Moreover, the congregation easily made its wishes known through those who were members of both bodies, and often took the initiative in accomplishing its objects by prompting the church to act, rather than by asserting absolutely its own coequal power, or even the power of veto. The perfect independency of each congregation in determining its own internal order, and managing its own affairs, was the cardinal and distinctive *principle* of Congregationalism.

This principle, as such, knows nothing of that division, or distinction, which has usually existed within the congregation, into two bodies; of church and society. Nor, where such two bodies exist, does it settle their relations to each other. But the usage has been, and more especially in former times, as I said, to allow the church not only to organize itself, and conduct its affairs in its own way, but to have habitual precedence, where the two had a joint interest or joint obligations. The liability of jar or opposition between them was reduced to a remote probability, by the fact that the leaders in both society and church were for the most part the same persons. The church, it will be seen, was an institution relatively of much more power and importance a hundred years ago than now. It was recognized as the heart of the religious organism, and the seat of its life.

Not unnaturally, therefore, the organization of the North Church occupies a more prominent place, and its doings are more minutely detailed upon the records of our early history, than the organization and proceedings of the society itself.

On the 16th of May, 1772, the First Church voted to grant the request of the fifty-two brethren and sisters, who asked a dismission that they might become a church connected with this society.

On the 19th of July, the day we commemorate, these fifty-two met at the house of the venerable Col. Benjamin Pickman, senior, for organization. Col. Pickman lived in the house now standing on Essex street, opposite to St. Peter street, built by himself, and at the present time owned by Mrs. Le Masters; its upper windows may still be seen rising above the row of one-story shops extending along its front; it was one of the most elegant houses of the town.

The Rev. Dr. Whittaker of the Third Church—afterwards "the Tabernacle"—a noted preacher, then at the zenith of a not long enduring popularity, attended and offered prayer. The church adopted the covenant of the First Church: the same to which, as members of the First Church, they had before subscribed: "hereby," they say, "recognizing and renewing the substance of the First Covenant entered into by our pious ancestors at their first founding a church in New England in this town, Aug. 6, 1629, professing ourselves, nevertheless, to be in charity with all men who love the Lord Jesus Christ in sincerity and truth." This covenant *was a covenant*, not a creed, nor containing a creed. It simply bound them to walk together in all the ways of God, "as he is pleased to reveal himself unto us in his Blessed Word of truth."

I do not stop to inquire whether they could be sure that they had the very covenant of Aug. 6, 1629, letter for letter. They believed they had the same, as, no doubt, they had substantially; as such they revered and retained it, adding only their broad profession of charity with all lovers of the Lord Jesus Christ.

To their acceptance of this elder covenant they add somewhat, to be sure, but rather in the nature of reiteration of a few of its obligations, than as adding new ones. While it is true, at the same time, that, incidentally, they show that they believed in God, as "Father, Son, and Holy Ghost;" in "the Holy Scriptures contained in the old and new testaments," "taking them for our [their] sole and sufficient rule of faith and practice;" and that they relied "upon the atonement purchased by the blood of the great Mediator for the pardon of our [their] manifold sins." Theirs was the faith of their time.

Within the next few months, and before the ordination of the minister, from twenty to thirty more members had been admitted to the church, making a membership of seventy-five to eighty persons.

At a meeting held on the 20th of August (1772), they voted that this should be called the North Church. The same day Thomas Barnard, junior, was formally chosen its pastor. John Nutting, who had held the same office for thirty-five years in the First Church, and Joshua Ward, who for nearly twenty years had been a deacon of that church, were chosen ruling elders, and Samuel Holman and James Gould, deacons. It was voted that the Lord's Supper should be administered on the last Sunday of every month.

The church and society were now fully organized. The meeting house was so far advanced that it was to be used for public worship on the next Sunday, though it required extemporized seats and other conveniences for the present. The minister had been unanimously chosen, and was their preacher already, though not to be ordained till the house should be finished. From August to the next January, the time of his ordination, Mr. Barnard preached regularly, and all the usual church rites were duly observed.*

The ordination of Mr. Barnard, which took place on the 13th of January, 1773, crowned with fruition the hopes of those who for two and a half years had been so steadily seeking his settlement as their minister; first, if it were possible, in the old church of their fathers; if not possible there, in a new one.

A little scene which occurred at the ordination must have touched all hearts.

Mr. Barnard's paralytic father, the senior pastor of the First Church, was present and when Rev. Mr. Diman of the East Church, who gave the Hand of Fellowship, had first welcomed the newly gathered church, and then its young pastor, to the communion of the neighboring churches, he turned to the elder Barnard, saying: "Reverend sir, we heartily congratulate you on the happy settlement of your son. How great is God's goodness! How doth he bring good out of evil, and turn afflictions into blessings! The uncommon disorder with which you have been visited and

---

*The first child of whose baptism in the North Church a record is found was Abigail, daughter of John Holman, presented August 30, 1772, the second Sunday on which the church was occupied. A month later, September 27th, there was a baptism of ten children, nine girls and one boy, which was probably the origin of the statement found in the *Salem Gazette* of October 27, 1772, that "Last Sunday (i. e. Oct. 25th), were baptized in the new Congregational Church in this town, ten infants, all females." Mr. William Gavet, for many years sexton of the church, whose death took place in January, 1856, at the age of 89, supposed himself to have been the first child baptized in the North Society; but in this, as we have seen, he was mistaken. He, together with other children of his father, Jonathan Gavet, was baptized in January, 1773.

taken off from your public labors was very grievous; but it has made way for the settlement of your son, thus near you, to comfort and cherish you in your declining age, and under your many infirmities; which is a very great favor of Providence to you. . . . And then there is this happy circumstance attending your son's settlement, that all his hearers are his friends who hear him with pleasure, and therefore with candor; which must also give him pleasure and likewise freedom in speaking, which is a favor that but few enjoy. And they are not only his friends but yours. They highly esteem you in love, as well as him, for your work's sake. And they have submitted to many difficulties and been at great expense to bring about this settlement. The Lord bless them and abundantly reward them for their kindness to him and to you. . . . We bless God, dear sir, . . . that you have the great comfort and satisfaction of seeing the public ministry, which you quitted with so much reluctance, carried on by your son, to the good acceptance and, we think, to the spiritual instruction and edification, of so many of your former hearers. As we condoled with you in your trouble, so we now heartily rejoice with you in this goodness of God to you."

A notice of the ordination, in the "Salem Gazette" of the week following, ends with the comprehensive remark that "The whole was carried on with propriety, elegance and solemnity. Genteel entertainments were provided in various parts of the town for the council, ministers, governors and students of Harvard College and all the company that were present at the ordination."*

---

* The sermon was preached by Rev. Mr. Williams of Bradford, afterwards Professor of Mathematics and Natural Philosophy in Harvard College, with whom Mr.

Mr. Barnard was to receive a settlement of sixty-six pounds, thirteen shillings and four pence; thirty pounds a year were to be paid to him besides, unless the proprietors should furnish him with a suitable house, in which case the payment of this sum should cease; and his "stated salary" was to be one hundred and thirty-three pounds, six shillings and eight pence; "but in case he be taken off his labor, and the propriety be obliged to supply the pulpit, then the salary" was to be "reduced to one hundred and six pounds, thirteen shillings and four pence." And further he was to receive "all the money that is contributed unmarked."

This unmarked money, of which frequent mention is found in the records, is explained by the custom which prevailed for many years of collecting the taxes for pews in the form, first of a weekly, then of a monthly and finally a quarterly collection taken in church, the sum being wrapped in paper and *marked* with the number of the pew, or the name of the occupant, or both; a regular account being kept with each tax-payer and pew, and the account adjusted at the end of the year. If it fell short, the deficiency was to be made up. If a surplus had been contributed, which was not at all unusual, it was credited on the next year's account. And as sometimes a stranger, or an occupant of a pew who was not a tax-payer, desired to contribute something, such sums were put in with no name or mark upon them. They were "the unmarked money," and were the minister's perquisite. Usually they amounted to very little;

Barnard had pursued his professional studies. The prayer of ordination and charge were by Rev. Edward Barnard of Haverhill, an uncle of the minister elect and brother of the senior pastor of the First Church. The first prayer was offered by Rev. Mr. Tucker of Newbury, who had succeeded Rev. Thomas Barnard, senior, in the ministry at Newbury; the other prayer by Rev. Mr. Swain of Wenham.

sometimes a few cents; sometimes a dollar or more; not unfrequently nothing. The amount for one whole year (1801) was $2.24; another year (1802), $3.47.

This society appears to have had no period of weak infancy. It was strong, confident and assured of its stability from the beginning. It boldly built a large meeting house, and sold nearly three-fourths of its one hundred and forty pews without difficulty and at once. Men of wealth sustained it with determination, and it had such credit from the start as to draw the doubting and hesitating to its support.

It had better than financial strength. It was instituted under the lead of sagacious and earnest men, who had had their character and capacity well tried in other positions of trust and honor. There were *good* men and women of their number, held in esteem alike for their probity and their charity. Among these names are many identified with the most honorable history of the town for the period; some of them known far beyond the limits of the town. The venerable Col. Benjamin Pickman, the first of four in lineal order who bore the same name and title, reputed to be, with a single exception, more extensively engaged in commerce than any other man in the province; a Judge of the Common Pleas; member of the Provincial Council; eminent for patriotic services and public spirit, such as to obtain public recognition and a handsome and valuable testimonial from the legislative assembly, while he was no less beloved for his private virtues; now drawing towards the close of a long, useful and generous life;—his sons, Col. Benjamin Pickman, junior, William Pickman and Clark Gayton Pickman, all successful merchants and much respected citizens,

whose names were familiar to an earlier generation, and are not yet forgotten in this community;—Col. William Browne, descended from a distinguished ancestry, well-educated, wealthy, benevolent and at the time a great favorite with the people; a little later a Judge of the Superior Court, and for a short time of the Supreme Bench, by executive appointment, though later still a loyalist and refugee;*
—Dr. Edward A. Holyoke, the widely-known and skilful

---

* Judge Browne was a descendant in direct line from the Samuel and the two William Brownes, who, with Benjamin, brother of the second William, were benefactors of Harvard College, and founders of the Browne scholarship in that institution. The Brownes were liberal patrons of good learning in the schools of Salem, as well as in the college at Cambridge.

This was not the only William Browne who was somewhat widely known. He had a cousin, William Burnet Browne, for whom he seems to have been mistaken by Mr. Ward, the editor of "Curwen's Journal and Letters," and by Mr. Sabine (who perhaps followed Ward) in his "American Loyalists." Ward, in his biographical notice of our Colonel William Browne (p. 504, 4th ed., 1854), rightly says that he was a son of Samuel Browne, but incorrectly adds, "and a grandson of Gov. Burnet." Colonel William Browne had an uncle, William Browne, the proprietor of "Ryal Side," who married a daughter of Gov. Burnet, and had a son, William [Burnet] Browne. This William Burnet Browne was a cousin, therefore, of Samuel's son, William. Mr. Sabine seems to have fallen into the same mistake (p. 180, of edition published in 1847).

In the commonness of the name a doubt was suggested to the writer, at one time, whether the William Browne who was one of the original members of the North Church, and Colonel William Browne, the loyalist refugee, and afterwards Governor of Bermuda, were the same person. Subsequent investigation left no room for reasonable doubt. Not only is he designated as "Colonel" William Browne upon the records, but his name which was prominent among the officers of the First Church before 1772, and among those of the North Church after that date, suddenly disappears entirely from the records at just the time when Colonel Browne left the country. Moreover, at the annual meeting of the proprietors, on Jan. 12, 1778, the collectors were directed " to apply to the Committee of Safety of this town, for all taxes now due on the pews belonging to William Browne, Esq." Colonel Browne's property was confiscated on account of his adherence to the royal cause; and under the circumstances an application to the Committee of Safety for the unpaid pew taxes, shows the political status of the pew-holder to be just that which Colonel William Browne held at the time. Add, that Colonel Browne had pews both in the First and North Churches, which were offered for sale after his departure, and we are justified in saying that there can be no question that Colonel William Browne, afterwards Judge, then refugee, and later still appointed Governor of Bermuda by the English Ministry, was the same who was among the original fifty-two persons dismissed from the First Church to form the North Church. His mother, Katharine Sargent, was also one of the original members of this church. She was a daughter of John and Ann Winthrop, and married after the death of her first husband, Samuel Browne, Colonel Epes Sargent of Gloucester, who removed to Salem not long after their marriage. Colonel Sargent died in 1762, and his widow continued to live near her son, Colonel William Browne, on Essex street, in a house which he built for her, next his own, in 1763.

physician, the courteous gentleman, the modest and exemplary Christian;—Samuel Curwen, the son of a beloved minister of the First Church, himself educated for the ministry, but diverted by ill-health to commercial pursuits; a captain under General Pepperell at Louisburg; a Judge of admiralty at the opening of the Revolution; a gentleman cultivated by letters and travel;—Francis Cabot, a merchant of reputation and a gentleman of large wealth and influence;—John Nutting, educated at Cambridge, sometime a teacher, who had been thirty-six years a ruling elder in the First Church, and lived to fill the same office for eighteen years afterwards in the North Church; for many years holding various and important offices under the Government;—Joshua Ward, the ardent patriot, long an officer in the First Church and in the North;—his son, Richard, active and prominent both in military and civil affairs;—Nathan Goodale, teacher and merchant;—the worthy Deacon Samuel Holman, who for forty years was one of the Standing Committee of the Proprietors and an officer of the church, deacon and ruling elder until his death, a period of fifty-three years;—Col. David Mason and Capt. John Felt, those sturdy patriots whose names soon after became connected with the cause of popular liberty from their part in the affair with the British Col. Leslie at North Bridge, in February, 1775;—and of younger men, Benjamin Goodhue, afterwards senator, and Dr. William Paine, Jacob Ashton, William Vans—these are some of the names that stand among the founders of the North Church and society.

The only time when, perhaps, the society may have felt that a serious breach had been made into its security and strength was at the breaking out of the Revolution.

At the first of it the leading men of the society were on the side of the Government. The minister inclined that way in the beginning, though not long. Col. William Browne, Joseph Blaney, Francis Cabot, Samuel Curwen, Benjamin Pickman (he who was Benjamin Pickman, the junior, at the formation of the church; his father had died in 1773), his brothers, William and Clark Gayton Pickman, Dr. Holyoke, John Nutting, Jacob Ashton, Weld Gardner, Jonathan Goodhue, William Vans, Andrew Dalglish, Henry Gardner, Nathan Goodale and James Hastie,— these were all disposed to support the Government; certainly not all, perhaps not any, with entire approval of the measures adopted by the Government, but from a conviction, shared largely by thoughtful men throughout all the provinces, that successful resistance would be impossible, and that the difficulties between the Mother Country and the Colonies might be composed by moderate and conciliatory counsels. The greater number of these loyalists finally fell more into sympathy with the tone of feeling around them, and in the end adhered to the American cause. A few, however, resolutely chose the other course and joined the royal standard and, when the storm burst, withdrew from the country, generally retiring either to the eastern provinces or to England. Samuel Curwen, William Browne and Benjamin Pickman were among the latter; and in the very interesting letters and journal of Mr. Curwen, written during the period of his expatriation, we have a vivid picture, if sometimes a sad one, of the struggles and heart-sicknesses which these exiles endured. Their hearts after all yearned for their early homes, and the homes of their people. In many cases impoverished, dependent, tossed between reviving hopes and new disappointments, as the fortunes of the conflict wavered, not altogether trusted by the Government whose pensioners they were, they wore away wearily the slow years of the war.*

Two or three votes found among the records of the proprietors seem to show that the resources of the society were much affected by the war.

At the annual meeting in 1776, a vote was passed to the following purport:—"Whereas, the difficulty of the times is such that, if a tax for the Rev. Mr. Barnard's salary was laid as usual, there is great probability that it cannot be collected; therefore voted that a committee [of gentlemen named] be desired to wait upon the Rev. Mr. Barnard, to know if he will accept, for the present, of a free contribution for his support in lieu of his salary." Mr. Barnard accepted this proposal upon condition that it should work no invalidity in the original contract at his settlement. And though there is evidence that he did not for a time receive the full amount of his salary under this arrangement, it was remembered afterwards, and partial or full restitution was made of the sum deficient; and from about 1795 a

---

* The Journal of Judge Curwen gives us also a pleasant glimpse of a fragmentary continuance of the fellowship of the North Church, in the years of their London exile. He makes frequent mention of social meetings with his old Salem friends; and often alludes to his Sundays, and his manner of spending the day. He became a regular attendant at the chapel of Theophilus Lindsay, the early and distinguished English Unitarian clergyman, who left a good living in Yorkshire from conscientious objections to some parts of the liturgy of the Established Church, which he afterwards altered for use in his London chapel. Mr. Curwen gives interesting notices of Priestley and Price, and other ministers of less note, whom he heard in London during his residence there. For Mr. Lindsay he came to entertain a very high regard, based upon his thoughtful discourses, and his beautiful christian life and character. He sometimes took with him, to his Sunday worship, his old friends and fellow-communicants of the North Church, Benjamin Pickman and William Browne; so, two or three, at least, of the brethren of the North Church met by the river of Babylon; and who shall doubt that there they sometimes wept (in secret) as they remembered the New England Zion, and the dear Salem of the West, and that they found it hard to sing her songs in a strange land?

regular annual addition of one hundred to three hundred and fifty dollars was made to his salary, and was continued to the end of his life; thus making his salary at the highest, however, but about nine hundred dollars.

Dr. Barnard's ministry continued from Jan. 13, 1773 to Oct. 1, 1814, the time of his death, nearly forty-two years; more than two-fifths of the century. He had had no assistant, though nearing the end of his sixty-seventh year, and left a fresh sermon partly written upon his table when he died.

If asked, for what ideas or what type of influence this church stood, during these earliest forty-two years, I should say, taking its pastor as its representative: first, it stood for the religion of a true humanity; a religion which made love to man the best expression of love to God; for that interpretation of Christianity which makes prominent its humane spirit. Dr. Barnard was a whole-hearted man. He loved his kind. He loved little children. Men of diverse tastes and various culture found themselves drawn to him. He won by his own genial, sympathetic and comprehensive manliness. You saw how friends gathered around him in the first instance in the First Church. They stood by him at the sacrifice of life-long associations and deepest rooted affections. The spirit that animated himself he evoked in others. He was a reconciler; not by studied compromises, but by native courtesy and magnanimity. His generosity of mind put generous construction upon other men's motives, and by the inbred honor of his character he held the confidence he gained. He proved that he had courage and sincerity, or he might have been cast aside as a time-server. He was a young man of twenty-seven only, when the Revolutionary War broke out. With such men in his society as Judge William Browne, Col. Benjamin Pickman, Francis Cabot, Judge Samuel Curwen, Dr. Holyoke and others, on the one side, and the Wards, Col. Mason and Capt. John Felt on the other; himself first leaning to the side of politic concession, even signing the complimentary address to Gov. Hutchinson, but afterwards joining the party of resistance with no equivocal or doubtful devotion, and publicly recalling some of the expressions to which he had previously subscribed, he seems, nevertheless, to have done all with such a frankness, conscientiousness and fearlessness, as to put his honesty and patriotism beyond question, so that he retained the friendship of those who became divided from each other.

In the affair of Col. Leslie at the North Bridge, he was conspicuous and characteristically the minister of peace. Among the various and sometimes conflicting accounts of the prominent actors and scenes of that day, there is a substantial agreement in mentioning Mr. Barnard's presence and active and successful efforts to prevent bloodshed. Leslie's force, three or four hundred strong, passed by his meeting house on their march through Lynde and North streets, to the North Bridge. The afternoon congregation had already been dismissed at the alarm that such troops were approaching, and Mr. Barnard lost no time in presenting himself to the British officer, who stood baffled and exasperated before the raised draw at the North River, and remonstrating against his threat to fire on the people. Young as he was, he bore the difficult part of pacificator among these angry, heated and hostile men, who, on either side defiantly declared their intention to yield nothing, with a self-possession and a persuasiveness in remonstrance, which finally succeeded. Col. Leslie gave his word of honor, at length, that if permitted to pass his men over the bridge, he would not go beyond a certain number of rods. The bridge was lowered and he kept his word. The mood of mind in which so many of the inhabitants had hurriedly and excitedly assembled leaves no room for doubt that there would have been serious collision and probably loss of life, if the counsels of forbearance had not prevailed.

I called a few weeks since upon the late Rev. Charles Cleaveland of Boston, who died at the age of one hundred years, wanting a few days. He joined this church in 1791, and from December, 1804, to December, 1806, was the clerk of the society. On my introduction to him as the minister of this church, he exclaimed: "O! I love the North Church! Good Dr. Barnard! Good Dr. Barnard!" and proceeded to express with enthusiasm his affection and reverence for that excellent man.

But Dr. Barnard was not merely the large-hearted man. He was a respectable scholar and loved the fellowship of literary men and good thinkers. He was a wise counsellor and his aid was much sought in the ecclesiastical councils of his time. He was a preacher of popular and acceptable gifts. Few ministers had more frequent proofs of this in the form of complimentary invitations to preach occasional discourses, abroad and at home; many of which were also printed. He delivered the Dudleian Lecture at Cambridge in 1795; preached before the convention of congregational ministers in 1793; before the Ancient and Honorable Artillery Company in 1789; and ordination sermons at the settlement of Aaron Bancroft in Worcester in 1786, and of Ichabod

Nichols of Portland, Maine, in 1809; besides many other discourses before charitable institutions and on days of public observance. A discourse preached on the death of Gen. Washington, in 1799, was published "by desire of the town" and it shows a warm and admiring gratitude for the character and services of that great man; a feeling which obtained repeated expression in his public discourses.

During the ministry of Dr. Barnard this pulpit and this society stood also for religious liberty. Not negatively only, by preaching practical religion and leaving dogmatic divinity aside, did the minister of this church discountenance bigotry and the over-valuation of theological schemes, but positively, earnestly, frequently, did he rebuke the spiritual assumption and uncharitableness which makes of one's own opinion, or of the interpretation of truth by one's own church, a standard for others' confessions. I presume that Dr. Barnard was in the earlier part of his ministry what was called then an Arminian, perhaps towards the end of his life a Unitarian. I speak guardedly, for though Dr. Channing so classed him, Dr. Samuel Worcester of the Tabernacle Church declared that he was not a Unitarian. Their different ways of defining "Unitarian" would probably explain the contradiction between them. Dr. Channing was not mistaken, in supposing that Dr. Barnard was, in his general habits of thinking, in sympathy with the liberal clergy of his time. I have heard a tradition that when once a parishioner said: "Dr. Barnard, I never heard you preach a sermon upon the Trinity," he replied: "And you never will." * It is very evident that the society at the time of

---

* Dr. Prince says of him, however, that though "his preaching was more practical than metaphysical," "he did not neglect to discuss any religious subject which he

his death in 1814 had had such teaching and was, in its whole organic life, so penetrated and moved by the spirit of religious freedom, that it was all ready to take, as it did take without a consciousness of change, its place among those churches which about that time were beginning to be known and to know themselves, as Unitarian.

One of the later and most interesting of the minutes entered by his hand upon the pages of the church record book, is the reply sent by this church to a communication from the Rev. Abiel Abbot and the society of which he was the pastor, in Coventry, Connecticut; an answer to the request that this church would send delegates to an ecclesiastical council to be held in Coventry, to advise them as to their duty under what seemed to them an arbitrary attempt of neighboring churches to exercise ecclesiastical domination over them, in clear violation of the vital principles of congregational liberty. This church declined to send representatives to a council in Connecticut, "thinking it not proper for us," they say, "to enter in ecclesiastical form another state, which, with the patronage of its civil government differs from us in its church discipline." This did not prevent their severe condemnation, however, of the interference of certain churches which had arrogated to themselves the power to dismiss a minister from his settlement without his own or his society's consent. But "we think," is their conclusion, "an ecclesiastical council formed of members only from this state, to take cognizance of your affairs, would not be a promising means under divine Providence to free you from the injuries of which you

---

thought would throw light on the scriptures, inform the minds of his hearers, and lay open the designs of God in the gospel, impress the minds of his hearers with reverence and love, confirm their faith and excite obedience."

complain, and to restore and establish the rights you claim as Christians. It might be seriously hurtful to you in civil process; which, in our judgment, must issue your aggrievements, or perpetuate them."

This letter was signed by Thomas Barnard, "by the desire and direction of the church." But it is evident, I think, from these last sentences at least, that it was not drawn up without consultation with legal minds; and a church on whose roll of members stood the names of Judge Putnam, Ichabod Tucker and Leverett Saltonstall, not to mention more, had no need to go elsewhere to find the ablest counsel for its guidance on questions legal-ecclesiastical.

Still, this letter was in the very vein of Dr. Barnard's most habitual thought and discourse. And it was well said after his death that "the influence of his name assisted to preserve the liberties of our churches from the abuses of power and the ignorance of misguided men."

Dr. Barnard, whose death occurred Oct. 1, 1814, was succeeded in the following April by the youthful John Emery Abbot, son of Dr. Benjamin Abbot, for half a century the distinguished head of Phillips Academy at Exeter, N. H. It would be difficult to make those of the present generation, and strangers to our history, understand fully the very great love and veneration with which this rare young man inspired his people; and which still make his name and memory dear to the hearts of his few surviving contemporaries. Less than twenty-two years of age when he was settled; assuming at once the full burden of pastor over a large society; and preacher to a congregation containing a large number of persons of high intelligence and culture; his health never vigorous; he possessed such graces of spirit, bore himself with such a modest dignity, preached with such a matured wisdom and moving earnestness, and gave himself so wholly and gladly to his work, that the remembrances and traditions of his brief and broken ministry of four years—barely two and a half of active labor and ended more than fifty years ago—are more distinct, marked and permanent here to-day, than would be expected from a ministry of a quarter of a century.

Before he had been two years here his health began to give way. A journey and short trial of a more southern air, in the fall of 1817, proved of no advantage,—it was thought did him injury. And though he preached once after his return, he continued from that time steadily to decline. In the next spring and summer, of 1818, he rallied somewhat, passing the season in his native town. In the autumn worse symptoms reappearing, he sailed for Havana, though very feeble, and passed the winter in and near that city. The warmer climate brought no restoration; and he returned extremely reduced to Exeter in June, 1819, and died there, at his father's house, on the 7th of October following.

Mr. Abbot was a good scholar and a conscientious student. But his highest power lay in the silent influence which ever went forth from a soul which had its conversation in heaven; a soul of deep religious sensibility; a character of stainless purity; a life which seemingly exhibited at once, in tranquil equipoise and harmonious activity, all christian excellences.

His early death, the fading out so soon of this morning light of beauty and promise, watched as it was by so many tearful eyes and sympathetic hearts, no doubt heightened that exaltation of sanctified love by which he became transfigured in the recollection of his people.

The coming of Mr. Abbot to the ministry of the North Church marks an epoch in its history, in that it was the first taking of an open stand by the society on acknowledged Unitarian ground. Gradually, perhaps unconsciously, the society and its first minister had long been tending to this point. The church had never imposed a creed upon its members; for neither the broad covenant of the First Church which it reaffirmed, nor the additional sentences which it put with it, made their subscription in any sense subscription to a creed. Even those phrases which incidentally disclosed the faith of the church in certain doctrines, which it then held but afterwards discarded, were never written to be used as a creed, nor were referred to as such, nor imposed upon any; and not till long after the church was largely composed of Unitarian believers, was it deemed of importance to change a word of them; for they knew this writing to have been drawn and signed, not as a statement of what was to be believed, but as an engagement to fidelity in certain duties to be done and certain practical ends to be sought. The church was always catholic in spirit and set sincerity of belief and simple discipleship above all forms of confession.

Congregationalism in Massachusetts up to this time had been a name without any necessary doctrinal significance. A church polity, simply as such, it drew up no system of divinity and prescribed no articles to be assented to. Individuals within these churches did such things abundantly. But, as men free to think and write their thoughts, they did it, and they had been equally free to think and write otherwise, if they had pleased, and Congregationalism, as a mode of church organization, government or fellowship, could not in consistency have cared or interfered.

The name Unitarian had not yet begun to be much applied, distinctively, to churches, but within these churches discussion had long been going on over the doctrines of the Calvinistic scheme which, by many of the leading men of the state, clerical and lay, were zealously denied and ably controverted. Mayhew and Freeman, and not a few others of the clergy of Boston and the neighborhood, had been open champions of the Unitarian faith in the last century. It has been said that as early as 1790, the general tone of thought in Boston was Unitarian. It was probably as true of Salem as of Boston. Drs. Barnard, Prince and Bentley, and, if prevalent traditions can be trusted, a rector of St. Peter's Church, contemporary with them, were theologically in close sympathy with the Boston clergy just named; while there were thoughtful laymen in all these churches, not a whit behind their pastors, as defenders of religious liberty and as loyal disciples of reason in the interpretation of Christianity.

The controversy waxed warmer in the early years of the present century. The views of different preachers were keenly canvassed and the lines of coming separation began to appear. William Ellery Channing, settled in the Federal street pulpit of Boston in 1803, though himself averse to polemic writing, gave a fresh impulse to the discussion by his inspiring discourses upon the immeasurable capabilities, hopes and aspirations, of human nature; by his bold and warning call to churches and Christians to stand fast in their Christian liberties — to come under no yoke of human creed or spiritual court; and by his constant appeal to the human reason and the human conscience, without whose authentication he urged that no religion could gain permanent credence and acceptance with reasoning and conscience-guided men.

Mr. Abbot had had his professional training in part under the guidance of Mr. Channing, in part also under the tuition of the elder Henry Ware; and had a warm friend in Henry Ware the younger. Sharing in the affectionate esteem of such men and of the younger ministers of the time trained in the same school of thought, such men as Frothingham of the First Church and Everett of the Brattle Street Church in Boston, his call and coming to this church pronounced, what had before been known but not so fully recognized, that this church took its place among those which made "Holiness, Truth and Humanity" their sufficient motto.

Mr. Channing preached at Mr. Abbot's ordination and Mr. Frothingham gave the Hand of Fellowship. The sermon made a deep impression. The subject of it was "Preaching Christ" (from Col. i, 28). In answering the question: "What are we to understand by 'Preaching Christ'," he announced, as his view, that "Preaching Christ does not consist in making Christ perpetually the subject of discourse, but in inculcating on his authority, *the religion which he taught.*" This sermon was soon followed by the well-known controversial pamphlets between the preacher and the Rev. Dr. Samuel Worcester of the Tabernacle Church in this city, and by the full opening of the question of separation or continued union between the "liberal" and "orthodox" parties in the congregational churches of Massachusetts, ending in separation.

A few months after the death of Mr. Abbot, the society and church gave a call to Rev. Henry Colman of Hingham to become their minister, but under such circumstances that it was declined. Mr. Colman was settled at the time over the Third society in that town; and a considerable number of influential members of this society regarded that which is now so common and so little questioned, the inviting of a settled minister by another church, as a breach of christian comity and good fellowship; and for that reason some resisted the action of the church and society in the matter and others took no part in the vote. A committee previously appointed for the purpose had, however, solicited the opinions "of the principal officers of the University at Cambridge and some of the most eminent clergymen of Boston" upon the question; and they reported unanimously, as the result of their inquiry, that the invitation could be extended "with propriety" and "with honor."

Five years after, Mr. Colman having left his parish in Hingham and a portion of the First Parish in this town having endeavored unsuccessfully to settle him as a colleague with their aged pastor, Rev. Dr. Prince, a new society was formed, principally from his friends in the First and North Church congregations, taking the name of the Independent Congregational Society in Barton Square, of which he became the first minister.

For a time the division of feeling, caused by the attempt to settle Mr. Colman and its failure, had a disturbing and depressing effect upon the harmony of the society. But within some six or eight months, fortunately, the minds and desires of the people centred with unanimity upon a gentleman who accepted their invitation and on the 14th of November, 1820, was ordained their minister and held the pastoral office for more than a quarter of a century and till his death, which occurred on the 26th of February, 1846,— John Brazer.

The period of Dr. Brazer's ministry was one of highest prosperity to this society, measuring prosperity by those tests which are most readily discernible; it was strong in numbers, ample and liberal in resources, united in action and attentive to the ministrations of the pulpit,— attentive because interested in them.

I know that to the severe judgment and sensitive spirit of the minister himself it often seemed otherwise. He deplored the little effect that his preaching seemed to produce. He estimated his success to be most moderate. He saw more distinctly what he had hoped to accomplish that had not been realized, than what he had done. But I take the judgment of those best qualified to say how it was and those facts I take which have their own voice, requiring no interpreter.

In speaking of the condition of the society while under his charge, I feel that I am so largely illustrating his work and the nature and extent of his influence that I need not attempt to separate them.

Thus it was, then, that the preaching of Dr. Brazer attracted hearers to his church, not by the surprises and excitements of a highly wrought oratorical manner, nor by rhetorical brilliancy, but by its ability, directness and power. It was marked by deep seriousness and by the grave dignity of the preacher's bearing and address; by the proofs of careful learning and studious preparation; by the clearness of his statements and the closeness and force of his reasonings, while all was presented in a style so conscientiously transparent and simple, that any mind capable of taking the thought was not hindered by ambitious phraseology, or obscure constructions, or confusing images.

Better than this, the honest hearer felt that he was honestly dealt with; that here the most difficult and most important office of the christian preacher was fulfilled, that, namely, of the monitor and quickener of the conscience and the faithful exactor of righteousness.

His preaching in the earlier part of his ministry, adapting itself to the state of religious thought and inquiry of the time, was more in the direction of doctrinal instruction for which his natural powers of mind, his strength in argument and his studious habits excellently qualified him. But, earlier and later, it was the natural tendency of his mind and moral nature, ever stirred by a quick religious sensibility, to give prominence to themes bearing upon personal conduct, the communings of faith and the soul's culture. To this, living witnesses can speak and the remembered voices of the dead bring testimony.

The venerated Judge Samuel Putnam of the Supreme Court of Massachusetts, in requesting a dismission of himself, wife and daughter to the church under the care of Rev. Dr. Lowell in Boston, in 1834, accompanied the request with expressions of grateful obligation to the pastor of this church, "for the very able and faithful manner in which you [he] have [had] discharged the arduous and very difficult duties of pastor and teacher," adding, "I desire also to manifest the deep interest which I now and ever shall have, for the peace and prosperity of the church and society, with which, for a great number of years, we have worshipped." No better testimony to the power and the elevated character of Dr. Brazer's ministrations could be adduced, than the character of the men whom he drew together to his instructions from Sunday to Sunday. Judges Putnam and Story and Cummins; Leverett Saltonstall, Col. Benjamin Pickman (the third in lineal descent who bore the title), Ichabod Tucker, John G. King and Frederic Howes; not to mention others less widely known, but scarcely less strong and disciplined in thought; trained minds like these; seekers for truth and its loyal followers like these, found here the wise and ripe teaching that carried them forward and helped them to be "men in understanding," while they heard also such an uncompromising summons to fidelity, as deepened their sense of accountableness for the right and religious use of every talent and ability they possessed.

But higher testimony than theirs have we to the pastor's faithful execution of his Master's commission, coming from an humbler class, who testify that to the poor the gospel was preached; preached not alone in words of hope and good cheer and unfaltering faith, but in acts of timely helpfulness and an ever open-handed bounty. Dr. Brazer performed well that delicate, but most christian and important duty of the minister, of bringing the rich and poor into closer sympathy and mutual regard; this, by the habit of bringing to the knowledge of the rich the opportunity and duty of doing good by their wealth among the unfortunate and needy and by acting as the almoner of the beneficent. It has been my privilege since I have entered upon these walks of ministerial service which he so long and so unostentatiously pursued, to hear many expressions of gratitude from lips now silent, and to come upon proofs at humblest firesides that there his memory is reverently and lovingly cherished.

As a visitor of the sick and a consoler and helper of those in trouble, he carried a quick and unfailing sympathy to the homes of his people. If he must fail to see any in his pastoral visits with as much frequency as he or they desired, it was the prosperous and happy, not the suffering, who waited for him to come.

Whether as preacher or pastor, he could not but be in earnest and impressive; indeed I know not where the qualities of the preacher which he exemplified have been better set forth than in his own words; or where the qualities which he set forth in words have been better exemplified than in himself.

In a sermon at the ordination of my friend who sits near, and a child of the North Church (Rev. Jonathan Cole), from the text "fervent in spirit," he says among other things worth quoting if there were time; "great results are sacrificed in a studied attention to details,— powerful impression in a pursuit of the minor graces of diction; the benefit of the many in an excessive deference to the refined taste of the few. Anything almost that has pith and point is better than this sentence-making, this tame and lifeless rhetoric." "Nor will the preacher, who feels the true dignity and importance of his office, freeze his words as they fall from his lips by his own apparent indifference to their import, or permit them to vibrate in a sleepy cadence, or to sink into a drowsy monotony. Nor when he speaks of themes that should strike and rouse the soul, will he speak as if he were performing a set task, but as if he were moved by a strong impulse to speak."

Once only I heard Dr. Brazer preach, in my youth, in the college chapel at Cambridge; and with what impression of his effectiveness in the pulpit is best attested by the fact that not only his fine dignity and enchaining earnestness of manner are well remembered, but that the lesson of the hour has not faded away in these thirty intervening years.

I am not ignorant of certain temperamental qualities, which at times interfered to some extent with an easy, free and close communion between Dr. Brazer and his people. He is pictured to me as a man by nature diffident and sensitive; not always accessible and at ease, and ready in conversation in all companies; and of a nervous excitability, perhaps, which made it difficult for him sometimes, not to betray those disturbances of feeling and changes of mood, of which others have no experience, or if they have them, which they are able to hide from notice. Of these little infelicities, comparative strangers, and those who knew him only superficially, sometimes made too much. But those who knew him more closely and sympathized more fully with his deeper spirit and controlling purpose, found them no bar nor embarrassment to their intercourse and communion with him, if indeed they saw them. In truth it is to be said of him, that they, who stood closest to him, knew him best, worked with him most intimately, and were themselves the most exacting judges of purity of character and personal fidelity, were the ones who most esteemed him and confided in him, and paid to him their most valued respect and affection.

Dr. Brazer I judge to have been, by mental constitution and habit, a conservative in his views of truth, his regard for ancient custom, his idea of the right social order, progress and reform. In the theological discussions of his time within his own denomination, he leaned to the old school rather than the new. As to the question of slavery and political changes in general, he shrank from disturbing existing foundations, and held by the conclusions of the past and fixed, rather than trust to the sea of the unknown and encounter the dreaded dangers of revolution.

His health began to fail, sensibly, as early as 1843, and he experienced much suffering; but he continued in the discharge of his duties till the first of the year 1846, when, on the first Sunday of the year, he preached his last sermon, from the text: "Whatsoever a man soweth that shall he also reap;" spoken of by those who heard it as "pervaded by a spirit of tenderness altogether beyond what was usual in his public services."

He left his home and people on the 19th of January, for a journey to the South, hoping that rest and change of climate would restore him. His illness was not considered as threatening a fatal result, and for a little while he seemed better; but he died at the house of a friend and classmate, near Charleston, S. C., on the 26th of February, 1846.*

I shall pursue the annals of our church and society no farther. I have reached the period of living ministers and of events remembered by the men of young and middle age to-day. To give more completeness to the record, I simply mention that Dr. Brazer was succeeded in the pastorship of this society by Mr. Octavius B. Frothingham of Boston,

---

* Mr. Brazer was born in Worcester, Mass., Sept. 21, 1789, graduated from Harvard College in 1813 with the highest honors of his class; was afterwards tutor and professor of Latin in the college, which honored him in 1836 with the degree of S. T. D. He died at the plantation of Dr. Benjamin Huger, in South Carolina, at the age of 56 years, 5 months.

who was ordained, March 10, 1847, and continued in the ministry here till April 9, 1855, when he resigned his charge to enter upon a new and wider field near, and soon within, the city of New York. Rev. Charles Lowe was installed pastor of this society on the 27th of September of the same year, and was compelled by ill health to withdraw from this ministry on the 28th of July, 1857. The present minister was installed June 5, 1859.

It has seemed convenient to divide the historical review we have taken into the periods of ministerial service, and the ministers themselves have stood out somewhat conspicuously in the sketch.

It would be interesting, if there were time for it, to make more full reference to others, men and women, whose part in the support and direction of the affairs of the society has been most important. Such as have not only kept up good courage in the minister by a ready seconding, but have done distinct and positive service in their own different ways besides; in Sunday School and choir, and in nameless ways, such as a man or woman of force and wisdom, who wishes to sustain and strengthen a church and do good, easily finds. A society is strong, and makes its power felt, in proportion as it has such members. It is feeble, without character, and of little influence, in proportion as it has them not. This society has never been without such a membership. The list of those whose active usefulness came within the first three-fourths of the century would be long. I have named several of them already, though not with the fulness of delineation which their liberality, constancy and efficiency would warrant. That family of Pickmans, for example. From the day when the church was formed, at the house of the first Col. Benjamin Pickman, to this, it has given the support of wealth, intelligence, character, and religious interest to this church. One of his sisters, at least, and two, it is believed, the widow of George Curwen and the wife of Ebenezer Ward, were original members of the society. Three grown-up sons, Benjamin, junior, William and Clarke Gayton, in the full maturity of their manhood, came with the father and mother and were, from the start of the enterprise, efficient coöperators in its establishment. Of the next generation was the third Col. Benjamin, the grandson of the first; lawyer, merchant, honored and respected citizen, Representative in Congress, liberal and enlightened Christian; and who, as president of the Board of Directors of the Theological School at Cambridge, gave the address at the laying of the corner-stone of the Divinity Hall in that place, and is remembered by those of you who have attained middle age, as having died here not quite thirty years ago. He was said by his pastor at that time to have been "a devoted friend of this church and society, where he has worshipped ever since they were founded." And his descendants are still with us. Of the same generation with him, and grandson likewise of the first Col. Benjamin, was the late Hon. Dudley L. Pickman, long a true friend of the society and whose descendants are still among the worshippers here. And so, too, are descendants of Clarke Gayton Pickman enrolled among the members of this congregation to-day.

I cannot trace every household minutely. I must not pass, without an additional word, however, Dr. Holyoke, a middle-aged man when this church was formed, and who lived to render it constant and valuable service for fifty-six years afterwards; one of its ruling elders for forty-five years; one of the committee chosen to build the first meeting-house; forty years an active member of the Standing Committee of the Proprietors; the first person on whom Harvard College conferred the degree of Doctor of Medicine; who, at one time, said there was not then a house in this town, to which he had not been called on some professional duty; who for many years stood at the preacher's right hand in the pulpit, on account of the deafness which, in his advanced years, prevented his hearing at the distance of his pew.*

I have already mentioned Deacon Samuel Holman, who held the office of deacon or ruling elder—a part of the time both—from the foundation of the church to the time of his death, fifty-three years; a member of the Standing Committee of the Proprietors thirty-six years; and Joshua Ward, chosen with John Nutting a ruling elder when the church was formed; Francis Cabot, during the earliest years of the society, a liberal member and an active officer in the management of its affairs; Jacob and Susannah Ashton, of whom I hear mention made as "pillars of the church," he, chosen a ruling elder fifty years ago; the brothers, Deacons Elijah and Jacob Sanderson, the first the elder brother, but the younger deacon; several among the more eminent lawyers of Essex County, and judges of the courts of Massachusetts and of the United States I have named before as worshipping here—Putnam and Tucker and Story and Saltonstall and

---

* Dr. Holyoke was known repeatedly to make a hundred professional visits in a day. But, extensive as his practice became at the height of his professional distinction, he acquired practice so slowly in the beginning, that he thought seriously at one time of leaving Salem for some more encouraging opening. It is recorded of him that "from the time he began his medical practice until his death, a period of nearly eighty years, he has never been absent from this town at a greater distance than thirty miles."

Cummins and King and Howes — and I mention their names again that I may take occasion to say that none of them were worshippers or hearers and nothing more, but that nearly all of them were found serving upon committees, and evincing their interest in other ways, in the welfare of the society, and their acceptance of the responsibility which membership in it involved. Ichabod Tucker's house was as well known to ministers as if it had been the house of a brother minister. His hospitality was wide and generous. He was a free, earnest and fearless inquirer into religious truth. He took a deep interest in the preaching of a liberal gospel, such as was represented by this church, and the society had in him a warm friend and steadfast supporter during a long life.

The name of Leverett Saltonstall I must not pass without recalling the long and faithful service he rendered here. Never pleading the engrossment of higher responsibilities, or more important cares elsewhere, numerous and exacting as his professional cares and public responsibilities often were, he was the trusted, willing and wise fellow-worker with the minister in all his labors. He was the devoted, punctual, and careful superintendent of the Sunday School; an attentive member of the choir; a sagacious adviser and an active worker in all christian and philanthropic measures; ready whenever the church, or the cause of truth, or the needs of humanity laid a claim upon him. And I might continue with a list of liberal-minded merchants and prospered business men, now gone, who have given of their means and of their willing helpfulness to this church from its beginning. Of the earlier I have named the chief; I might mention more, the Wests and Gardners, Joseph Peabody, Ichabod Nichols,

Gideon Tucker and others. It were well worth while, if there were time, to speak of the women also, whose intelligent interest in christian studies, and whose philanthropic impulses have here raised and kept high, the standard of educated reflection, religious thought, and earnest living; such women as Miss Burleigh, the Misses Ashton, Miss Plummer, Mrs. Nathaniel Peabody and the Misses Savage,— to mention no more.

Many of you have listened, very likely, for names which you have not heard, but which you expected to be called, when the story of the North Church was to be told. But I have intended no complete enumeration; far from it. I have written down some of those names which I found recorded, or have heard about and known familiarly, especially among the oldest and the first, for their being at the founding of the church, or early in the counsels of our fathers, and foremost at the business of church building here.

One characteristic of this society I have already noticed as appearing during the ministry of Dr. Barnard, which, I think, can be traced throughout its history; a true catholicity of spirit, showing itself in a uniform hospitality for various opinion, and a disposition to judge men by the standard of character rather than that of creed; adopting, indeed, the standard of Jesus; "by their fruits ye shall know them."

I have said that Dr. Barnard exemplified this spirit. Whatever his own creed—and every man has a creed—he would as little have thought of requiring another to have the same, as he would suffer another to require conformity in him. His protest against church assumptions and individual dogmatizing was constant and effective. He demanded freedom

for all. His sermon at the ordination of Mr. Bancroft in
Worcester was a just expostulation against the irrational attempt to bring free minds, earnest in the pursuit of truth,
all to like conclusions and a level sameness in their specula-
tions; and against the wrong done to truth, and to the soul
itself, by enforced uniformity.

This spirit has been kept alive in this church, I believe, all
along its way, and was never more truly characteristic than
to-day.

I suppose it is true that the prevailing thought of the
society, and the general color of its tendencies and prefer-
ences, whether relating to social, political, or religious
questions, have been what would be called conservative;
the more honorable and noble, therefore, its devotion to
intellectual freedom and mental integrity, and its careful and
jealous maintenance of the right and duty of private judgment, and of fidelity to the individual conscience.

Let me not claim too much. I do not claim that this was
an absolute and perfect catholicity, or even a toleration without inconsistency or flaw. The passions and prejudices of the
hour always ebb and flow through church doors, as elsewhere.

When the First Baptist society was about to settle its first
minister, Rev. Mr. Bowles, in January, 1805, I find it upon
the record that they asked for the use of the North Meeting
House for the services of his ordination; and it was granted.
But the newspapers* tell me that our neighbors went, after
all, to the Tabernacle Church for their service. Was it
because they learned that the vote opening the North
Church to them showed twelve dissentients? At any rate,
let us not hide it that such was the fact.

---

* "Salem Gazette," Jan. —, 1805.

I find upon the outside of a pamphlet in the library of the Essex Institute—the proprietors' record makes no allusion to it, though the statement must be received as none the less authentic—that the use of the church was solicited for the funeral solemnities which were to be observed in Salem, on the death of the American officers, Capt. James Lawrence and Lieut. Augustus C. Ludlow, who lost their lives in the engagement between the frigates Shannon and Chesapeake off this coast on the first of June, 1813. "The use of the North Meeting House was requested," says the note of Mr. Crowninshield, "because it has many advantages over every other in town, particularly on account of its size and the fine organ which it contains." The committee of the proprietors made answer that they "had no authority to open the house for any other purpose than for public worship." And it was true that a vote stood on the proprietors' book "that the house should be opened only for public worship." But it had been before, and was afterwards, opened on many public days, and if the proprietors had been as generally democratic in politics as they were federalists, there is little reason to doubt that the committee could have found sufficient authority for granting its use on this occasion.

In the period of its later history, a period of unexampled latitude of inquiry, I believe that the living ministers who have served in this place will bear their united testimony that, diverse as have been their own interpretations of truth and duty, and their administration of the Teacher's office, and with whatever of individual objection their instruction upon any theme may have been received, that objection has seldom taken the form of an expressed wish, or *consent*, even, that the minister should be guided by any conclusion but his own; and the general voice has been clearly, unmistakably, constantly encouraging to entire loyalty to every innermost and fixed conviction.

Conservative, if this church has been, after a sort, it has always had its pioneers searching forward with earnest questionings into the new fields of religious truth. Samuel Curwen was a Unitarian in 1775-6, when the society generally were not. Ichabod Tucker and Frederic Howes were free critics, in 1815, of the phraseology of the covenant of 1773, and of many points in the prevalent theology of the day, long before these had been generally abandoned. And I need not tell you what a kindly shelter this church has given to all serious and reverent questioning, however free, in these later years.

It is my joy, my pride—I hope not an unpardonable pride—that I can bear this testimony; that this society seems to have had and to have that steadiness and patient self-possession, which comes from freedom only; from courage to prove all things; which has come, I may say, from an experience more than commonly wide and instructive; from having a faith that has been made to know the strength of its own rooting; and has found it too deep and fast to be torn away by the conflicts of opinion; a faith which sinks past and below all human opinions, including its own; sinks into the spirit of God and so beds itself in the life eternal, that it has no fear that it can ever be moved.

He was a true prophet, I like to think, who wrote of you once: "Animated by a spirit of conservatism which does not dread reform, and by a liberality which is also cautious and wise, you will help to guide the progress in whose advantages you will share."*

We say sometimes that the future is not within our control. Spoken of the future event, in its detail of form and time and order, this is true. But of each future seen as revealing the persistency of forces that are never idle; seen as a stream flowing unbroken from the fountain of past causes lying deep in the recesses of the human will and the human motive, each future thus stamped with a distinct character of its own, and having a manifest unity with its own past; seen as such, nothing is plainer than that each future, say our future, is largely within the directing will of the souls standing on their own ground and on their own feet to-day; for that Providence which we recognize in history makes use at every stage of the free human will, and works through it, on towards its own unchanging ends.

We can see that the beginning of these hundred years was charged largely with the very religious thought and life that constitute the life-blood of the best being and activity of this hour. We hope there is growth and believe there is; but it is the same tree.

As surely is it in our power to pass down to the children of that generation which shall occupy our places a hundred years forward such a positive, strong, vital current of religious energy, prophetic fire and courage, moral sturdiness and irrepressible seekings for the face of God and the well-being of mankind, as shall then be traceable back to this day.

We study history, in part to learn how to make it, and in

---

* Rev. James Freeman Clarke, in a letter declining an invitation to the pastorship of the society.

part to learn how to be made use of by it; how to discover its lines of movement, that we may fall in with them and be wrought humbly into its sublime and endless building.

> "The new is old, the old is new,—
>
> * * * * * * *
>
> The eternal step of progress beats
> To that great anthem, calm and slow,
> Which God repeats!
>
> Take heart!— the Waster builds again,—
> A charmed life old goodness hath;
> The tares may perish,— but the grain
> Is not for death."

EXERCISES

AT

NORMAL HALL,

INCLUDING

ADDRESSES

AND

CORRESPONDENCE.

EXERCISES AT NORMAL HALL.

After the exercises at the church, the members of the North society with their invited guests assembled at Normal Hall on Broad street, for a collation and social entertainment, the hall being opened to them for the occasion by the courtesy of Professor D. B. Hagar, Principal of the State Normal School, and with the consent of the Committee of the State Board of Education having charge of the building.

The tables were laid with elegance and abundance by Mr. E. P. Cassell, and were decorated with flowers in great profusion and variety.

Shortly after two o'clock the President, the Hon. GEORGE B. LORING, called the company to order, and asked their attention while the Rev. J. T. HEWES, of the First Church, invoked the divine blessing, as follows:—

Our Heavenly Father, we thank Thee for all Thy gifts. We thank Thee that we are permitted to gather here upon this memorable occasion and unite our hearts, our sympathies and our memories in one common feast of thought. We pray Thee, bless this occasion unto us all, bless all connected with our churches, and all the families who are represented here to-day. Bless also the memories of those who have gone from our sight, but whose memory and character we cherish in our hearts at this time, and may we feel it is good for us to have come here, and may its influence go with us throughout our lives. We ask all this as disciples of Jesus Christ, Thy Son. Amen.

After an hour spent in festivity, the President, Dr. LORING commenced the intellectual exercises of the occasion with the following address:—

ADDRESS OF THE HON. GEO. B. LORING.

I assume the duties which have been assigned me on this occasion, my friends, with mingled emotions, with a crowd of various memories and with renewed respect for all the associations, old and new, by which, in my mind, the North Church in Salem is surrounded. Although my connection with this society is of comparatively short duration, I cannot remember the time, when its name did not convey to me the thought of a warm religious faith, great integrity and ardent devotion to the best purposes of life. Born among the theological incidents of Essex County, in one of its most theological towns, and in the midst of some of its warmest theological endeavors, taught at my father's fireside to know the sacrifices of the New England clergy, and called upon to listen to the traditions of Liberal Christianity here, I can never forget the imposing attitude in which this church stood before my youthful mind, with its scholarly pastor and his cultivated flock. To my ancestors, of all the generations that I ever knew, the name of the North Church was sacred. And I now hold and prize, as a precious family inheritance, the well-read Bible and devotional volumes, which consoled and comforted the founders of this church and their fathers before them. This occasion, therefore, is to myself full of interest.

But to you also who sit here, indeed to all the thoughtful and devoted Christians of this christian community, this event is interesting and suggestive. A century of the deepest thought, the boldest speculation, the most vigorous action, the most rapid change, the most thorough and permanent progress, we trust, constitutes the lifetime of this church. In the great efforts and events of that period of time just now closing, the worshippers here have, in various ways, performed an important part. The severity of the first collision between the patriots of the Revolution and their oppressors was modified by the soothing and conservative words of your first pastor; it was a child baptized at this altar, who, in manhood, sustained the honor of Massachusetts in her early political struggles; it was the bold and stalwart and sagacious pillars of this church, who established the early commercial renown and prosperity of this city; and to the statesmanship and jurisprudence of our land, have its pious sons made liberal and valuable contributions. Not always revolutionary perhaps, it has always been faithful and prudent and wise. Open-minded at least, when not restless nor audacious, it presents an admirable illustration of the power of a charitable religious faith to remove all obstacles to man's advancement, from the repose of conservatism to the vigorous and somewhat uneasy ways of even healthy reform. And while it has held that intimate relation to the highest mental and material effort of its century of life to which I have referred, it enjoys the remarkable distinction of having furnished, in its infancy, Armenianism and pacification to the councils of the first war for American freedom and, in the strength of its manhood, Unitarianism and a chaplain to the service of the last; illustrating, in this way if in no other, its capacity for progress, and its growth in vigorous thought and valuable endeavor. That it has discharged its duty well, therefore, who can doubt? That it has performed its part in the great work of liberalizing the christian faith, and warming the christian heart, and enlarging the christian mind, and making wide the entrance to the christian church, as it has passed on from the formalities and fears of its first pastor to the mild courage, and solicitous liberality and abiding faith and practical philanthropy, which characterize him who now fills the place once occupied by Barnard and Abbot and Brazer and Frothingham and Lowe, in its progress "from strength to strength," let us all believe, and remember with pride and inspiration.

Prepared for each advancing occasion, by that liberal christian faith, which recognizes the mercy as well as the justice of the

Almighty Father, and true to that broad charity which, founded on divine love, looks with a forgiving eye on human infirmity, what a parochial paradise the North Church has been, from the beginning of its century until now! From its sacred walls no pastor has yet been driven. Fortunate, I know, in its selections, it has, I am sure, exercised all the kindness and consideration which a pastor could desire and, as a natural and consequent reward, its people have received the best its pastors could bestow. While I cannot for one moment believe that this record will either embolden the pastors or embarrass the people who come after us, I trust it will serve to teach a lesson of mutual responsibility, and of that gentleness towards each other's faults, and regard for each other's virtues, which can alone make a really high-toned christian society, and secure and develop a really useful parish minister.

And now, my friends, what a dear and sacred procession passes before us! Oh! that we could recall for one moment that sainted assembly, to whose entrance to the heaven of peace and rest, this church was the shining portal! As we gather around their altar and our own, what a pure and radiant company surrounds us, the old and the young, the strong and the gentle, dearer than ever now that they are free from the tarnish of earth, and now that they beckon us on to their blissful abode. Time and the centuries may make more illustrious records, but none so tender, none so exalting as the chapter of joys and sorrows, of conflicts and victories, written by a christian church in the life and labor of a hundred years. There may be more stirring annals, but there are none more purifying and ennobling than those which tell of a pastor's devotion and a people's love; of the heroism of the suffering and bereaved; of the power of great faith and trust in God; of the sweet associations which surround the altar; of that sublime aspiration which, rising above the conflicts of opinion, builds a broad and universal church on earth and rejoices that there is but one congregation in heaven; of that spiritual and triumphant church, whose corner-stone is the " charity " which " never faileth." To the future of the North Church we submit this as the lesson of the past, while we pray for the prosperity of that Zion of charity and love, which shall be "the joy of the whole earth."

And now, my friends, I know of no occasion in which a people like ourselves are not happy to greet the muse. We have a church poet among us, and I call upon the Rev. CHARLES T. BROOKS, who will now read to you a poem. Mr. Brooks then read the following

RHYMED REMINISCENCES.

Is there a place, in these impetuous times,
For sentimental, retrospective rhymes?
Will the express train of this rushing age
Accommodate a floral pilgrimage?
Can Poetry or Piety beguile
The iron car of Fate to stay awhile,
And let its favored prisoners pause an hour
To rock in Fancy's barge, or rest in Memory's bower?

There are, who say, In this new morning's blaze,
Why rake amidst the dust of buried days?
Not in that heap shall truth, the diamond, lie,
The future shows it sparkling in the sky!
On! is the word; — your antiquarian lore
Is idle, childish pastime — nothing more!
Heed not the tale, O friends! a larger thought
To musing souls by earth and sky is taught.

The modern traveller in his dizzying car
Sees calmly that alone which lies afar:
To scan the nearer things he vainly tries —
They speed too fast for his bewildered eyes.
Relieved, his vision rests where, far and fair,
The landscape stretches in serener air.
How oft my heart leaped up with mute delight,

When, as a boy, I journeyed home at night,
To see, while trees and lights behind us fled,
The moon and stars ride with us overhead.
So with the things of time — like dreams they glide —
The eternal things are ever at our side.
The present moments sparkle, fade and flee —
The past is part of God's eternity.

Once, in a tropic clime, I sailed away
From a steep coast across a tranquil bay,
When lo! behind the fast receding shore,
Up rose the inland hills, and more and more
Lifted their greeting summits, green and clear,
And made the friendly land seem following near
So, as we voyage o'er the sea of time,
The past looms up, mysterious and sublime,
Lifts its fair peaks into the tranquil sky,
And with its greeting, follows as we fly.

When summer-nightfall veils the landscape o'er,
From upland meadow to the murmuring shore,
How sweet, to men who sail the darkling seas,
Low voices borne from land on evening's breeze!
So from afar, o'er Memory's mystic deep,
Like sounds from home, melodious whispers creep,
Of souls that wait on some far inland shore
To welcome back long absent friends once more.
Oft on the sea of life these tones we hear,
That make that distant shore seem strangely near.
A spirit's breath is in the quivering breeze
That sweeps the invisible wind-harp of the seas;
A spirit's voice breathes out a plaintive strain,
With sweetest cadence in each sad refrain;
A song of songs, where all the heart has known
Of grief or gladness blends in every tone.

"Dame Memory," (so majestic Milton sings,
In speech that like a silver trumpet rings)—
"Dame Memory and her siren daughters"— nay —

No flattering, false, deceptive sirens they!
Though oft across life's waves their mournful smile
The pilgrim's fond, reverted glance beguile,
Though, by the magic of their soothing strain,
Springs tender pleasure from remembered pain,
Though, over days that faded long ago,
Their tender music flings a moonlight glow,
That moon with no delusive glory gleams;
Forth from a hidden sun that lustre streams,
And every joy that has been, prophesies
Of bliss that shall be in unfading skies.

O pale and pensive Memory! thou, no less
Than Hope, thy sister, art a prophetess!
Men picture thee alone amidst thy dead,
In fruitless wailing o'er the days long fled,
With tearful eyes that passionately yearn
To wake a life that slumbers in the urn;
While bright-eyed Hope with sun-tipped pinion flies
To hail the life new-streaming from the skies.
Young Hope — Old Memory: so the poets feign;
But is it so? Are not these daughters twain
Of God, like those two sons of light, twin-born —
The Star of evening and the Star of morn?
And what though Hesper in the sunset skies
Looks a mute solace for the day that dies,
Doth not that gracious herald point the way
To ever-dawning, never-dying day?
Aye, Memory *hopes* — she hopes and prophesies;
Of life eternal she too testifies;
She is the evening star whose tender light
Heralds the day of God, that knows no night;
The farewell smile of day in western skies
Greets the far East, where soon the sun shall rise.

Hope — Memory — blessed pair! how sweetly gleams
O'er life the lustre of their mingling beams!
There comes, e'en here on earth, full many an hour,
When, by the stress of thought's transfiguring power,

Some joy or sorrow, with absorbing sway,
Swells to an age the limits of a day:
And lo! the sun stands still o'er Gibeon,
While softly, from the veil of Ajalon,
The lingering moon looks forth — and moon and sun
Like rose and lily, weave their lights in one;
Moonrise and sunset — Hope and Memory — blend
To make the Heavenly day that knows no end.

The past is not all *passed*, not wholly dead!
Our life still echoes to its voice and tread.
The soul awakes — and lo! like phantoms glide
The living shapes that bustle at our side;
The while our *dead* dwell on an inner mount,
Made green forever by the living fount,
Where this imposing world's tumultuous roar
Dies in faint murmurs on an inland shore.

What is your boasted Present Hour, and where?
Ye seek to clutch it, and it is not there!
The Past, the Future — these, in friendly strife,
Make the perpetual present of our life.
On that vast sea, the rushing flood of Time,
Where ages, years and moments sink and climb,
'Twixt the last ridge and the next moment's brow
Comes the brief instant dreamy souls call *now*,
And deem a foothold firm to stand upon;
Yet, ere the mind can grasp it, it is gone!
The only true and real *now* abides
On the soul's rock above the rushing tides:
That Mount of Vision, where from Memory's mien
The veil falls off, and Hope's own eyes are seen.

The Past is nothing, sayst thou? Rather say,
The Past is everything; naught else shall stay.
For hear this truth, O soul, by reason taught,
And heed this truth, O man, with wisdom fraught:
The Past, one day, all Time shall gather in;
What has been, **is**; what will be, will have been.

O friends, who gather here this festal day,
On Memory's altar pious gifts to lay,
Say, do your hearts confess, the Past is dead?
That aught once precious to the soul has fled?
Oh no! the good old times, the good old men,
If once they seemed to perish, live again.
The men of reverent soul and thoughtful mind,
They have not passed away and left behind
Their name and memory only here below;
Their presence fills our hearts with kindling glow.
The white haired sires who rose on childhood's eyes,
Like hoary mountain peaks in purer skies,
That seemed in august majesty to stand
And catch the vision of the promised land —
Those old white heads — like lamps of lambent light,*
Pillars of fire to guide through this world's night,
The eyes of love that on our childhood smiled,
The lips of wisdom, faithful, firm and mild,
The careful hands that led our wayward feet,
Morning and evening greetings, soft and sweet,
These are not lost, these have not vanished; no!
They were no cunning juggler's mimic show!
Parents, preceptors, pastors, were a line
Of Prophets pointing to the Love Divine:
A group of shining ones — no shadowy band,
Still beckoning onward to the sunny land,
Where still they walk, arrayed in robes of white,
And bid us with them walk the fields of light.

To-day how real and how fresh appears
The faded history of a hundred years!
A hundred years! — though few the living men,
Whose memory runs through threescore years and ten,
Yet we, who haply in our boyhood saw
The old *centennial men*, with wondering awe,

---

* I think this comparison is a reminiscence from one of Theodore Parker's printed prayers.—C. T. B.

Saw in their eyes, and seem e'en now to see,
The lifetime of a former century.

We see thy new-cut frame, "Old North," arise;
We hear thy new-hung bell salute the skies,
We see the manly Barnard's placid form
Amid the Revolution's gathering storm.
Hark to the roll of Sabbath breaking drums!
Up Lynde street now the bristling column comes
I see the startled congregation pour,
Curious and anxious, from each swarming door.
Men, women, children, parson in his gown,
All to the river-side are hurrying down,
And there is seen a sight I wonder much
Has tempted no historic painter's touch.
This way and that the fiery colonel flies,
With flashing sword and fury flashing eyes;
Our placid, kindly pastor stands the while,
Aplomb, with quiet words and quiet smile,
Helping right well the *logic of events*
Across the river with his calm good sense.
For lo! that side the stream is played the game
McFingal's muse has handed down to fame.
For neither blood-red coats nor bloody threats,
Nor brandished swords, nor gleaming bayonets
On foemen's guns can strike with proper awe
Those daring boys astride the bridge's draw,
Who, mindful of the ancient saw, *before*
The horse was stolen, shut the stable door,
And when the iron prey he sought is gone,
Will let the *seizer* cross his Rubicon.

Old North! thy tender years were then but three;
War rocked the cradle of thy infancy.
Who is there living now that saw that day,
Heard that first muttering of the coming fray?
That congregation God has gathered in,
Where shall be heard no more earth's battle din.
Gone is the house of God that felt the jar,

That Sabbath noon, of War's approaching car.
Gone? nay, its place shall know it never more,
Haply one day shall men in vain explore
To find the place itself where once it stood,—
Still more, a vestige of its ancient wood;
Yet through all transmigration safe to-day
Its form abides and shall abide for aye.
Where — in what realm — do still these eyes behold,
As once, with childish gaze, in years of old,
They looked upon that holy, homely place,
The old square pews and each familiar face?
Say, in what world that reverend pile still stands,
Alike defying time and human hands?
Unchanged by sudden whim or slow decay,
Lives that old house in memory's light to-day.
Oh for some Goldsmith now, in vivid hues
To paint the scenes that mock my feeble muse!
Once more, old sounding-board! reverberate
And ring and roar while thee I celebrate!
Stupendous wonder lifted up on high!
Ponderous paradox to childhood's eye!
Enormous bulk suspended in mid-air,
A sword of Damocles, by a wooden hair!
Each urchin watched with mingling hope and dread,
To see it fall plump on the parson's head!
And that dark hole beneath the pulpit stairs,
That still almost, at times, my memory scares!
What if the "tidy-man,"* bad boy! should hale
Thy trembling body to that gloomy jail!
—But soft! half lost through memory's gallery-door,
My thoughts one flying phantom half restore:
'Tis thou, old Father Boyce! risen from the dead,
The well-known old bandanna round thy head,
And the knob-headed pole — the magic wand —
The dreaded ensign of thy stern command:

---

*Corruption of *tithing-man*, the same person having, probably, once been sexton and tax-collector.

Full many an urchin of the gallery crew
Feared that long sceptre — aye, and felt it too.
Like rifle's crack I've heard the blow come down
With a sharp ring upon some culprit's crown.
— The vision fades — old Boyce slips through the door —
Another, brisker step is on the floor;
But, quick-eyed, nimble-tongued and slight of limb,
Old William Gavett was a boy to him.
Little old man, thy image leads a train
Of funny recollections through the brain.
It marks the time, when doubts began to grow,
If bodily shivers fanned the spirit's glow,
I see thee stand beside thy oven-door
With hospitable hands to feed once more
The foot-stove borne along the icy street
With its *red comfort* for maternal feet;
Where filial feet that could not touch the floor,
Dangled and kicked till the long hour was o'er,
The last prayer closed and seats slammed down again
With what queer Hood might call a *wooden Amen*.*
— Again across the field my magic glass
I slide, to let another figure pass.
What grave, gaunt form now stalks before my eye —
O prince of organ-blowers, Philip Frye!
That suit of black, that sober Sunday face,
Threw o'er thee such a sanctimonious grace,
That strangers sometimes have been known to err,
And take the blower for the minister.
— But what a change when Monday morning came!
Can this — I often wondered — be the same,
The very self-same Philip, that I meet
Mincing and simpering down through Essex street?
The long-tailed Sunday coat of black displaced
By a blue jacket of the shortest waist;
The Sunday visage too is laid aside,

---

* Hood, in his "Music for the Million," describes an angry man as slamming a door to with a *wooden Damn*.

The air of holy reticence and pride:
The Sabbath spell is off — with common men
Lo Philip is a man *— yea boy, again.
But soon as Sunday morn again comes round,
The reverend Philip at his post is found,
Where in the pauses of his holy toil,
As if anointed with invisible oil,
He looks from out his cell complacent round,
Rapt with the memory of the solemn sound,
With large, contented eyes that seem to say,—
"Have we not done the music well to-day?"
* * * * * * * * *
But tender memories rise meanwhile and cast
Their sacred shadows o'er the deathless past.
The home where first we tasted heavenly love,
The church that brought to view a world above,
To these the heart comes back, where'er we roam,
"True to the kindred points of heaven and home!"
How sweet a memory his, on whom, as child,
The gentle face of sainted Abbot smiled,
Who feels to-day, though fifty years have fled,
That hand of benediction on his head!

Ah, all too soon for us that gracious light
The veil of death removed from mortal sight —
Removed — not quenched; — from heaven, with purer beams.
Along our path through memory's air it gleams.
And many a one, whose young eyes scarcely saw
The *look* of that sweet face, for very awe,
Feels that remembered *presence*, mild and calm,
Breathe o'er his soul a summer morning balm.

Then came to us that gifted one,† whose mind,
Graced with ripe culture and with taste refined,
In fervid feeling's glow devoutly wrought
The lucid links of energetic thought.

---

* The classic allusion here will of course be understood.
† Dr. Brazer.

Well could he point with wit the shaft of truth,
Stir the ambition of ingenuous youth,
Rebuke the worldling's vain and shallow sneers,
And show Heaven's rainbow-light on sorrow's tears.

One picture waits for this poor pencil yet —
Who that beheld the sight can e'er forget? —
When, punctual as the Sunday morn appears,
That form unbowed beneath its hundred years,*
And at the pastor's side devoutly stands,
As if to hear with him the Lord's commands.
So a calm mountain rises white with snow,
While at its feet streams gush and roses glow;
The evening beams that play around its head,
On other worlds a morning-sunlight shed.
Serene old man! when sank thy honored head,
A hundred years were numbered with the dead;
As melts a snow-white foam-flake in the sea,
A century melted in Eternity.
Nay, from the sacred place where once with awe
In the prayer-hour thy aged form we saw
Stand with bowed head and reverential air,
A century still looks down upon us there,†
And with a voice of old experience cries:
Fear God, love man, be temperate, just and wise!

With thee my song shall close :— O patient friends,
'Tis well that here my broken music ends.
So its last moan the shattered sea-wave makes,
When on the monumental rock it breaks.
Haply may these poor words, my stammering tongue
Upon its native air hath freely flung,
To the rude clang of memory's wayward lyre,
In some true heart awake a smouldering fire,

---

* Dr. Holyoke, who in his last days used to stand, often even through the sermon, with his ear close to the preacher.

† "Forty centuries are looking down upon us."—Napoleon at the Pyramids.

And reëukindle there the faith sublime,
That hears through all earth's din the Eternal City's chime.

Peace to my lingering song! and peace to thee,
City of Peace! of Pilgrim memory,
Sweet home and sacred shrine, old Salem town!
Add new bright centuries to thy old renown!
Well may he be forgiven, a child of thine,
Whose hand presumptuous would to-day entwine
Amid thy chaplet green one fresh-plucked flower,
That may not long outlive the passing hour.
No words could ever give fit thanks to thee,
For all that thou hast given and been to me!
A child's warm blessing on thy fields and skies,
Thy rocky pastures dear to childhood's eyes,
Thy fresh blue waters and fair islands green,
Of many a youthful sport the favorite scene,
North Fields and South Fields — Castle Hill — Dark Lane,
And Paradise, where memory leads the train
Of her transfigured dead, whose relics lie
At rest where living waters murmur by.*
A blessing on the memory of the line
Of statesmen, saints and sages, sons of thine!
A blessing, last of all, on thee, old North!
From thee may Peace and Love and Light stream forth!
May Learning and Religion, Grace and Truth,
Shed here the glory of perennial youth!
May Faith and Freedom here join hand in hand
To lead thy children to the promised land!
Dear city of our fathers! may their God
Still guide and comfort with the staff and rod,
And in the cloud and fire lead onward still
Our faltering footsteps up the heavenly hill!

The President then called upon the Rev. S. C. BEANE, of the East Church, to read the first hymn in the programme. That

---

* In the beautiful cemetery of Harmony Grove, washed by the North River.

hymn, continued the President, was written by that most estimable of clergymen of whom Mr. Emerson once said that he was a man of genius, JAMES FLINT, D. D. I am fortunate in calling upon Dr. Flint's successor to read it.

The audience then united in singing the following hymn to the tune "Federal Street":—

> In pleasant lands have fallen the lines
>   That bound our goodly heritage:
> And safe beneath our sheltering vines
>   Our youth is blest, and soothed our age.
>
> What thanks, O God, to Thee are due,
>   That Thou didst plant our fathers here;
> And watch and guard them as they grew,
>   A vineyard to the planter dear.
>
> Thy kindness to our fathers, shown
>   In weal and woe through all the past,
> Their grateful sons, O God, shall own,
>   While here their name and race shall last.

THE PRESIDENT.

My friends, I think Salem is getting on famously. The tune that has just been sung was also written in Salem, by a Salem man. Beginning, therefore, with the poem by Mr. Brooks, the hymn by Dr. Flint, and the music by Gen. Oliver, I don't think Salem ought to be ashamed of herself. You have heard allusions made to Mr. Abbot. We have here a contemporary of his, who preached in his pulpit between the time of his call and his ordination, one of the most stanch and faithful ministers of the Unitarian Church — the Rev. JOSEPH ALLEN, D. D., of Northborough.

ADDRESS OF DR. ALLEN.

I have many pleasant memories connected with the good old town of Salem, and especially with the North Church, and one of its ministers. It is now almost threescore years, fifty seven years, I think, for I believe it was in 1815—that I was invited by my friend, John Emery Abbot, to supply his pulpit after he had received the call to this church, and before his ordination. It was in March and the following April that I sojourned among this people, at the house of Ichabod Tucker, well known in that day, whose hospitality I enjoyed and whose memory is dear to me, as is that of his accomplished lady and the other inmates of his family. I well knew John E. Abbot. He was my contemporary, somewhat younger than myself; but we pursued our theological studies at the same time and partially in the same place, he residing in Boston and pursuing his studies under the direction of Dr. Channing, but coming over to Cambridge frequently, and enjoying with us the wise sayings and instructions of the venerable Dr. Ware and President Kirkland. It was not long after his ordination that I was called to the town of Northborough, to be the minister of the town, not of the church. I invited my friend, John E. Abbot, to come and give me the Right Hand of Fellowship, which he accordingly did, and it is published with the other services of that occasion. Soon after his ordination his health became infirm, and at last he was obliged to relinquish his labors, which he loved so truly and which he performed so faithfully and so acceptably, and was laid upon a sick bed. I visited him in his sickness and conversed with him, when he supposed, and we all did, that there was but a step between him and the grave. I preached for him one Sabbath while he lay sick, at his request. I visited him after the services, and had a very beautiful conversation with him. I remember especially the discourse, which was not then printed, but which was given to me in manuscript, on the recognition of friends in the future life, and I thought then, and have thought since, that he was one of those I should hope to meet in that better life, to renew the acquaintance and friendship, which was so soon broken by his early death. After his decease I formed the acquaintance of his successor, Dr. Brazer, and exchanged with him several times, during his ministry. I well remember, too, the old minister of the First Church, Dr. Prince; with him also I exchanged pulpits. I do not remember his contemporary, Dr. Barnard, though I presume I often saw him at Cambridge, where ministers formerly congregated on Commencement Days. I remember on one occasion, when I went into the pulpit, I saw before me an aged man, who had come into the place that he might the better listen to my discourse, the venerable Dr. Holyoke. I came here again when he had reached the age of a hundred years, hoping to see what I never had seen, a man who had completed his century; but I learned then that he was on a sick bed. He died a few days after, and one of my sons, who was born about the time of his decease, was named for him. You will see, therefore, that I have been acquainted with Salem for more than half a century. At one time I had in my family six of the seven sons of Stephen C. Phillips, who were members of my household, and pupils under my care. I want to say in closing that I am happy to be here, that I received the invitation to be present with a great deal of pleasure, and that although I was not here at the commencement of the exercises, yet I felt a deep interest in the discourse of Mr. Willson, whom I have known for many years. It has been to me a feast of good things, and I shall always bear in remembrance this pleasant occasion.

THE PRESIDENT.

I know I speak the voice of you all, when I say to Dr. Allen that the obligation is entirely on our side. We who live in Salem, and who entertain the faith of the fathers here, as we believe it, have confidence in the law as well as in the gospel. We have the pleasure of having present with us on this occasion the president of the National Unitarian Conference, Hon. E. R. HOAR, of Concord, who, while he has assured me, that he desired to pronounce a benediction, may assure himself that we only ask his benediction, for whom he addresses must profit.

ADDRESS OF JUDGE HOAR.

MR. CHAIRMAN AND MY FRIENDS: I have nothing to say to you except to join in the benediction to which your chairman has alluded. I am sorry to say I have not yet reached the christian maturity and venerable age when it can be said of me, as perhaps might have been said of our friend who last addressed you, Dr. Allen, "his presence itself is a benediction." I have nothing to say except to offer my warm sympathy with the object of your meeting to-day, and to express to you the delight with which I have attended the services and listened to the discourse of Mr. Willson, which was charming to my ears throughout, though it rivalled the most able of his predecessor's attempts in its length, and perhaps would have shocked some of them by its wanting a text.* Why, my friends, we have of late been getting so national in our views in this country, we have had so much cause for it in one way or another that when I walked into that quiet and darkened church this morning and heard that story of New England life of a hundred years ago, I seemed to be breathing a new atmosphere. The full fragrance and flavor of New England life seemed to come back to me.

These church relations of our people, — the Established Church of Massachusetts — though as popular and absolutely democratic as any of our civil institutions, have given more to the character of New England than anything else we have had. I look some-

---

* In the delivery, the text and introductory remarks were omitted.

times with respect, sometimes with admiration, upon modern improvements. I am a friend of Sunday Schools, and I have no doubt but that they do good; but there is no Sunday School instruction that ever produces the effect upon the heart and mind of the child, that ever trains up such men and women, that ever gives such character and strength to the community, as does that attending church from early childhood, Sunday after Sunday, with father and mother, in those old square pews, better perhaps than the modern ones, under the eye of father and mother, and there acquiring the habit and feeling of reverence before the understanding can catch the import of the long sermon; and the influence of these associations has been carried westward, and thus New England character and influence have been diffused across this continent.

Your church has attained undoubtedly a very respectable age, and one that it is becoming and well to celebrate, but I almost feel, as some thoughts come across my mind, as if I was a contemporary with it. The minister under whom I grew up to manhood and who was my minister until after my marriage and I had got some way along in life, was settled over our parish only six years after your parish was founded; and the only physician I ever had occasion to employ until I had got nearly old enough or wise enough to do without them altogether was a classmate of, and of about the same age as my minister. The parish of which I am an humble representative, is two hundred and thirty-seven years old; we look upon you, therefore, nearly as a man in advanced age looks upon a hearty youth, just celebrating the attainment of his majority. You have got through the season of trial and of experiment, and may now be fairly expected to go forward and make your mark in society, and be admitted to the full responsibilities of adult years. In this conspicuous position, in this good city of Salem, which has been always so famous for the quality of its people, I have no doubt that your light will shine

like a city that is set on a hill, and that you will be as prosperous
in the future as you have been in the past. I was gratified to
hear of the condition of the society in one respect, and sympathized very strongly with you when I heard from your presiding
officer that you had never *got rid* of a minister. I believe, too,
that the strength and prosperity of a christian society is very
much promoted by regarding the relation between minister and
people as similar to that between husband and wife, as one not to
be changed; and I am happy to tell you, to encourage you in the
good work on which you have entered, that the society to which
I belong (during the two hundred and thirty-seven years of its
history), never yet parted with a minister except to the service of
his Master on high. But, my friends, this is a family gathering,
and, except for the briefest expression of sympathy and gratification, certainly no one outside your own circle has any right to
take up your time.

THE PRESIDENT.

New England has sent many influences West, many men of
many minds, and many industries, but she has sent nothing, I
think, of more value to the West than the Unitarian thought of
New England. At any rate we know of nothing more valuable.
We have here the pioneer of that service, one who, in the early
days of Unitarianism, took up his abode in the western wilds, and
has been a faithful servant there ever since. I am happy to
introduce to you the Rev. WILLIAM G. ELIOT, D. D., of St. Louis.

ADDRESS OF DR. ELIOT.

You will pardon me, dear friends, if my response is very
brief, for to tell you the truth, among these venerable antiquities
I feel that I have no place, no standing at all. It is true that
I am old enough for any purpose, and that I can remember more
than half the term of years which the North Church has lived; but

in the ecclesiastical relation, as well as in the social, I have lived all my life, I may say, in the midst of youth. I have always been with a growing community, and the church with which I am connected—it grieves me to say that I am not called its pastor now,— has had thus far but one pastorate, and the thirty-seven years of my ministry is the church's life-time; so that, far from having attained anything like a respectable old age, we are in early infancy yet. Whenever I come here to these old communities I feel lost, almost oppressed, by the steadiness, the staidishness, so to speak, of everything around me. Why, almost thirty-eight years ago, when I went to St. Louis, it was not half so big as Salem was then; now it has 350,000 inhabitants. It is all youth, it is all effervescence, it is all change, though there is a good deal of strength and manliness coming into it every day. But when I ask myself where does it come from, I feel compelled with pride to look back to these old centres of thought, to these old centres of education, these grand old centres of patriotism, and to say, it is from these that we get our life blood, it is this which is making us strong. And when you hear of the wonderful strength of that western country, never forget that it is for you still to be sending an inspiration there, so that our mind shall keep pace with our body, so that our growth shall not be only of this world, but that it shall belong more and more to the world of ideas, to the world of progressive thought; so that, in short, we shall reconstruct in the West a better New England than New England itself has ever known. Thirty-seven years ago I came to Salem, and have only been here once since, and that was twenty-five years ago, and only for two or three hours. I came, as some of you remember, to ask help to build a church in St. Louis, which you generously granted; and now, returning here after this long interval, I am glad of an opportunity of thanking you for the help you gave us in our time of need. With this expression of gratitude for the favor of so long ago, added to my thanks for a day of great enjoyment, I heartily wish you, God speed!

THE PRESIDENT.

I have no doubt when Judge Hoar alluded to the antiquity of the society at Concord and the age of his pastor, Dr. Ripley, he thought he had got Salem in a spot where it would be difficult for her to get out. Now I wish to inform him that the First Church, the mother of the North Church, is two hundred and forty-three years old, and still lives, beating the church at Concord, I am happy to say, by six years. We have, moreover, had a centenarian in our church, which I do not believe the church at Concord ever had; and I am sure that under the modern modes of life, if it never had one, it never will. Let me introduce to you one of the former pastors of the First Church in Salem, in Essex County, the first church in the centre of civilization we believe, the Rev. THOMAS T. STONE, D. D.

ADDRESS OF DR. STONE.

I am much afraid I shall be obliged to content myself with an apology, if for no other reason, that I am fearful the few words I would like to say will not be heard by the audience. I will, however, say a word which may possibly reach a few ears. I was thinking, as the possibility of being called upon occurred to me, that I should be obliged to confess that my chief affection must naturally be for the mother rather than the daughter. I have never ceased to feel a strong attachment to the First Church from the remembrance of its earlier history, from the experience which I had during my ministry there, and the friendships which were then formed, and from all the associations which have grown up with it. And this attachment to the First Church, notwithstanding it originated there, has extended through the whole city; it will remain forever in my memory. At the same time I have some recollections of the North Church. Fifty-three years ago, in the fall of the year 1819, I entered upon my senior year at

Bowdoin College, and had a friend who was brother to Mr. Soule, the present principal of Exeter Academy and at that time an assistant. I well remember one day when we were walking together, that he read to me a letter he had received from his brother at Exeter, giving an account of the death of John Emery Abbot. I may say also as a pleasant recollection of him, that some years before I entered college he had graduated there, and traditions of his pure and beautiful character were handed down to the time my college course commenced; so that really I have known him longer than most present. I remember particularly the impression left upon my mind in regard to what Mr. Soule reported as the last words he uttered,— words sanctified by the lips of him whose name it is our joy to bear — "Father, into thy hands I commend my spirit."

There is no other one, of whom I have any special knowledge, who has been in the ministry of that church before the time that I became myself connected with the First Church in this place. Since then, one of my earliest remembrances is of one who has been referred to here to-day, a friend with whom I have been in sympathy and affection during the whole period of my ministry, and whom I have retained in memory to this hour, Octavius B. Frothingham.

Like those who have spoken before, I feel I have nothing to say beyond these imperfect reminiscences, for my boyhood was spent among the hills and valleys of Oxford County, Maine, and it is not for me to say anything at all about my later years. But these very reminiscences must of course assure you, as they must remind myself, of the age to which I have reached, and of how short a time I have to pass here on earth. Not only was I born and educated in a place so remote from you, but I was born and trained in the midst of ecclesiastical associations and sympathies far from these with which I am now surrounded, so that you may consider me as one who has been imported into the ecclesiastical circle in which I now stand; and whilst I rejoice in whatever relates to truth, yet there is to me nothing so sacred as the grand assertion of spiritual freedom, of perfect, unqualified, unlimited liberty of thought; and I trust you will pardon the words of an old man just closing his course, if he urges upon all who are united in the sympathies and the remembrances which gather around this day, the importance of cleaving with unyielding tenacity, to the very last, to the great idea of freedom; never suffering it to be in the slightest degree impaired, weakened, diminished, even limited.

THE PRESIDENT.

The American Unitarian Association has done a great work in this country in the planting of churches in the new and remote sections, and in endeavoring to liberalize the thought of those young and vigorous communities. One of the most efficient agents of that association, the Rev. CHARLES H. BRIGHAM, is present with us to-day, a scholar and a teacher from whom we shall all be glad to hear.

ADDRESS OF THE REV. C. H. BRIGHAM.

Well, ladies and gentleman, or brethren and sisters rather, I suppose that would be your best title, considering that this is a religious gathering, I shall have to say, as Judge Hoar has said, that I have nothing to say, because this seems to me a time of reminiscences only, where we should tell stories about the old church. Now I would like to tell you some old stories about Mr. Barnard's ordination, but unfortunately for you I was not there, or about the little matter at the North Bridge, but unfortunately again, I was not there to see it. My recollections of Mr. Barnard are mainly in the name of a young man from Salem who was in college and whose name was Thomas Barnard West, who was a very good youth, and who was in a class which had some difficulties and troubles. But I suppose his goodness came from the name he bore. I can recollect Dr. Brazer a good many years ago. He used to exchange with Dr. Lowell, and old Dr. Lowell's people rather liked the change, for though he had a very different voice, and one to which they were not accustomed, yet he always preached good strong sermons, and made the children understand what he was talking about, and got a very strong hold upon the men and women of the church. That is the only reminiscence of the old ministers that I can give you. I can give you some valuable ones of those who have been connected with the church for twenty-five years past. Here is your pastor, with whom I am very well acquainted, and then when I was in Europe I travelled with Mr. Frothingham and with Mr. Lowe, two others of your ministers, and if there ever was a man who could calm down the quarrelling Arabs and make them behave themselves, that man was Mr. Lowe; and if there ever was an agreeable companion in Switzerland, it was Mr. Frothingham, who used to let me ride up hill while he walked, and let me walk down while he rode, which suited me very much.

I am continually reminded of Salem at the West, for just as far as your Salem is from Cambridge, just so far from the Michigan University there is a Salem. The university excels Harvard in numbers, and about once a week I see a man who comes down from Salem to talk to the boys, and tell them about his money. He gives liberally, and about the only thing he really loves to talk about is what the town of Salem did during the war, when the draft was made, and they all subscribed so liberally that there was no draft at all, and he boasts of the money he gave himself. The students there ask me about Salem, and they have an idea that there were witches in Salem at one time. Salem witchcraft is the very first idea they get hold of, and I tell them that if they want to see the witchery, they must come down here and go out on Essex street some Sunday afternoon, when all the young ladies are out, and then they will see the true witchery of the nineteenth century. Some of them, too, have an idea that there is a queer old house that everybody ought to go and see with its seven gables, and people say it is the old house of Hawthorne, and think of it sometimes as the place where a dreadful murder was once committed, but we will say nothing about that.

My friends: I have nothing left to say except to thank you and my friend Mr. Willson for the privilege of being here. If you come to Michigan, and it is a pleasant day, I will drive you to Salem, where forty or fifty years ago there were plenty of Indians, and where even to-day the bears are not all gone, but where in hard winter they sometimes unfortunately find themselves in pits and traps set for them by the inhabitants.

THE PRESIDENT.

The relations between the Unitarians of the old country and the Unitarians of this country have always been very intimate. She has furnished us with good literature and also with good men; and I congratulate you and myself that we have a gentleman here to-day who learned his first lessons in Unitarianism in England, who can tell us about the movement there, and who has furnished the literature of our denomination with a rich supply of refined thought and elevated sentiment. I present to you with great pleasure the Rev. Wm. Mountford.

ADDRESS OF THE REV. WILLIAM MOUNTFORD.

The Unitarians of England and those of America have a common ancestry, not merely as to blood, but politically and religiously. We are much more intimately connected than is commonly known. The founders of the first churches in Salem, Plymouth, Boston, Dorchester, Roxbury, were mostly of the same Puritan connection, and the same temper generally, as were the two thousand clergymen of the Established Church who, in the year 1662, forfeited their livings rather than violate their consciences, and disown the headship of Christ by submitting themselves to the act of uniformity as to public worship, which had been made law over their heads by an unscrupulous parliament and a poor, faithless, almost perjured king. It is from these men and others of like mind, that the Unitarians of England derive their religious ancestry and, very commonly also, even their lineal descent. After thirty years of grievous persecution, the people who had been ejected from their churches were allowed to build chapels for themselves; and it was their peculiarity, as distinguishing them from all other dissenters, that they deliberately and strenuously repudiated the use of a creed, or any other bond in common than acceptance of the Bible.

In so many of the earliest churches of this region, there has been a development of that spirit which was in John Robinson, at Delft-haven, when he said his last words to the future founders of Plymouth; for he spoke of his persuasion, of God's having still much fresh truth to burst forth from his Holy Word. Many more persons than did would have followed after the early settlers of New England, but they were prevented by one cause and another, and some of them by the Government, and among the latter class, it is said, was Oliver Cromwell. As compared with what their friends in England had to undergo for many long years, your forefathers had not such a very hard time, while taking possession of broad acres and getting their own way as to Church and State.

It was from England that Dr. Bentley of this city got much of his sympathy as a Unitarian, and generally it was from English writers that American divines got initiation into Unitarianism — writers, such as Hopton Haynes, the intimate friend of Sir Isaac Newton, and Duchal the preacher, with whose writings Dr. Channing was well acquainted. Dr. Franklin presented a quantity of books to some little town in New England — Franklin I think — as a public library, and of the books a curiously large proportion were theological, and of those that were theological, a striking proportion were by English Unitarians. The father of William Hazlitt was the author of two volumes of good sermons; he was a zealous Unitarian, and a great good man as to Church and State in England, by the way of opposition. For two or three years, while his son William, the celebrated essayist, was a little boy, he lived hereabouts; was familiar with Kennebunk, and preached occasionally at King's Chapel in Boston. The first christian congregation in America, gathered together as Unitarian, was in Philadelphia, and it was in connection with the preaching there, of Dr. Priestley; and of the earlier members of that congregation, several of the chief were English Unitarians. The Unitarian congregation at Washington had English people among its first members, and its first clergyman was an Englishman, who had been a Unitarian minister at Birmingham, in England. Dr. Priestley was also from Birmingham; he was, ecclesiastically, a refugee; as, in a way, was many another Unitarian, who migrated to this country between the years 1790 and 1820. Before Dr. Priestley came to this country he had been driven from Birmingham by a mob, and not without the connivance of the magistracy. His house, library and laboratory had been burned; the houses also of some of his more immediate friends; his chapel and two other places of Unitarian worship. After his expulsion from Birmingham he went to London, but there he got no peace, and it was in the bosom of Pennsylvania that he found rest at last and died. Since then, however, and recently, by the repentant public at Birmingham, and elsewhere in connection with science, monumental testimonials have been erected to his memory. Of the connection between England and the Unitarians of America, I could readily adduce many more illustrations; but from what I have said you can see, that though the Unitarians of England are, by time, but like distant cousins, yet that they and you, by origin, are of the same old household of faith. I will add one thing for its singularity. The grandfather of a schoolmate and friend of mine, Mr. Russell, was a fellow-sufferer with Dr. Priestley, and he undertook to accompany him to America; subsequently, in quieter time, he went back to Birmingham; but while he was in this country he would seem to have been much more at home, religiously, in New Haven than in any other city of New England.

Perhaps in no country in the world has there been as much improvement, ecclesiastically, as there has been in England during the last fifty years; though, to be sure, the commencement was from very low down, and from what was very bad indeed. I remember the time in England, and I was more than ten years old then, when no person could be a member of a municipal government, be a mayor or alderman, be an officer in the army or a justice of the peace, be a member of the Cabinet or an exciseman connected with the Customs, without his producing a certificate, for which he had paid a fee to an Episcopal clergyman, showing that he had taken the sacrament in a church connected with the Establishment. At a later time even than that, it was not possible for Unitarians, nor even for Trinitarian dissenters, to be married, except at the Episcopal church and by an Episcopalian clergyman. Nor was there any legal registry as to the birth of children, except at the Episcopal church. I remember the time when horrible things happened in London, because of the fewness and smallness of the burial grounds which there were for an enormous population, growing every year at a tremendous rate. The bishop of London, in the House of Lords, resisted a Bill for terminating the horrible, shocking use of some of the little church-yards in London, with a view to the employment of cemeteries in the suburbs; and as to this opposition, he was resolute, except on condition that, wherever a person died, a sum should be due to the Episcopal clergyman, equivalent to a burial-fee, and on the payment of which, the friends or executors should be free to carry the body away and bury it as they pleased. It is even now less than thirty years since an assault was made, involving the tenure of almost every Unitarian church in England and Ireland. But it was stopped by the Prime Minister of the time, Sir Robert Peel; who introduced a bill into Parliament, by which Unitarians were emancipated from the disqualifying effects of an old persecuting law, by which, formerly, every person, for impugning the doctrine of the trinity, was liable to fine and imprisonment, and for doing it a third time was liable to the confiscation of all his property and to be imprisoned for life. Sir Robert carried his Bill through Parliament triumphantly and amidst the acclamations of the leaders of all parties, and yet also against an opposition, more numerous as petitioners, than was ever made against any Bill or any law. When I was a youth, I was offered an education at Oxford, one of the great national universities. But my way was barred by the Episcopal church — the church Established by Law as the phrase used to be. At that time, a young man might have had a birthright title to a scholarship and been the best candidate of the year, as regards literary and moral qualifications; but he could not be matriculated, without signing the Thirty-nine Articles. A man could not even begin the study of theology, at the university, without having first avowed and signed his belief in those Thirty-nine Articles. Of abuses and oppressions, such as I have been referring to, the larger part, though far from all — but the larger part — are now abolished. Now is not that a great advance as to church-matters? Well, it is really, that is to say for England.

Those Thirty-nine Articles! What multitudes of hypocrites they have made in England! What souls in vast armies, they have straitened and tortured in conscience! Oh, that some man of wide personal knowledge, somebody like Dean Stanley, would write on the subject his reminiscences and experiences, before it is too late! What flippancies he would have to tell of, and what agonies! It is said that Theodore Hook, being asked at Oxford by the vice-chancellor whether he was prepared to sign the Thirty-nine Articles, replied "Oh yes! Forty, if you wish."

We are getting now to understand that there is no knowing well what a man is theologically, by simply what he can sign or say. It may very well happen sometimes that the more a man knows, the less there will be by which he would willingly swear to abide. And again, the same truth, in one man's mind, may be no better than a prejudice, while in the mind of another person, it may be like a quickening soul. We are getting to understand that signing and assenting, and that even without meaning any harm, is a very different thing from believing; and it is what many a man has been a party to, who had no more soul of belief than the pen he wrote with, whether goose-quill or steel. Any man can sign, in a way, the Articles of the Church of England, for instance; but understanding them, as the framers meant exactly, is not quite so easy; and believing in those articles by a right discernment of the logic which they involve, and by the best helps reasonably accessible from learning human and divine,— to that, probably, in all England there are not five hundred persons competent, and on the Episcopal bench, not eight, as it would seem.

People talk so strangely about faith and believing! What would be the gain as to science, or the world's progress, if every boy on going to school should be made to subscribe his belief in the elements of geometry as developed by Euclid! Faith, every earnest soul is competent to — on the most important points, religiously; but faith as to conclusions drawn from metaphysics, faith as to such things in any proper sense of the word, is what few people can profess without making themselves ridiculous. Of the merely conjectural, or of the unknowable, however plausibly expressed as to seemingness, what is got by exacting or giving a profession of belief? Obfuscation moral and mental — that is all.

It is not what creeds and history a man can swallow that is

good; but what he can inwardly digest and have his soul quickened with. To profess an article of faith is what, apparently, in a light way, most people are able; but thoroughly to understand it is something not quite so common; and inwardly to digest it, so as to live by it — think, hope and pray — that may be something still more rare. Horne Tooke would have us think, that believing a doctrine is our having such a sense of it intellectually and morally as that it can be be-lived by us. It is the believing temper, or rather it is the temper which grows on a man with believing; this, that is so rarely looked to, is the ultimate true test as to creeds, professions, pretensions, inquiry and conviction. Not will merely, nor recklessness, nor arrogance, nor loud voice in statement, helps a hearer as to belief, but soul only,— the soul, that is alive with the wisdom of the past, and sensitive as to the future — the soul, as it quickens with the Divine Spirit, and throbs, too, with its fleshly connections.

No doubt, the constitution of free churches has its exposures and liabilities, like everything else that is human; but they are no more than what are capable of being readily treated among people of any honor, not to say even of christian grace. But I have been asked, what security has a free church against the inanities and vagaries of some conceivable clergyman. There is the Bible! And twenty creeds could not make it more binding, or plainer. And besides, after all, why should ineptitudes, and ignorance, and crass ignorance be accounted a greater scandal to Liberalism than it is to Orthodoxy, or than when it is preached in white sleeves? As to preaching, there are no better guarantees than common sense and good faith, and truthfulness even simply as to the text, "We preach not ourselves, but Christ Jesus the Lord: and ourselves your servants for Jesus' sake."

But now, yet another word still as to church freedom: and for comfort I prefer to argue it as though on foreign ground. At the present time, in the Church of England, the ablest man theologically, next perhaps after Dean Stanley, is Professor Jowett, now known perhaps by some higher title. His work on the "Epistles of Paul" is a fine, scholarly production. As to interpretation, it is old Unitarianism, mostly; but it has a grace of its own. Certain special passages in his work having been complained of, he was summoned by the vice-chancellor of Oxford to renew his subscription to the Thirty-nine Articles, which he did at once. Two days afterward, in the London newspaper called the "Times," were published, in parallel columns, the passages in his two volumes which had been complained of, and also such extracts from the Thirty-nine Articles as they were supposed to conflict with. And plainly the two columns were in flat contradiction. The complaining Dr. Golightly, with his companion, added something like this: "What is a safeguard worth as to the Church, when a man will publish in two serious volumes, what he will practically repudiate within a fortnight, and yet still continue to go on publishing and selling?" True enough! Quis custodiet custodes? The old trouble! But yet Dr. Jowett might say, "Always are we to be ruled by fools? Am I, because of my knowing more than some other people, and being wiser than the old creed-makers of the dark ages, to forego place, honor and advantage, and turn dissenter, and get down into the dirt?" There is something in that; and let it go for what it is worth. But how about the persons who have stayed outside the university of Oxford, with all its wealth and high places, because they were unwilling to enter it dishonestly? It is a curious sign of the times that Dr. Jowett should be able to be the Head of a college in Oxford, and be ready to sign the Thirty-nine Articles any day, and yet publish the works he does, and get the kind of praise he gains. He is to be pardoned, perhaps, because of extenuating circumstances, but still more certainly he is to be pitied. The sadness of such a case, and there have been hundreds and perhaps thousands very like it — I say, the sadness of such instances is evidence as to the wisdom which waited on the foundation and development of the North Church in Salem.

Oh the wisdom more than worldly, as to which the founders of your church had some sense! For in an ordinary way how could they have anticipated, what yet they were providing against, as to friendly meeting — this flood of knowledge which has been pouring in upon us, since Newton was wondered at, and ceased from this world? What could they have known of the way in which this earth was about to unbosom herself as to her secret history, as concerning time and make? How could they have foreseen such facts as the discovery of that ancient and, to a certain degree, authoritative manuscript, connected with the Scriptures, called Sinaitic? What could they have foreknown of the speculative effects of having the universe, through science, widen round us so familiarly, as that we mortals on our earth can feel ourselves but like the occupants of some one out of — what the Psalmist may have meant when he said "The chariots of God are twenty thousand?" How could they have foreseen, what yet is so absolutely certain, that even theology itself would have to be born again; born not of the will of man nor of creed-makers, but of the Spirit — in Christ Jesus, a new creature? All honor to the men who were ahead of their age, and whose faces were set aright as to the coming dawn!

The coral insects begin building from the floor of the ocean; they shape for themselves little cells that become their tombs; and with building cell upon cell, and tomb upon tomb, slowly the surface of the sea is reached. And prompted by an instinct greater than what might suffice for their little lives, these insects build up islands and rampart them about, against seas wild with the whirlwind; islands where man can land and live, and which the orange can perfume with its scent, and brighten with its golden fruit. And a hundred and two hundred years ago the founders of churches, free as to what are called creeds, acted from a perception of right, and yet also more wisely than they knew, as to the future. For what could they possibly have anticipated as to what was to be after them, with the widening disclosures of science and history and archaeology and also experience? "The Bible," they said among themselves, "the Bible is our creed, open always for study by all the light that time may let in upon it, or the heavens vouchsafe." Wise master-builders, they! And now Protestant churches, bound by the creeds of preceding centuries, can live only by ignoring their fetters, or else by a debasing tampering as to the meaning of words and phrases! All honor again to the good men who forestalled all that, as to peril!

And now as the successors of these honorable men, what is due from us? Distinctively, honesty and simplicity as to profession, and reverence and carefulness as to the study of the Scriptures; and could I say, also, leadership in the church as to thinking? But that last thing is of the gift and call of God, and not of mere fleshly willing. And yet if we were as good, as to time and circumstance, as our forefathers were, it is from among us that teachers should rise, who might be competent to the philosophy of the Scriptures as to revelation, and who might interpret concurrently the marvel of Christ's resurrection and the marvellousness which does so clothe the lily of the field, and which lies latent through the winter in every acorn about to become an oak, and in every grain of mustard-seed which in Palestine is to become a tree, whereon the birds can alight and sing. And if our school of thought were as well open to light as it ought to be, apparently it might be in connection with us that the earliest teachers would be heard as to that rainbow of promise which the sun of science makes in even the fogs which accrue from earthly change and decay.

And now I will say, by way of a moral, that because of pride in ancestry we are liable to spiritual apathy, and perhaps at the last to find ourselves glorying in mere negations. There have been times when denial, ecclesiastically, was almost as grand as the prophet's "Thus saith the Lord." But those times are past, and to-day boys of sixteen are very often ready to deny and dispute anything religiously, and a community like yours, as to education, has all the notions of Strauss and Buchner in the air, as it were, and latent in the minds of the children. Free-thinking is nothing now as a peculiarity, except as it explores the way to the temple of truth, and now and then ushers a high-priest of thought into the holy of holies, and prepares us all for the 'lively oracles' of a living God. The liberty which does not ennoble us and quicken us as religious thinkers, we are unworthy of. For thinking, in a church, can be straitened and enslaved not only by old, complicate, intricate creeds, but also by prejudices unconsciously entertained, or by inherited predispositions of feeling or by the subtle management of perhaps two or three persons more bigoted than scrupulous.

What the better are you for being Unitarians, unless there abide in you that spirit of truth which is guidance, and prompting and willingness as to all truth?

In England, on such an occasion as this, there is a Sentiment which is never forgotten—Civil and Religious Liberty, all the world over! and in olden times, when George the Third was king, it was, no doubt, familiar to your forefathers as a post-prandial toast. "Blessed is the nation whose God is the Lord," says the Psalmist, and happy are the people who are strong in the same great truths which their fathers lived by! Happy the persons all, who can triumph in the same great cause, which their forefathers loved and struggled for!

Oh! those words that come to mind so forcibly to-day: "Your fathers, where are they? and the prophets, do they live forever?" Yes, they do, all of them forever and ever, withinside of the spiritual and invisible; and in those spheres of being which collectively we call heaven; and from within which, it is possible that they may be cognizant of us, at this very moment — like as it is written as to some of the incidents of revelation " Which things the angels desire to look into." Alive forever! Yes, they are, and even in this world, in a way, they survive themselves, in the true principles which they elaborated, in the institutions which they founded, and in the continuation of the churches, forth into which went their earnestness. " Other men labored, and ye are entered into their labors," or you ought to be. They who strive for the right, and who live faithfully by what light they have, follow after the great army of martyrs and confessors, to find, on passing the gateway of death, that they have been sharing in a struggle with sin and darkness, greater perhaps and more wonderful than they had ever thought.

There is plan and purpose in the world's ongoing, as much as there ever was in the shaping of our earth. For every sowing in tears, there is always somewhere, at sometime, a harvest of joy. No man lives all to himself; and no man dies merely to himself. Striving, hoping and believing—that is the temper, as to which through nature and through Christ, God would be shaping us. Clouds and darkness are round about him; but justice and judgment are the foundations of his throne. Oh, there is no knowing at what rate swings the slow pendulum which regulates the course of human progress, nor what the circumference is of that face, round which creeps the finger which indicates the hours of reform and advance. Nor can a guess be hazarded as to that millennial hour, when again the morning stars will sing together, and when the angels of heaven will cry "The war of man with man, and of creed with creed—earth's warfare is accomplished: and the kingdoms of that world have become the kingdom of our Lord and his Christ." But with every sunrise it is nearer earth—that blessed time! and with every pulse that throbs our veins, it is nearer to us—that coming time! And oh, it is so surely nearer to us, with every good life that is finished, and with every good and perfect thought that comes down from above, into a good man's mind!

THE PRESIDENT.

I am happy to say there is in our family a robust sister. The First Church did not send forth the North Church alone, but she also established a branch in the town of Marblehead. I have the pleasure of introducing to you the Rev. JOHN W. CHADWICK, of Brooklyn, N. Y., who will respond for that branch.

ADDRESS OF THE REV. JOHN W. CHADWICK.

MR. PRESIDENT, LADIES AND GENTLEMEN: Once upon a time Parson Brazer, of the North Church in Salem, and Parson Bartlett, of the Unitarian Church in Marblehead, had arranged for an exchange of pulpits and when the Sunday morning came and the time for the services had arrived, Dr. Brazer, I think, got to his post in good season, and the Marblehead people were duly edified by his preaching. But the people of the North Church in Salem came to church and the time came for the services to begin, but no minister appeared. After waiting about fifteen or twenty minutes beyond the usual time, and wondering very much what had happened, Parson Bartlett, who was always a person of rubicund and florid appearance, arrived, looking somewhat more florid than was his wont. No explanation was given but the parson went on with his services with as much composure as he could command. It was afterward discovered that he had undertaken to walk from Marblehead to Salem (and at that time I may say the Sunday omnibus was not regarded as a means of grace) and, to save as much time as he could, he walked "across-lots." Mr. Hale has a sermon he is fond of preaching about the way of the transgressor being hard, the transgressor being the man who goes "across-lots." On this occasion the way of Parson Bartlett was particularly hard, for he was chased by a bull. It so happened, however, that he was in the close vicinity of a stone wall, and he climbed over; the bull came on with such tremendous velocity that as he went over the wall, he went over the parson too, and did not discover for some time that the parson was not ahead of him. By that time the parson had got back over the wall, and over the bull went again. And so it went on for some twenty minutes, the "artful dodger" being now on one side of the wall and now the other side, the contest growing continually more lively and exciting, until the owner of the bull, by some happy conjunction of affairs, happened to discover what was going on, and sent some one to call off the bull, and the parson proceeded on his way rejoicing. The moral of which is, that under the circumstances I think I should be justified in "dodging," for two reasons, one of which is that this is the first warning I have had that I was to speak at all. Mr. Willson said something about coming prepared to sing, and I have sung with the rest. Another reason is that these speeches have gone on so long and so pleasantly that we have come to that time when it is always proper to say that "so much has been said and so well said that I will not occupy your time." I was glad to have the President date me from Marblehead, for I was somewhat in doubt when I found he was aiming at me whether I was here as a representative of Marblehead or as a representative of Brooklyn, and certainly it is as a representative of Marblehead I am here in my thought, because as I sat in the church and heard the pleasant words of the speaker, singing that pleasant song of departed days, my thoughts were thoughts of Marblehead and not of Brooklyn. My heart almost condemns me for having allowed Parson Bartlett to appear before you in a ridiculous aspect at a time when almost everybody was afraid of the minister. I am sure I never was afraid of him, for it was always a very pleasant time when he came into the house, except when I was sick and he would order me some medicine, for you must remember, he was a physician of bodies as well as of souls. The town people generally used to think his medicine was orthodox, whatever they thought of his creed; perhaps, because they got the medicine for nothing. My thoughts were of him and all his kindly pleasantries, and of one other who only a year or two ago passed beyond this life, and with whom year after year I entered into "close communion." So that as I heard your preacher talk of Parson Barnard and Mr. Abbot, of Mr. Brazer and Dr. Prince, the names did not seem at all unfamiliar to me because I had heard my good grandmother talk of them so often that I felt I really knew them. There was one sermon, too, that she was very fond of reading to me, by Dr. Prince, with the beautiful text, as she thought, "In the day that I make up my jewels." Through her, therefore, I entered into communion with these people. As I listened to Mr. Willson's address, I wondered with what eyes they would regard us from their heavenly seats, we who are working in their places, but by such different methods and such different ways, and thinking this over I was glad when the key of explanation came from Mr. Willson's own lips; when he told us that the corner-stone of their preaching and of their hold upon the people was the liberty, the humanity, the holiness and love they taught. So I felt we were with them. We are doing our best in our way, and we are with them in the most essential way of all. Being in this Normal School building reminds me of that motto of Dr. Pierce of Lexington, "Live to the truth," and I am sure if we of this day and generation are true to our light, to such light as is given us, working on as faithfully and steadfastly as we can, doing our work in our own way, there is nothing existing in this world or in any other that can separate us from the love of Christ that was in those men and women of the elder days, who constitute with us one family in earth and in heaven.

THE PRESIDENT.

The relations that existed between the distinguished men of the time when the Rev. John Pierpont sang his great song in Boston, and when the liberty-loving people of Salem listened with so much gladness, have continued to this day. I am happy to introduce to you the Rev. GEORGE L. CHANEY, minister of the Hollis Street Church, Boston, a society that was old before this church was born. Mr. Chaney came from Salem.

ADDRESS OF REV. GEORGE L. CHANEY.

MR. PRESIDENT: There are three blessings for which I desire to give thanks. First, that I was born in Salem; second, that I went away from Salem; and third, that I have returned to it to-day.

You remember the old tribute which the wandering sons of Salem were wont to pay to their native town:—that it was a good place to have come from. But as often as we come back to the old city her motherly love makes us feel that it is an equally good place to return to. That we never know our blessings till they take their flight is nowhere better shown than in the experience of a Salem exile from home.

Just as people who have most to boast of fall into self-disparagement, so it has long been a practice, among the rising generations at least, to laugh at the slow gait and drowsy habits of the good old mother city that bore them. But a very short acquaintance with other towns and life in other countries opens our eyes wonderfully to the advantages we had at home. How should we know until we had tried other places that every city did not have a grand parade ground in its centre, with a green-coated company of valiant elm trees keeping perpetual guard around it? Or how were we to learn that the old museum was a Salem specialty? That only here could a man be at home in all the world without leaving his native city? We should have regarded it as local prejudice if any one had claimed for Salem the possession of a peculiar institution in the Essex Institute or the Athenæum. These nurseries of science and letters were so much a matter of course in our youthful life, that any Salem boy taken to Timbuctoo or Terra del Fuego would have innocently asked the way to the Institute or Library, not conceiving of a land in which these things were wanting.

Then there were the ships, the merchants, the barques and brigs of every clime, the stately Custom House, making a long arm of Derby Wharf to catch and treasure all the products of the world; the magnificent poor-house, as the old conundrum had it, "just like your head — because it was on the Neck"; the real home houses of the citizens, each with its yard and garden, where better things than the perishing flowers that grew there were planted in the young folks who made those flowers their care; and, last of many graces, there was the beautiful resting place of the dead, one of the earliest signs of the high level to which christian civilization was advancing in the new world.

It is not surprising that a city thus open to communication with foreign countries and thus supplied with the apparatus for receiving, preserving and transmitting knowledge from generation to generation should have nurtured thoughtful people. It is not surprising that she should have come early to broader views of religious truth and more comprehensive schemes of christian activity than were common in other cities. I take equal pride in the thought that here were consecrated the first missionaries, and here were some of the earliest defenders of a gospel too humane to omit one of God's creatures from his saving purpose and declared power in Jesus Christ, his Son.

It is impossible for a man who comes in contact with humanity in many nations, and finds it the same under all its disguises of color, language and dress, to accept any plan of salvation, which cannot survey beyond his native city. Every seaboard town in active communication with the Indies, or the Mediterranean, is always exposed to liberal infection. No quarantine can keep out the heresy that man is man, and although in ignorance, sin or shame, still an object of providential love and care. Thus it happened of necessity that churches of humanity were formed and maintained in this cosmopolitan city. One such church has called us together to celebrate its one-hundredth birthday. We have listened to its record of service, its story of long-tried fidelity to truth and God's humanity under the guiding inspiration of the christian gospel. In every street of this city, homes have been visited and hallowed by its sacred ministries. In sickness and in health, in sorrow and in joy, this church has been the faithful partner of the homes united to it. Commerce and trade have felt its call to honorable dealing. The courts of justice have been more just for its maintenance of the just cause. Corrupt politics have felt the lash of its indignant rebuke, and ancient wrongs have sought in the grave a refuge from its strong attack. Proud as we are of the literary renown and commercial enterprise that have distinguished our native city, have we not, in the memories that throng the church and that pursue us wherever we assemble on this day, deeper cause for devout pride and thanksgiving? For what were stores of knowledge or stars of genius or fires of enterprise in us or in any people, unless governed by religious principles? What, indeed, but the material for ruin to their possessor and his unfortunate companions! Religion gives to every other gift or accomplishment its safe direction. And as the rocket sprinkles the sky with a rain of innocent splendor, or carries fire and destruction over the earth, according to its pointing, so human talents depend upon the divine hand of religion to uphold and direct them.

But, Mr. President, I have another claim upon your indulgence than that of my nativity or my calling, both of which, as you see, I am not slow to magnify. I cannot forget that I am the minister of a church which had attained a vigorous majority when your church was in its cradle. You must have heard of its old-time minister, the Rev. Mather Byles, the ministerial wag and tory of his day. I take no stock either in his wit or his treason, for both of which he got his due in being expelled from his church. But I recall a story of him which may do service in illustrating my final word of congratulation. Dr. Byles was so open a tory that he was constantly watched by a guard, who used to walk up and down in front of his house to see that no mischief went in or out. The doctor playfully called the guard his observe-a-tory. One day being in want of something at a neighboring store (sermon-paper, perhaps), Dr. Byles persuaded his guard to do the errand for him, agreeing to take his place during his absence. So the doctor was seen walking up and down in front of his house, with gun a'shoulder, keeping watch over himself.

I used to fear, Mr. President, that such would be the end of the liberal church; every minister and every church and every man with gun a' shoulder, keeping watch over himself — the last result of individual isolation. In such a gathering as this, how vain the fear! In this commemoration of a hundred years of work well done, we give a pledge of sympathy in the work of the future. A hundred years to come, may the churches that stand for freedom in the choice of the christian religion and consecration in its practice make one brotherhood, and on this day, 1972, may they meet to repeat this festival with greater fulness and even grander cheer than have been ours to-day!

The PRESIDENT then read the following letter from THE SALEM UNIVERSALIST SOCIETY, as showing the sympathy which persons of different denominations feel towards each other, and especially as evincing the friendship of this sister church, of another and yet a kindred faith; that church being represented on this occasion by its pastor, Rev. E. C. BOLLES.

Salem, June 15, 1872.

Francis H. Lee, Esq.,

My Dear Sir:—In parish meeting, held June 10, 1872, it was *Voted*, that the accompanying letter of congratulation be adopted, and that a copy be sent by the clerk of the First Universalist society, to the secretary of the committee of the North Church and society, for their centennial celebration.

Very truly yours, T. H. Barnes, *Clerk*.

"TO THE NORTH CHURCH AND SOCIETY, SALEM.

Dear Brethren:—We have learned through your invitation to our pastor that you are to observe on the 19th of July next, the centennial anniversary of the founding of your society and church. We would not lose this early opportunity of conveying to you our congratulations. We rejoice that you have thus completed a century of church life, and through fathers and sons have so long and so well upheld the interests of liberal religion in this community.

It is a matter of even greater pleasure to us that the hundredth anniversary finds you ready and in earnest to add another chapter to the story of the devotion of the past.

We would join you, therefore, in the pleasant thoughts of this memorial day, and beg you to remember that we are with you not only by the bond of neighborhood but by that of fraternity as well."

THE PRESIDENT.

I regret that the eloquent pastor of this church extending a kindly hand to us has been called away. I should have urged him to remain had I known he was about to leave. I know of no better service I can perform than to ask another son of Salem to respond for the Universalist Church. I ask the Rev. Mr. White of Keene, N. H.

ADDRESS OF THE REV. WILLIAM ORNE WHITE.

You will pardon me, sir, for thinking that here is an excellent opportunity for me to act upon what Rev. Mr. Chaney has just told us about "Mather Byles." For, at this late hour, what better can I do, than in emulation of that ancient worthy, to "mount guard over myself?"

Having had no premonition of the sentiment to which I am expected to respond, I am, nevertheless, very thankful for the privilege of saying, that in my own immediate neighborhood, we Unitarians and Universalists have very pleasant fellowship, one with another. Upon the shelves of our Universalist brethren, you can often find the volumes of Channing and Ware and other leading Unitarians, side by side with those among their own writers who are closely allied to us in liberal thought, and in great and beneficent work. Let us all unite in cordially wishing our Universalist friends increasing success in the new century of effort upon which they have recently entered.

It is tantalizing to think, sometimes, how near you come to escaping your fate. I was just thinking, as you called upon me, sir, that two minutes more from each of these excellent gentlemen who have spoken, and it would have been out of the question for you to have called upon me at all, without drawing unduly upon the next century.

Do we not find, in the absence of some of our friends, in this intense midsummer's heat, a sad warning against our being so prone to act upon the familiar saying, "It will be all the same a hundred years hence?" What could have set this people out to form their church on the nineteenth of July? As we miss familiar sons of Salem who are in their "tent on the beach," or climbing the mountains, we can call back, across the cliffs of the century, to Thomas Barnard and his friends, "It was *not* all the same a hundred years hence!" Even so small a matter as fixing the day of your being "set off" as a church made a difference, a hundred years afterwards, in our celebration.

I feel a little like a child, as well as a guest, of the North Church to-day. For although a son of the old "First Church," with which my maternal ancestors were identified, I can recall with much pleasure my brief connection with the North Church Sunday School, just before such a school was established in the parent church. How much grace and dignity Hon. Leverett Saltonstall lent to it as its revered superintendent! My own teacher was that excellent man, the late E. K. Lakeman, whose genial presence and kind words it is always a pleasure to recall.

My earliest remembrance of anything is the marriage of a beloved relative, at which Rev. Dr. Brazer officiated, when I was between three and four years old. How gracious was his way of greeting his young friends upon the street! How vividly can we recall those plaintive cadences which gave such effect to his reading of the one verse of the hymn! Again and again, upon his exchanges with our own minister, I remember the fearful solemnity which marked his reading of the words:

> "And now, my soul, another year
> Of my short life is past;
> I cannot long continue here;
> And this may be my last."

Of Rev. John E. Abbot, the most distinct impression I have received was from the faithful friend who accompanied him in his unavailing journey to Havana, and who said of him, referring to his period of comparative health, "wherever he was, whatever he said, even though he were chatting cheerfully with you at 'a party,' *he always seemed to be in heaven*."

It so happens that Keene, which has been my home for more than twenty years past, is the town to which Rev. Asa Dunbar retired, after seeming to stand as a stone wall between the elder Thomas Barnard and his son. How brief was his term of service in the First Church! His declining health soon threw him into the profession of the law, which he honorably pursued for a few years in Keene, and then died, at the age of forty-two. Had he, or his past friends in Salem, foreseen the brief and chequered years that remained to him, and the long and brave career of the young Barnard, may we not feel that the disruption which was occasioned by the rivalry of these men and their friends might have been prevented?

But in that case where should we have been to-day, and where my opportunity of thanking your committee for their kind invitation, and yourself, sir, for the privilege of expressing the pleasure which I feel in being here?

The following hymn was then read by the Rev. GEORGE BATCHELOR, of the Barton Square Church, and sung by the company:

> Great God, we sing that mighty hand
>   By which, supported, still we stand;
> The opening year Thy mercy shows;
>   That mercy crowns it till it close.
>
> With grateful hearts the past we own;
>   The future, all to us unknown,
> We to Thy guardian care commit,
>   And, peaceful, leave before Thy feet.
>
> In scenes exalted or depressed,
>   Thou art our joy, and Thou our rest;
> Thy goodness all our hopes shall raise
>   Adored through all our changing days.

CONGRATULATORY LETTERS.

The President said he had two or three pleasant letters, indicative of the kind feelings which old friends had after they had left the city. He then read the following:—

YORK, ENGLAND, June 21, 1872.

My Dear Mr. Willson: — Your letter reached me just as I was leaving London for a short tour northward, and I take my first leisure to thank you for the invitation to join in the approaching centenary of the "North Society." Most gladly would I, if I could, leap the space that separates Old England from the New, to be one of the gathering that will meet to renew old ties and to refresh themselves with the memories that hang about our loved church.

I have visited during the week one of the colleges in Oxford that had just celebrated, two days before, its *ten hundredth* anniversary. It was good to think that, amid all the changes and revolutions of those thousand years, so valuable an institution had preserved an unbroken life, and had twined about itself rich associations with every portion of so long and varied a history; and I was glad to be reminded by your letter in my pocket that, in our country too, there are some among the best institutions we possess which, if they cannot claim so great antiquity as that, are relatively to the period of our national life almost as old.

Let us make much of their anniversaries when they come round, and may they be dearer and stronger the older they grow.

My own connection with the society covered only two out of its one hundred years; but when I recall the rich experiences and the consecrated friendships that are to me inseparably associated with the church, I realize the more how much that is precious must have accumulated about it to the multitude of souls it has welcomed and nourished during all the hundred years. How much I should like to look in upon your celebration. I should meet many whose faces and forms are almost the same as when they greeted me eighteen years ago. There are others whom I knew as children and who are grown I suppose wholly out of my recognition; but I should like to look in their faces and take them by the hand and see how far they have realized the anticipations I used to like to form about them when I was privileged to look on them as members of my flock.

But very many of those who were nearest and dearest to me during my ministry have left this earth and will not be with you— I am almost startled when I count them over and see how many they are. Inasmuch as I am forced to be among the absent ones I take a kind of solemn joy in thinking in what a company I am; for whether the absence is occasioned by a difference of continent or by difference of sphere may be less of a distinction than we are apt to suppose. I think it would be hard to find anywhere in the world truer exemplifications of the christian life than we had among those dear departed ones, whose loveliness and unselfish devotion to duty and religious fervor give now an odor of sanctity to the church they loved so well; and what a testimony they give to the value of that form of religious faith which has borne such precious fruit! May their memory stimulate us and make us strive that it may work in us also the same perfect work!

May God bless you in your ministry, and bless the people— who in every true church are ministers too— and may you and they so labor together as to help on the kingdom of righteousness and truth and love.

I am ever sincerely yours,

CHARLES LOWE.

PORTLAND, MAINE, July 16, 1872.

My Dear Mr. Willson: — It is a great disappointment to me, that I shall not be able to be present at the centennial celebration of the North Church. I should not allow any light thing to detain me from it; for I would not willingly neglect so filial a duty; but an engagement of long standing, and involving the convenience of others beside myself, takes me out of communication with Salem for a week to come.

I trust that the occasion will be successful in renewing the recollections which are too good to be allowed to perish, and that the elements will be as propitious as the occasion, that the thermometer may not see fit to celebrate the centennial by itself rising to one hundred degrees.

My chief contribution, if I could be as present as I am in desire, would be an interest loyal to the old church. My memories of its history go too little way back, and are too largely personal to be of value to others, though to myself they are a part of the most precious things in my life; and yet, though one of its younger children, I can touch directly or indirectly along the whole span of its century's life. The church was founded in the dark days just before the Revolution, — an act of faith not the least memorable among the many historical events in the history of Salem. It is ninety-seven years since some of the parishioners of one of my predecessors at King's Chapel came down to Salem in their red coats seeking powder, and found Mr. Barnard standing at the old North Bridge. The clerical dress and manner of that noteworthy figure among the worthies of the old town, were a tradition still, — the beautiful youth of Abbot, all fragrant with piety, was an inspiring memory not yet dim, twenty-five years ago.

Dr. Brazer's kind, scholarly presence I well remember, and have to confess that one of my earliest impressions of him is as standing at the door of the pew where I was just emerging from a sound sleep, and smiling benignantly on his small parishioner who did not then dream of one day himself exercising a soporific influence on future hearers.

The old church I never knew except in its degradations when painted carpets hung up to dry, where the fathers and mothers in that Israel used to come up to their holy place; but the present church, if I can judge others by myself, must be to many who have gone forth to the ends of the earth, as stately and venerable as any cathedral, with its gray tower and green-mantled walls.

The North Church has had a succession of men of rare and various gifts in its ministry. For many of its children, the voices of its living ministers, present and past, are mingled in the best things which we have in this world to remember; yet the best things which that pulpit said to me in the forming years of life could not speak more eloquently than it used to speak by its silence. That mahogany tower whose beauty seemed to surpass any other carven work spoke as a symbol, and the best testimony of the church was the testimony of the undying words of the New Testament which it has written above its preacher's head as the law of his utterance and the pledge of its own faith and fidelity.

Much has changed in the hundred years, but the freshness and truth of those words, and of the gospel whence they are drawn, have surely gained by the testimony of a century's added life.

The christian lives that have been lived, loving, helpful and strong, in the North Church, and the faith that has been nourished there, are evidences not to be gainsaid, that the Christianity which the church was instituted to teach is real, and that the substance of its faith is fact and truth. Shall we not also take them as promises that the old church will still have work to do and will do it, in the years to come, for God and for Jesus Christ, reconciling the old truth with the new vision?

Yours faithfully, HENRY W. FOOTE.

JAMAICA PLAIN, July 18, 1872.

GEORGE B. LORING, ESQ.

*My Dear Sir:—*I have delayed answering your kind invitation to join the North society in celebrating the one hundredth anniversary of its organization till now, in the hope that I might find myself able to accept it. But as the day is at hand and the intense heat continues, I am compelled at the last moment to acknowledge the honor of the invitation with gratitude and to decline it with great regret. Believe me, I should greatly enjoy being with you. My associations with the North society are all interesting and agreeable,— extremely so. My acquaintance with it covers more than a third of its entire history. Forty years ago, when I became minister of the church in Barton Square, the North society contained in its membership as noble a list of men and women, adorning their positions and illuminating the spheres of their various activity, as any parish in the commonwealth could then boast. I recall their presence to-day, as your preacher will do to-morrow, with equal reverence and affection. I remember, with a heart which yearns towards them across the interval of years that separates us, the most gracious cordiality with which they received me, a mere youth, to their refined and charming homes. I can never forget the amiable and courtly Col. Benjamin Pickman, at whose table I was a frequent guest; nor his exceedingly modest but highly cultivated brother and sister, William and Rawlins who, in their tastes and studies, impersonated the best genius of literature, and in their character the simplicity, sincerity and charity of the gospel of Christ. Who that knew him will ever forget the commanding figure and the massive intellect of Dudley Pickman, or his fine powers of conversation? The meek and diffident Frederick Howes rises into this group, a studious man of rare attainments, matched, perhaps, by no other in the society unless, perchance, by a lady of his own family. There is another name which will not fail to be remembered with tenderest interest on the occasion; and I could form no better aspiration for your proceedings than that they might be animated by the spirit of that grandest of men and best of Christians, Leverett Saltonstall.

But I am sorry I began to refer to names because the list is so long, and so many in the same and in less conspicuous walks rush to my attention only to be passed by. Besides the Peabodys who will be fitly commemorated, there is one most friendly face which I love to recall,—that of a neighbor who I suppose never had a christian name, and in respect to whom we were always violating the injunction, "Call no man *master*," for we never called him anything else but "Master Cole." At the remembrance of these persons and their families and of so many others equally worthy, all the venerations of my heart leap up and mingle with those which I bear towards so great a number in all the parishes of your good city, my long-time and most pleasant home.

Please give the hearty love of their old friend to the North society assembled to-morrow, and believe me,

With sincere regard, yours very truly,

JAMES W. THOMPSON.

PROVIDENCE, July 3, 1872.

FRANCIS H. LEE, ESQ.

Dear Sir:—I deeply regret that I cannot accept your friendly invitation to attend "a celebration of the centennial anniversary of the founding of the North Church and Society in Salem," to take place on Friday, the 19th inst.; but the semi-centennial anniversary of the founding of the Rhode Island Historical Society, of which I have been twenty-two years librarian, occurring on the same day, I cannot, as a member of the committee of arrangements, with propriety, absent myself on that occasion.

Your note of invitation revived pleasant memories of the years of my ministry in Beverly and of the fraternal intercourse I held with the clergy of your city and vicinity. The Ministerial Association which embraced the names of the venerable Dr. Prince, of Brazer, Flint, Thompson and Upham, of Salem; Thayer of Beverly; Sewall and Bigelow, of Danvers; Robbins, Pierpont and Swett, of Lynn; and Hamilton and Waite of Gloucester, combined in no common degree, high scholarship, devoutness and geniality. Certainly, I have never known a body of men in which the spirit of brotherhood was more strongly developed, or who were more devoted to the work of their profession.

* * * * * * * * *

The mention of these and other names awakens many recollections of men and events in your goodly city of which I may not here speak. And while, in conclusion, I rejoice with you in the honorable record of a century of your society's life, accept assurances of my best wishes for its future, and my earnest prayer that its prosperity may be perpetuated until the church on earth shall be merged in the church of the first born in heaven.

Very sincerely yours,

EDWIN M. STONE.

Mr. Willson next read extracts from a letter from S. Endicott Peabody, Esq., who removed a little more than a year ago from Salem to London, England, prefacing the reading by a grateful mention of the deep interest which the writer had always shown in the welfare of the society, and the valuable services he had rendered in the Sunday School, and in other positions. The letter had not been written for public use, but it might be presumed that the writer would not object to the introduction of a few sentences as a greeting from an old friend with whom the society had parted most reluctantly. Mr. Willson also observed that the letter contained substantial pecuniary aid towards the expenses of this celebration of the society's one hundredth anniversary.

22 OLD BROAD STREET,
LONDON, June 18, 1872.

My Dear Mr. Willson:—Your friendly note just received reminds me most pleasantly of the day of jubilee which is at hand for the old North Church, with which for four generations my family have been identified. . . . Whether it will ever be my good fortune to be again an active member of the good old congregation I cannot know, but I never enter a church on Sunday without seeing before me, not only the familiar walls of the " Old North," but all the forms and faces of those whom I have known with various degrees of intimacy from earliest childhood to a very mature manhood. . . . .

With the sincere hope that the celebration may pass off most agreeably to all who will have the happiness to participate in it,

I remain, cordially and gratefully yours,

S. E. PEABODY.

THE PRESIDENT.

I now desire to introduce to you a venerable son of Salem, the Rev. Mr. HODGES.

ADDRESS OF THE REV. R. M. HODGES.

I esteem it a privilege to be present on this memorial occasion. Let me pay a tribute of gratitude to the Author and Preserver of my life, for the kind providence which has upheld and blessed me in being even unto this hour.

Mr. Chairman, I regard it as a special favor to be invited to contribute, in ever so humble degree, to the grateful emotions of this festival. I am not, as you are aware, a member of this family in the great communion of Christians, but at an interesting period of my life, my best affections were strongly attached to the ministering servants, and to the public ministrations of the church which was here gathered one hundred years ago to-day. My recollections of Dr. Barnard bring with them, sentiments of reverence, of gratitude and love. He did a favor for me which makes his memory dear to me. He was a venerable man and the dignity and urbanity that distinguished his demeanor sat gracefully upon him, for they were the heritage of a succession of worthy progenitors.

Of the saintly Abbot, I have no words in which to clothe my conception of his pure and devout character. It was my privilege for about a year to be his pupil in theological studies and christian training. His teachings and his example I regard as legacies that will never lose their value, and which are presented in a revived light and with renewed emphasis by the observances of this day.

Though debarred the honor of being affiliated to the North Church, I may claim with satisfaction the prerogative of being a son of Salem. The place of one's nativity, in these latter days, has come to be regarded as not an immaterial point in the history of one's life. It has recently been declared, in the interest of no inconsiderable authority, that if one were not born in Boston, it had been better that he was not born at all. This is an unpleasant dilemma, to say the least, for a majority of mortality to be placed in. Although subject to the bereavement of this declaration, having first breathed the air of Salem, I do not consider myself as altogether out of the pale of humanity, inasmuch as my better half was born in the specially favored city, and to that circumstance and the basis of it, I am ready mainly to attribute the happiness that has crowned my days.

I am glad, Mr. Chairman, that I am alive to-day, if it be only a moiety of existence, that I may speak in honor of the place that gave me birth. The merchants of olden time, the Grays, the Peabodys, the Crowninshields pass in review before me, reminding me of magnanimous thoughts and generous deeds. The physicians of former days, the venerable Holyoke, venerable for years, the unequivocal Treadwell, firm and decided, the imperturbable Oliver, calm and unimpassioned, are still held in grateful remembrance for the confidence which their skill inspired, and for the ability which their sympathetic affections gave to bear, with fortitude and patience, suffering and disease. And then, the Storys, the Saltonstalls and the Kings, have they not imprinted their names on the jurisprudence of the commonwealth in ineffaceable characters? The servants of Christ and preachers of his gospel, Prince, Bentley and Barnard, Worcester, Hopkins and Emerson, Emerson still living and reverently alive in all true hearts, and Bowles, Ballou and Turner, Fisher and Griswold, have they not all been more worthy of their high calling, and have not their words and deeds given purity and dignity to the records of ecclesiastical history?

Other names, in other walks of life, I am aware, are worthy of respectful notice on this occasion. The names of Bowditch and of Pickering carry with them their own eulogy. But there are two gentlemen, both of them members of the church in whose honor we are assembled to-day, whom I would not fail to pass unnoticed. They are Thomas Cole and Jacob Newman Knapp, both of them holding high places in the now distinguished office of guiding and disciplining the intellectual powers of the young. I doubt if any man in any community ever left a more desirable or a more useful impression upon the minds of so many young ladies, as did the genial and kind-hearted teacher of the school in Federal street, near the Tabernacle Church.

Of Mr. Knapp, although I was not one of his pupils, I am not afraid to speak words too strongly eulogistic. He was a representative man. He felt deeply all beneficent interests, and exerted himself to advance them in honor. Wherever he went, he carried with him a salutary influence. When you were in his presence, you felt that you were in the presence of a friend, an earnest friend to the advancement in power of humanity. Educated to be a minister of the gospel, without any affectation, in his intercourse in society he exerted a beautiful and beneficial influence. I have always classed him with the sainted John Emery Abbot. It is such men whose memory gives dignity and grace not only to this occasion, but to every occasion that confers honor on humanity.

Mr. Chairman, music is regarded as a great moral force. It quells the stormy passions. It gives peace to the troubled mind. It is the handmaid of devotion, preceding and following it with the most grateful effect.

May I not claim for Christianity that it is not only an exponent for love, but that it instigates it. This occasion, which in its primal meaning is in honor of Christianity, ought to be dedicated to the highest power of Christianity. If Christianity is a moral power, creates love, it ought not to be held subordinate to any other power, for where love is, there is peace.

Let me close with one word in tribute to the memory of Dr. Ichabod Nichols. He was an eminent son of this society. He was preëminently a scholar. He was conscientious in the use and improvement of his powers and affections. I have never known a man who labored so assiduously in the intricate recesses of the works and words of God. The *truth* was to him the supreme good, the most valuable of all possessions. His "Hours with the Evangelists" is a work of consummate power. It shows with whom he delighted to hold communion. Any community, any individual, may well be proud of holding relationship to such a man.

I have not said a word with reference to our peculiar form of religion. I believe it to be in accordance with the teachings of the evangelical scriptures. After a brief life of study, a life somewhat protracted, I am willing to leave it as my testimony, that the interpretation of the word of God, which Dr. Channing has left on record, is the true interpretation; not on the authority of Dr. Channing, but on the authority of the Holy Spirit.

THE PRESIDENT.

I am reminded of the educational interest of our community, of the hospitality of those who are interested in this institution; and I am further reminded that we have been cordially met on this occasion by the Episcopalian denomination of this place. I call upon Mr. D. B. HAGAR, the teacher of this school and a representative of the Episcopalian faith, to make some remarks.

ADDRESS OF MR. D. B. HAGAR.

Mr. CHAIRMAN:—You have taken me so completely by surprise that I scarcely know how to begin, and I fear you will think I scarcely know how to leave off. The scene before us is a very strange one in this place. I am accustomed to command here, to ask questions, to examine and to endeavor to convert those who come here to what I consider ways of truth. I think the object would be altogether too large to undertake to convert this present assemblage to my views, and it might not prove very successful. I might possibly run through the church catechism, but I fear there would be a great many mistakes. Therefore I shall attempt nothing of the kind. It has been a great pleasure to me to be able to contribute in any way to the pleasures of this occasion, and I was very happy indeed to use my influence to secure for your use the hall in which we are now assembled. I endorse with all my heart one of the leading doctrines of your denomination, and that is, the right to liberty of thought. I believe it is not only a person's right, but I think it should be deemed by him to be both a privilege and a pleasure to think for himself and at the same time to respect the opinions of other people. It has been my good fortune to be associated with members of the Unitarian denomination; for many years some of my most warm and confidential friends have been among the clergy and laity of the Unitarian church. We have lived together without fighting one another;

we have lived very happily indeed. And I esteem it a very great privilege, and it has been a source of profit to me, that I have been enabled to associate with those who hold different views, so different from those which I hold myself. I simply wish to express the gratification I have felt in listening to what has been said, and I can only wish great prosperity to those engaged in doing what they honestly believe to be good and right.

THE PRESIDENT.

I had almost entirely forgotten an important part of the old North Church, the laity, the pillars on which the clergy lean. I introduce to you the Hon. CALEB FOOTE.

ADDRESS OF THE HON. CALEB FOOTE.

MR. CHAIRMAN:— You well know that I am entirely unprepared for this call. If I were as felicitous and ready in eloquence as the chairman of the day I should be proud and glad of the opportunity. As it is I can only borrow at second hand or third hand the quotation from Mr. Hale, and say that "so much has been said," etc. I shall therefore only propose a couple of votes of thanks. I wish to ask you, the members of the congregation here present, to pass such a vote to our beloved pastor for the extremely beautiful, interesting and valuable discourse which he gave to us this forenoon. If it is your pleasure to pass such a vote please express it in the usual manner. [The motion was unanimously carried.] I also wish to propose a vote of thanks to the gentleman who has so acceptably, so eloquently, so readily and appropriately conducted the services of this afternoon, for which I think we are under great obligations to him. If you unite in the sentiment with me you will please so express it. [This motion was also carried, *nem. con.*] And so, Mr. Chairman, the pleasant duty which I assumed, in lieu of a speech which would have been unseasonable at this late hour, is satisfactorily concluded.

Mr. Willson said: I do not propose to speak of the questionable advantage just taken of me, and which calls me to my feet. [Mr. W. having just been conspiring with Mr. Foote to bring on a vote of thanks to the Chairman, but finding himself somewhat astonished at the unexpectedly wide scope of the latter gentleman's motions.] But being up, I am glad of the opportunity which you have given me to say a word in explanation of the absence of Rev. Mr. Frothingham from our festivities to-day. He was expected to be present until a very late day, and to me it is a matter of sincere regret, in common with all his many friends, that he is not here. He promptly accepted the invitation of the committee to meet us, but a few days since sent a note saying that he was on the point of leaving New York to journey in the direction opposite to Salem, and that it was doubtful if he would be able to return to attend these commemorative exercises.*

I desire to express to you, my friends, before I sit down, something of the gratitude which I feel, but which I cannot fully express, for the extreme kindness with which you have received me more than once to-day, and which is indeed a kindness which you have never, on this day, or any other, withheld from me. For these thirteen years — years marked indelibly by changes in many of your households, by no little change in you and me, and by changes memorable indeed and eventful to the country we love — for these thirteen years I have tested your friendship, to find it forbearing, steadfast and true; and it is my great happiness

---

* The absence of Mr. Frothingham on this occasion caused much disappointment. It left a gap in the pastoral reminiscences of many of the middle-aged members of the society which was seriously felt. His ministry covered a period of intense thought and radical inquiry upon religious questions in which he took a leader's part, and of which the influence will long be seen.

I take the liberty to introduce here a portion of a private note received from Mr. Frothingham since the day of centennial commemoration: "I was very sorry to be absent from your fine occasion in July. But the journey from Sharon Springs in the hot weather, on purpose for that alone, was more than I could face. I ought to have written you a letter to be read, and a sentiment too; unhappily, the thought did not occur to me till a few hours after the time of grace had gone by. The day seemed to spring upon me unawares. Friends spoke of the occasion to me afterwards in terms of great satisfaction, making me sensible that I was the loser by not being there."

at this moment to believe that I have had your confidence, all the way; not the less that you may not always have given consent to my opinions, or even agreed with me as to the line of duty. And now, congratulating myself, that it is my exceeding good fortune to come in the right place, in your line of ministers, to enjoy the honors and satisfactions of this day, I give place to the Chairman from whom you are waiting to hear.

RESPONSE OF THE PRESIDENT.

It gives me great pleasure, my friends, to be here on this occasion. I certainly am very grateful to you for the kind manner in which you have received my name. I am not accustomed to speak on occasions like this, and if I have conducted myself in a way that has been satisfactory to you, I shall consider it to be entirely owing to the inspiration of the admirable sermon to which we listened this morning. I have had excellent support on every hand, and I assure you that the occasion has been to me of the deepest and most profound interest, recalling as it has to my mind all the associations of my childhood and youth, bringing before me continually the faces of those who imparted to me good counsels and religious instruction in the commencement of my life. No man can tell until he has passed through some form of trial and suffering the value of those early principles taught him by his parents. Then it is that the religious faith of his fathers becomes to him of inestimable value, and then it is that he learns to love those in whose care and keeping he is accustomed to repose his religious faith. I am gratified that I have lived to see this occasion, and that you bestowed upon me the privilege of presiding here. I am sure that one of the privileges of my life will be that my name will pass down with others in this church as one of those who aided, in a small measure, the faith, the fidelity, the honesty, and the religious fervor of our ancestors. Now, my friends, I will call upon you to join in singing the doxology, and that will close the services of this occasion.

DOXOLOGY.

Old Hundred.

From all that dwell below the skies,
   Let the Creator's praise arise;
Let the Redeemer's name be sung
   Through every land, by every tongue.

Eternal are Thy mercies, Lord;
   Eternal truth attends Thy word;
Thy praise shall sound from shore to shore,
   Till suns shall rise and set no more.

BENEDICTION.

SOME MEMORANDA

OF THE

CHOIR OF THE NORTH CHURCH OF SALEM;

Its Members, Organs, Hymn Books and Music.

BY

HENRY K. OLIVER.

SOME MEMORANDA OF THE CHOIR.

Upon matters connected with the musical department of the parish, the records are meagre, nothing being found therein till 1795, twenty-three years after the organization of the society. Under date of Dec. 17, 1795, a vote was passed at a meeting of the "Committee of the proprietors of the North Meeting House," held at the house of Joseph Hiller, Esq., E. A. Holyoke being moderator, " that sixty dollars be appropriated for the purpose of instructing young persons belonging to our society in the art of psalmody." A Committee of three, Benjamin Pickman, Esq., Deacon Samuel Holman and Henry Rust, was chosen to carry this vote into effect.

By vote of the proprietors, Jan. 7 and 8, 1798, Dr. Barnard was requested "to improve [make use of] Dr. Watts' Psalms and Hymns in the public worship, together with Tate and Brady's [which was then in use] if the same be agreeable to him and the church."

The church, acting thereon,

Voted, "That for the future this church will make use of the Rev. Dr. Belknap's collection of Hymns in our public worship, in the stead of that collection we have hitherto employed, ... provided this alteration shall be agreeable to the proprietors."

The Church were willing to change, but preferred Belknap to Watts, and apparently also differed from the proprietors in not wishing to retain Tate and Brady.

NOTE. — By record of April 11, 1796, Messrs. Northey and Rust were a committee to see to repairs of the bell "lately broken." A new bell, weighing 1,000 pounds, was afterwards procured "by subscription." Its note is B. middle line of Treble Clef. It was cast in England, and by vote of the committee was to be placed "on the top of the tower," apparently in a cupola erected on said top after the original spire had been taken down. The church then stood on the corner of North and Lynde streets.

On the 5th of February following, the proprietors voted to concur with the church in the above vote, only modifying the proposition "to improve Dr. Belknap's collection," by adding, in partial adherence to their first vote, " together with the psalms now in use." Perhaps this desire on the part of the proprietors to keep Tate and Brady, along with the new book to be introduced, and the counter desire of the church to dispense with it, caused the whole matter to be dropped for the time. The records make no farther reference to the subject till Jan., 1803, except that the proprietors voted in January, 1799, " not to act" upon a proposition which had been made, to add Dr. Watts' Psalms and Hymns to those already in use. On Jan. 23, 1803, the proprietors having submitted to the church, anew, the very proposition embodied and adopted in their vote of Feb. 5, 1798, — after discussion, an undecided vote, an adjournment, more conversation, and another vote, it was declared by the pastor that : " It appeared [to be] the determination of the church to concur with the proprietors of this house in the introduction of Dr. Belknap's Hymns and Psalms into public worship in connection with Tate and Brady's Psalms."

As the pastor could read from either collection, at his pleasure, however, no doubt Tate and Brady were soon quietly superseded by Belknap.

At a meeting of the Proprietors' Committee, held at the house of Jacob Ashton, on the evening of Aug. 29, 1800, it was

Voted, To recommend to the proprietors "to consider what measures they will take to provide a suitable place (either by building or otherwise), where such persons belonging to the society as are desirous of being instructed in psalmody, may conveniently meet for this purpose."

The proprietors adopted this recommendation and authorized the Committee to carry it into effect. A sub-committee, consisting of Messrs. Elijah and Jacob Sanderson and Benj. Watkins, were intrusted with the matter, who, after due consideration, decided that a building of two stories, instead of one, as originally contemplated, would be preferable, and so advised the proprietors, who, at their meeting of Jan. 12, 1801, accepted the suggestion and authorized the erection of the building, the cost thereof not to exceed the sum of seven hundred dollars. Land for the purpose was leased of James Odell, and a passage way thereto of William Luscomb. At a meeting of the Parish Committee, Jan. 12, 1801, the same sub-committee were directed to agree with and employ some person or persons suitable therefor, to take charge of and to teach psalmody to such persons as attend public worship at the North Meeting House, in the new house built by the proprietors therefor, and to draw on the treasurer for the expense attending the same. This "new building" was situated near the First Baptist Church, on the Odell estate, on the corner of a passage way leading from Federal street to Bridge street, and a passage leading from the first passage way to North street. It was subsequently removed farther down the second passage way, and now stands, as a dwelling-house, next above the gasometer. It was occupied, at one time, for a day school by William Biglow (H. Coll. 1794), afterwards Master of the Boston Latin School[*] from 1805 to 1814, and subsequently by Samuel Haraden Archer (Dart. Coll. 1818), from 1819 to 1835.

The proprietors, at their meeting, Jan. 25, 1803,

Voted, "That forty-five copies of Dr. Belknap's Collection be purchased at the expense of the proprietors for the use of the choir."

At a meeting of the Committee, Sept. 22, 1803, Col. Pickman and Mr. Elijah Sanderson were chosen a sub-committee to request Mr. Samuel McIntire and Mr. Josiah Peabody, to apply to Mr. Samuel Holyoke, or some other person, and request him to assist them in keeping a singing school for the society.

---

[*] Then standing in School street, on site of the Parker House. Master Biglow was a good classical scholar, a great wit, but severe in discipline. A common word of encouragement was "Study, boys, study, and fill up the gap where brains are left out."

This Mr. Holyoke, a graduate of Harvard College, 1789, was a son of Rev. Elizur Holyoke (Harv. Coll. 1750), minister of the East Parish of Boxford, Mass., and a cousin of the late centenarian, Dr. Edward Augustus Holyoke (Harv. Coll. 1746), of Salem. He was born at Boxford, Oct. 15, 1761, and died at Concord, N. H., Feb. 22, 1820. In his day, he was a much celebrated composer and teacher of music, writing generally for the church, and in the faulty style then in vogue. His music is now wholly out of use, having few of the elements of endurance that characterize the church Chorals of Germany and England, after the models of which later American writers have written, whose compositions show a vastly increased knowledge of the principles and laws of counterpoint and harmony. His most celebrated work was a large Collection of Hymn Tunes called the "Columbian Repository of Sacred Harmony." This was a very extensive collection of Sacred Music, containing 472 quarto pages and 750 pieces, including the whole of Dr. Watts' and of Dr. Belknap's Psalms and Hymns, to each of which a tune was adapted, as well as to some of the "particular" metres in Tate and Brady's. Published by Ranlet, Exeter, N. H. At a meeting of the Committee, Aug. 12, 1805, a sub-committee of five persons, Messrs. Benj. Goodhue, Samuel Putnam (afterwards Judge P.), Ichabod Tucker, Samuel McIntire and William P. Symonds, was chosen "to regulate the singing in time of divine service."

The first hint of an ORGAN is noticed in the record of a meeting of the Parish Committee (Messrs. Samuel Holman, Abijah Northey, Elijah Sanderson and William Ward), August 29, 1806, when it was

Voted, "That the clerk notify a meeting of the proprietors to be held at the Meeting House, on Monday, Sept. 8, to know if they will appoint a Committee to dispose of the Schoolhouse belonging to the proprietors, and appropriate the proceeds towards the purchase of an Organ, if wanted for that purpose," that is, if said proceeds be wanted to make up the amount needed, over and above the subscription.

At a meeting of the proprietors on Monday, Sept. 8, 1806, it was

Voted, "That the building belonging to the proprietors, which has been improved for a singing school, be sold, and the proceeds thereof in whole, or in part, be appropriated, if wanted, towards procuring an ORGAN for the North Meeting House," and "that the standing Committee be authorized to carry the vote into effect."

It was further

Voted, "That whatever Committee may be appointed by the individual subscribers towards the aforesaid Organ, in aid of the sum realized from the sale of the school-house, be authorized to draw out of the treasury, the whole or a part of the sum which said sale may produce, and unite it, if wanted, to the sum raised by subscription for procuring the Organ and placing it in the Meeting House."

At a meeting of the proprietors, at the house of Abijah Northey, June 3, 1808, it was

Voted, "That Ichabod Tucker, Esq., Mr. Samuel McIntire, Mr. Leverett Saltonstall and Capt. William Ward, be the Singing Committee for the said proprietors, and they are requested to take charge of the Organ when completed, and to regulate the singing in said society as they may judge most proper for the purposes of devotion and praise."

Voted, also, that "The treasurer be authorized to hire the sum of four hundred and fifty-seven dollars and eighty-five cents, to discharge the balance due by the Committee of the Organ as per account rendered in this day and examined."

This instrument was made by John E. Geib & Son, of New York, 1808, builders of some celebrity in their day. The son was a musician of some considerable note, and a maker of Piano Fortes. This Organ had two full manuals, from GG to F, omitting GG sharp; but the bass of the upper manual (swell) was "fixed," the keys being immovable, and without pipes, so that the bass of the Great Organ had to serve for the swell also. Originally it had no pedal bass. The stops were, in Great Organ (56 notes),— Open and Stopped Diapason, Principal, 12th, 15th, Sesquialtera, Dulciana, Trumpet, and blank Viol di Gamba; in Swell (extending from tenor G upwards, 38 notes), Open and Stopped Diapason, Principal and Cremona. Its touch was exceedingly hard, even affecting skill in fingering. In 1832, Messrs. Hook, Salem men who, starting in a small shop at the corner of Essex and Sewall streets, and afterwards removing to Boston, achieved the very highest and most merited celebrity as Organ-builders, made some repairs, changes and additions. They took out the old diagonal bellows, and put in one of more modern make, with feeder and reservoir, added an octave and half of pedals with a double Open Diapason of 16 feet pipes, added a Flute stop in place left blank for Viol di Gamba in Great Organ, and greatly eased the very hard touch. Good (but only that) for its day, its tones were not smooth nor agreeable, and its un-facilities would greatly trouble a modern organist. These changes were made while the instrument stood in the old church, corner of Lynde and North streets. Some repairs were made prior to the above, by William Goodrich, Organ-builder of Boston.

On the Sunday of the first playing of this Organ, Dr. Barnard preached a sermon on music, his text being "And when they had sung a Hymn they went out to the Mount of Olives." He spoke of "the stately Organ that now adorns this House." The opening of this instrument must have been quite an occasion, a full choir of volunteers having been trained to give some special music; among which was Dr. Madan's then well-known, and now shelved, Anthem, called "Denmark," Before Jehovah's awful throne.

On the Committee for procuring this Organ, were two gentlemen long identified with the music of the parish, Messrs. Tucker and Saltonstall. They were both lawyers, the former occupying, for many years, the office of Clerk of the Courts of Essex County. He was a prominent and much respected member of the society, distinguished for his interest in its welfare, and well remembered as the "minister's host," his house in Chestnut street (now Mrs. Thomas Cole's), being a home for those who supplied at exchanges or other occasions. He sang in the Choir for many years. Mr. Saltonstall was very largely and successfully engaged in the practice of law, and often placed by his fellow citizens in offices of honor and trust. He represented Salem in the Legislature of the State many times, was its first Mayor (in 1836), and a member of Congress, from the district, from 1840 to 1844. Eminent in his profession, respected and beloved by the whole community, and ardently attached to the society to which his religious convictions led him, he gave it his most earnest service and sustained its interests with unflagging devotion. A polished and accomplished gentleman, of marked and attractive face and figure and dignified bearing, of genial disposition and warm sympathies, "none knew him but to love, nor named him but to praise." He had an admirable bass voice, with exquisite musical taste, and great skill in performance; and, except when absent from home on professional or public duties, always occupied a seat in the Choir, and joined earnestly and devoutly in the praise-service of the church.

The other member, Mr. McIntire, a player on the double bass and violoncello, was a noted architect and mechanic of his day, and of rare taste and skill in his special business. He planned the old Tabernacle, the South Church, on Chestnut street, always admired for its fine proportions, and very many of the old and stately residences of the wealthy Salem merchants of his day.

By a vote passed at a meeting in June, 1821, it appears that the subject of a change in the Hymn Book was contemplated, and a special Committee was appointed upon the subject, consisting of the Hon. Joseph Story (H. Coll.), the celebrated jurist, one of the judges of the Supreme Court of the United States, Hon. Leverett Saltonstall and Hon. Ichabod Tucker. This Committee, at a meeting of the proprietors, January 14, 1822, reported in favor of substituting, in place of Dr. Belknap's, the collection known as "Sewall's," recently printed in New York, as "in the opinion of the Committee, compiled with great judgment and taste, and containing a suitable variety of sacred poetry by the best authors." The Committee added, that Rev. Mr. Brazer, the then pastor, "had perused the book and was satisfied with it." The recommendation was not adopted, and the subject was recommitted to the same Committee, with the addition of Messrs. Frederick Howes and Benjamin Pierce. This new Committee, at the annual meeting of January 13, 1823, reported "that in our opinion a change is desirable; but we think it inexpedient, at present, to recommend any particular substitute, and pray to be discharged from any further attention to the subject." [Signed, Joseph Story, *Chairman*.]

The notification for the annual meeting of March 19, 1827, contained the following clause: "To consider and determine upon the expediency of discontinuing the use of "Belknap's Collection of Psalms and Hymns," and of obtaining some other collection instead thereof." At that meeting, at which Hon. Dudley L. Pickman presided, it was

Voted, "That the Committee chosen at the last annual meeting be authorized to procure a suitable number of copies of 'Sewall's Collection of Psalms and Hymns' for the use of the church and society, printed with good type and on good paper, and handsomely, but not expensively, bound."

Subscription copies were to be paid for by the subscribers, and the rest by the treasurer.

This was the introduction of this collection, which was used by the society up to 1850.

Col. Benjamin Pickman and Messrs. Dudley L. and William Pickman were wealthy and influential citizens of Salem. Col.

Pickman's house stood on Essex, opposite St. Peter street, Mr. D. L. Pickman's on Chestnut street (now Mr. Benjamin Shreve's), Mr. Wm. Pickman's on Essex below Beckford, now Dr. G. B. Loring's.

In 1829, by vote of the proprietors' Committee, though no record thereof appears, Henry K. Oliver (Harv. and Dart. Coll., 1818), then Master of the English High School of Salem, was appointed Organist and Choir director, at a salary of two hundred and seventy-five dollars. His first thought of organ-playing came from a suggestion of Hon. Mr. Saltonstall, in a conversation on church music in 1822, intimation being given that, after qualifying by a course of study and practice, he could probably have charge of the Organ and Choir of the North Society. On this hint, he commenced study with Mr. Thomas Cooper, organist of St. Peter's Church, who, with his brother, Mr. Samuel Cooper, ranked among the best organists of the day. Compared with the present time, players were very scarce. Mr. Cooper removing to Boston, Mr. Oliver succeeded him at St. Peter's in 1823, removing in 1827 to the Barton Square Church, and thence to the North Church in 1829, where he continued the next following twenty years. During nearly all this time the Choir consisted mostly of volunteers, though salaried singers, mainly sopranos, were employed. Among these for about thirteen years, from 1837 to 1850, was Miss Catharine S. Mallet, afterwards Mrs. Henry Lemon.

This lady, a sister of Miss Sarah Mallet, organist of the North Church from 1826 to 1829, first came to Salem in 1827, as leading soprano soloist of the Mozart Association, and organist of St. Peter's Church, succeeding Mr. Oliver. This Association, consisting of about one hundred members, comprising the best talent of the city, devoted itself to the study and practice of the works of Handel, Haydn, Mozart, Beethoven, etc. It gave many concerts and greatly improved the musical knowledge, taste and skill of Salem. Mr. Oliver was its President and Conductor.

Mrs. Lemon, now residing at Newton, possessed a voice of great power, with a richness, fulness and delicacy rarely surpassed. Well instructed in the art, and with admirable appreciation of what she rendered, she never failed to make a deep and most favorable impression. She particularly excelled in Oratorio and sacred music. Most estimable in private life, she was a general favorite, and her own annual concerts always commanded a full house and hearty welcome. When permanently engaged at the North Church, she was ably seconded by Miss Ellen M. Swan, now of Boston, an alto of the very best quality, and a most excellent singer. The music of the church during all this period was of rare excellence. Miss Mallet died at Bangor, Maine, May 25, 1872, having been for many years, the organist of the Unitarian Church in that town. They were daughters of Monsieur Mallet, a French gentleman of much respectability, who came to this country with Lafayette, and served in the army of the Revolution to the end of the war. He then settled in Boston as a teacher of music, declining to receive any pension. He was among the earliest publishers of music in Boston, the friend and business partner of the celebrated Dr. G. K. Jackson, and predecessor of Graupner,* the famous double-bass player, whose music store was in Franklin street.

Mr. Adrian Low, one of the old and valued members of William Manning's corps of famous coach drivers on the Boston and Salem line of stages, and a faithful and trusted express messenger, was, at this time, a leading bass singer. His sudden disappearance, never accounted for, will be remembered by our older people. Mr. Henry Lemon, now of Newton, a baritone, was also a member of the Choir at this same date.

Nothing noteworthy in the musical history of the parish appears in the records till the year 1835–36, when the subject of a new church edifice was agitated, resulting in the erection, by subscribers, of the present stone building on Essex, west of North street.

---

* All these men are well remembered by the writer.

At a proprietors' meeting held on the 27th of May, 1836, it was

Voted (though not without some opposition), "That the old Meeting House, land, and appurtenances, the bell, organ, and clock, shall be sold for the most the same will bring."

A Committee of five persons, Messrs. John G. King, W. H. Foster, Nath'l Saltonstall, Geo. Peabody and Emery Johnson, were intrusted with this sale. The committee for building the new church purchased the old Organ at $706.50. The instrument was afterwards set up in the new building where it remained till 1847–48, when the subject of a new instrument was agitated.

By a vote at the annual meeting of the proprietors, April 11, 1847, Messrs. Francis Peabody, Geo. Wheatland, and John C. Lee, were appointed a Committee to consider the expediency of making certain alterations in the interior of the house and of purchasing a new Organ. At a meeting June 10, 1847, Col. Peabody, in behalf of the Committee, made a report favoring certain alterations, and the purchase of a new Organ, whereupon it was

Voted, "That the fund belonging to the society, which was bequeathed to it by the late W. W. Palfray, together with the proceeds of sale of old Organ, be applied by the special Committee towards procuring a new Organ, and towards certain proposed alterations in the pulpit, and in the interior of the church."

This appears to have been done, and a new and larger instrument, being the same now (1872) in use, was procured and set up. It was built by Simmons and McIntire of Boston, and set up in 1848. The main part of this instrument is about twelve feet long, with two wings added, of about four feet by three on each side, falling back from the main body. This main body, containing the wind-chests and swell, is about six feet deep, with three towers of pipes, the centre fifteen feet high, the end ones twelve feet high, with a very handsome front showing the gilt pipes of the diapasons. The following is its schedule.

GREAT ORGAN GG to F	SWELL.
Open Diapason 57 pipes	Open Diapason.
Stopped Treble and Bass 57 pipes	Stopped Treble and Bass.
Principal	Double Stopped Diapason.
Twelfth	Dulcino.
Fifteenth	Picolo.
Sesquialtera	Hautboy and Tremulant.
Clarabella	Pedal Bass of 20 pipes from GGG upward.
Dulcino	
Flute	
Couplers connect	

The bellows are not in the body of the instrument, but in a casing suspended from the ceiling of the room in the tower, back of the Organ, a large trunk conveying the wind to the wind-chests of Great Organ and swell. The blower stands in an open space between the rear of the Organ and this room. The instrument, though not of the highest order, is a vast improvement over its predecessor. Its foundation stops are not quite evenly balanced, and its fancy stops not smooth, nor reaching clear down the keyboard.

Hitherto, the Choir appears to have consisted mainly of volunteers, excepting that the organist was paid a fixed salary which had gradually risen to $275 per annum. The other expenses were for Organ-blower, Music books, and a leading Soprano singer. By vote of the proprietors at their annual meeting April 29, 1850, the cost of the annual music was limited to $500, to be raised by taxation. At the same meeting, Sewall's collection of Hymns was exchanged for a book called "Hymns for the Sanctuary," as recommended by a Committee, consisting of Messrs. Frederick Howes, Thomas Cole, and Caleb Foote. This book continued to be used till about 1869, the latter portion of the time, in conjunction with Dr. Lowell Mason's Selection of Tunes for Congregational Singing, the society having decided to introduce that form of praise service. In 1848, Gen. Oliver removed to Lawrence as

Agent of the Atlantic Cotton Mills, and was succeeded, after a short interval, by Dr. J. F. Tuckerman.

Between 1846 and 1862, the following votes are found on the records on the subject of the church music.

Dec. 28, 1846.—The proprietors voted that the Piano Forte, now in the school-room (rear of the present church), be " placed in the charge of their Committee, to be disposed of if they shall think it expedient." (This instrument had been bought some years before, and placed in the vestry then underneath the church building, a room afterwards abandoned on account of its extreme dampness. This room had been used for Sunday School, Choir and other meetings.)

May 8, 1854. — *Voted*, unanimously, "That the thanks of the society be presented to Dr. J. F. Tuckerman for the skilful, appropriate, and very satisfactory manner in which he has conducted the musical services of the society during the time the same has been under his charge." —

May 1, 1855.—A letter from Dr. Tuckerman was presented at a meeting of the Proprietors' Committee, as follows. —

SALEM, March 17, 1855.

To the Committees of the Proprietors of the North Church.

Gentlemen:—The removal of Mr. L. Saltonstall, Jr., Bass,* from Salem, which will shortly terminate the constant and able service which he has rendered in the Choir of the society for several years past, obliges me to suggest the necessity of an appropriation (of say $125 per annum), for the salary of a bass singer after the 1st of April next. With this addition, the expense of the music may be estimated as follows: —

Salaries now paid (not including Bass), ...	$500
Add for Bass voice	125
Allowance for repairs of organ tuning, music, etc.,	75
	$700

which sum I hope will be allowed.

Allow me to suggest that the discipline and training of the Choir have suffered for want of a more decided organization than now exists, and to

---

* Son of Hon. L. Saltonstall.

advise that its immediate Director be intrusted formally by your Committee with the power to engage the several members, as well as to apportion salaries and disburse the same by drafts on the Treasurer, not exceeding the limits of the annual appropriation.

I am, respectfully yours,
J. FRANCIS TUCKERMAN.

These suggestions were adopted by the Committee, and full power in the premises delegated to him as Director.

At a meeting of the Committee, Oct. 3, 1855, after the ordination of Mr. Charles Lowe, the following vote was passed:

"That the thanks of the Committee be presented to Dr. Tuckerman and other members of the Choir, and to those who volunteered their services in the orchestra, for their highly acceptable performances at the installation of Rev. Mr. Lowe on the 27th September ultimo. John H. Nichols, *Clerk*."

Votes of thanks to Dr. Tuckerman were also passed by the proprietors at their annual meeting of April 28, 1857, and May 3, 1858. At their meeting of May 7, 1860, on motion of Mr. H. L. Williams, it was

Voted, "That the members of the North Church desire to place on record their high sense of the valuable services rendered by Dr. J. Francis Tuckerman, for many years, in conducting the Choir of the church, and at the same time to express their sincere regret at the discontinuance of his connection with the church, offering their best wishes for his present and future welfare."

The Secretary was directed by vote to forward to Dr. Tuckerman a copy of the above. To this a reply was received expressive of a grateful sense of the recognition of his services, and cordially reciprocating the good will of the Committee.

The aid of Dr. Tuckerman was invaluable in the musical services of the society. It was rendered wholly gratuitously on his part. Himself an amateur of most uncommon taste and skill, a composer of much merit, with a sweet, well-trained and commanding tenor voice, and admirable administrative capacity as a leader, he brought the music of the church to the highest order of excellence, and his loss from the parish was very deeply regretted. He afterwards took charge of the Choir at "Grace Church," (Episcopalian).

He wrote for the Choir the tunes known as *Danvers*, *Beckwith*, *Contrition*, *Supplication*, *Chelsea* (L. M.'s); *Lambeth* (S. M.); *Ashburton*, *Saltonstall*, 7s; "*The Lord is my shepherd, I shall not want;*" and several chants, all possessing very great merit. He married Lucy, daughter of Hon. Mr. Saltonstall.

At the annual meeting of May 1, 1861, the charge of the music was placed in the hands of Gen. Oliver (who had returned from Lawrence to Salem), Caleb Foote and Joseph Cloutman, the former of whom took charge of the Choir, as successor to Dr. Tuckerman. His new service as Organist and Director he rendered gratuitously.

At the annual meeting of April 28, 1862, it was

Voted, "That the thanks of the society be presented to Gen. Oliver for his successful efforts in lessening the expenses of the music, and in instructing the members of the Choir and the children of the parish during the past year." A similar vote was passed at the annual meeting of April 28, 1863.

At a meeting of the proprietors, April 26, 1864, Gen. Oliver proposed, that if the proprietors assent, he will continue in charge of the musical affairs of the church, provided full power be given him to hire and discharge singers, and to control the general organization and management of the Choir, doing all without charge for personal services. His proposition was accepted. Committees on music were elected in 1865 and 1866, the same power, however, being with Gen. Oliver who was chairman of the several Committees chosen.

In 1865, though no record to that effect is found, the parish adopted Congregational Singing.

During the time of his officiating in the management of the

Choir, he wrote many Hymn tunes for its use. Among them *Federal Street, Harmony Grove, Chestnut Street, Merton, Norman, Frothingham* (on occasion of Rev. Mr. Frothingham's ordination, to a hymn written by his father, Rev. N. L. Frothingham, of Boston),* *Chadwick, Walnut Grove, Salisbury Plain, Walgrave, Vesper, Downing, Morning, Elkton, Algernon*, several Chants, and the Motets, "*Lord of all power and might*," "*The Lord shall comfort Zion*," "*How manifold are thy works O Lord*," "*Holy Lord God of Hosts*," with other compositions, most of which were subsequently published and used elsewhere. Some of these were written before his removal to Lawrence in 1848, and some after his return.

His organ-blower for many years was Philip Frye, now dead, a most skilful inflator of the bellows. This, in the old Organ, was a double apparatus with two handles, between which, in the rear of the instrument, the blower stood, alternately working one handle up and the other down, somewhat like the beam of a steam engine. Dr. Holmes well describes the labor of this "brother-player" in his humorous "Organ-blower," which is so exact and true that it is inserted here.

> "O brother, with the supple spine
> How much we owe those bows of thine!
> Without thine arm to lend the breeze,
> How vain the fingers on the keys!
> Tho' all unmatched the player's skill,
> Those thousand throats were dumb and still.
> Another's art may shape the tone,
> The breath that fills it is thine own."—
>
> Not all the preaching, O my friend,
> Comes from the church's pulpit end!

---

* At the ordination of Mr. Frothingham the musical performance was conducted by Gen. Oliver at the Organ, Miss Frost, of Boston (for the occasion), Soprano, Miss Swan, Alto, Mr. B. S. Whitmore, Tenor, and Messrs. William Brown and B. F. Baker, Bassos. The tune "Frothingham" was then first sung, and a Motet by Charles Zeuner to the words "How beautiful upon the mountains," a composition of very great merit.

> Not all that bend the knee, and bow,
> Yield service half so true as thou!
> One simple task performed aright,
> With slender skill, but all thy might.
> Where honest labor does its best,
> And leaves the player all the rest."

Gen. Oliver always made it a point to thank his faithful helper at close of service; for what were the player without the blower, as the former was once made to feel, when, in the midst of playing a Hymn tune, the Organ ceased, with a dying wail! On running to the rear to find the cause, he found his helpmate, wearied with rising and sinking [the Hymn was a four verse, six line Long Metre, with the thermometer at 90° and a summer afternoon], had dropped into "sound" slumber — and,

> In sleep serene and calmly laid,
> Oblivious of the needed "blows;"
> With deep-drawn breath and full, he played
> The diapason of the nose; —
> So full, so rich, and all so clear and strong,
> The echoing pipes the snorting strain prolong.—H. K. O.

The Choir of the North Church has always been fortunate in its members, having had among them many persons from the best educated and most prominent families of the parish. As well as the writer can recollect, there have belonged to it at various times down to the year 1873: —

Ichabod Tucker, Esq., Tenor, H. Coll., 1791.
Dr. Nathaniel Peabody, Tenor. Father of Mrs. Nath'l Hawthorne, Mrs. Horace Mann and Miss Elizabeth Peabody.
Hon. Leverett Saltonstall, Bass, H. Coll., 1802.
Oliver Parsons, Esq., Tenor.
* Dr. Charles G. Putnam, Bass, H. Coll., 1824.
* Mrs. Joseph Augustus (Putnam) Peabody, Soprano.
* Mrs. Charles G. (Putnam) Loring, Soprano.
* Mrs. Francis B. (Putnam) Crowninshield, Soprano.
Joseph Richards, Esq., Tenor. Father of Mrs. Theodore Tilton, of New York.
Nathaniel J. Lord, Esq., Bass, H. Coll., 1825.

---

* Son and daughters of Hon. Samuel Putnam, Judge of Sup. Court of Massachusetts (H. Coll., 1787). His house was No. 138 Federal street.

150 MEMORANDA OF CHOIR.

George Peabody, Esq., Bass. H. Coll. 1823.
Gen. H. K. Oliver, Bass and Organist, H. and Dart. Coll., 1818.
Benjamin Tucker (nephew of Ichabod, Esq.) Tenor, H. Coll., 1821.
Dr. Edward S. Lang, Bass.
Mrs.   "   "   "   Soprano, } Sisters.
Mrs. Edward Brimmer,   "   }
Solomon S. Whipple, Esq., Bass.
Mrs. "   "   "   Soprano.
John Chadwick, Esq., Bass, Cashier Exchange Bank.
Mrs. John Chadwick, Soprano.
Samuel B. Buttrick, Esq., Counter Tenor.
Col. Joseph Sprague, Bass, Aid to Gov. William Eustis.
Hon. Caleb Foote, Bass, Editor Salem Gazette. Mrs. C. Foote, Soprano.
Henry Lemon, Esq., Baritone.
Edw. H. Payson, Esq., Bass.
Mr. Benj. Shillaber, Bass.
Mrs. Horace Mann (daughter of Dr. Nath. Peabody), Soprano.
Miss Elizabeth Peabody (daughter of Mrs. J. A. Peabody), Soprano.
Mrs. H. Lemon, Soprano (sister of Miss S. Mallet, organist).
Mr. Adrian Low, Bass.
Miss Ellen M. Swan, Alto.
Mrs. Harriet M. Badum, Alto.
Miss Elizabeth Donaldson, Soprano.
Mrs. John C. Lee, Soprano.
Ebenezer Shillaber, Esq., Bass.
Mr. Samuel N. Glover, Bass.
Dr. Edward Barnard, Tenor.
Miss E. M. B. Brooks (sister of Rev. Chs. T. Brooks, H. Coll., 1832), Alto.
* Mrs. John Webster, Soprano.

* Mrs. Stephen Field, Soprano.
* Mrs. William F. Nichols, "
* Mrs. John Frost, Soprano.
George Francis Chever, Esq., Tenor, H. Coll. 1840.
Mrs. Benjamin S. Whitmore, Soprano.
Horace P. Farnham, Esq., Bass, H. Coll. 1843.
Miss Emily P. Farnham, Soprano.
Mr. Benj. S. Whitmore, Tenor.
Stephen Wheatland, Esq., H. Coll., was leader of the music in the years 1846 and 1847.
Dr. J. Francis Tuckerman, Tenor, H. Coll., 1837.
Mrs. J. Francis Tuckerman (daughter of Hon. Leverett Saltonstall), Soprano.
Mrs. Benjamin S. Whitmore, Mezzo Soprano.
Col. Henry Merritt (Mass. Vols. Killed at Newbern, 1862.)
Mrs. S. F. Govea, Soprano.
Mr. J. A. Newcomb, Bass.
  "   E. A. Bennett,   "
  "   Jos. Newell,   "
Leverett Saltonstall, Esq., Bass.
Mr. Stephen P. Driver, Tenor.
  "   Geo. A. Fuller,   "
  "   Cyrus L. Hayward,   "
  "   Charles H. Stanton, Bass.
Mrs. Mary E. Dixey, Alto.
Miss M. E. Smith,   "
  "   Fanny E. Paine, Soprano. } Sisters.
  "   Eleanor V. Paine,   "   }
Miss Elizabeth S. Merritt (daughter of Col. M.), Soprano.
Mrs. William L. (Nichols) Kinsman, Soprano.
Miss Mary E. Aldrich, Soprano.

The present Choir, 1872-73, consists of

Misses Lucy B. Willson, M. Louisa Webb, Mary M. Brooks and Mrs. Anna B. Richardson, Sopranos.
Mrs. F. H. Lee, Miss Mary E. Webb, Altos.
Hon. Lincoln F. Brigham, Dart. Coll., 1842, Chief Justice Superior Court of Mass. Hon. George B. Loring, President Mass. Senate, 1873, H. Coll. 1838. Mr. Robert W. Willson, H. Coll., 1873, Tenors.

Gen. Henry K. Oliver, Ex-Adj. Gen. and Treas. of Mass. Solomon Lincoln, Jr., Esq., Barrister. Augustus J. Archer, Esq., Merchant. Mr. Francis H. Lee. Prof. Edward S. Morse. Mr. Henry M. Brooks, Treas. F. R. Lead Co. Mr. Arthur W. Foote, H. Coll. 1874, Bassos.
Miss Louisa A. Goodwin, Organist.

---

*Daughters of Capt. James Buffington.

The several Organists have been

John Hart	from 1808 to ——	Henry K. Oliver,	1829 to 1848.
Thomas Cooper,	—— to 1821.	George J. Breed,	1848 to 1857.
Rev. Joseph Mueascher,	1821 to 1823.	Frank Upton,	1857 to 1866.
Marshall Pratt,	1823 to 1824.	Manuel Emilio,	1867 to 1868.
Peter C. L' Ouvrier,	1825 to 1826.	Louisa A. Goodwin,	1868 to ——.
Sarah Mallet,	1826 to 1829.		

The several Music Books used have been

Salem Collection, edited by John Appleton, of the firm of Cushing & Appleton.
Village Harmony.
Bridgewater Collection, edited by Judge N. Mitchell and Bartholomew Brown.
Handel and Haydn Collection, edited by Lowell Mason.
Boston Academy's, edited by Lowell Mason.
Ancient Lyre, edited by Charles Zeuner.
American Harp, edited by Charles Zeuner.
Carmina Lucia, edited by Lowell Mason.
Greatorex, compiled by Greatorex.
Massachusetts Collection, edited by Geo. J. Webb.
Mozart Collection.
Beethoven Collection, edited by Ives, Alpers and Timms.
Church and Home, edited by Gould and White.
Kreissman's Anthems, August Kreissman, Songs of Zion.
Baumbach's Motets, edited by Baumbach.
Oliver's Collection, compiled by H. K. Oliver.

At present (1872), the only book used is the "Hymn and Tune Book," published by the American Unitarian Association, and used for Congregational Singing (the only music now in vogue in the service) by both Choir and congregation. It was formerly the custom at the opening of the service, for the Choir to sing a short anthem, motet, or chant, generally from the books of Zeuner, Baumbach, Oliver, or Gould & White. This was continued until the introduction of the "Hymn and Tune Book," published by the American Unitarian Association, Jan. 1, 1869. The service (held in the forenoon only) now consists of a Voluntary on the Organ, a Hymn tune, Prayer, Reading of Scripture, Hymn tune, Sermon, Prayer, Hymn tune, Benediction, Voluntary. The afternoon is given to the Sunday School, at the Vestry in rear of the church.

THE CHURCH:

COVENANT; EARLY MEMBERS AND OFFICERS; MINISTER'S LIBRARY; SUNDAY SCHOOL; EXTRACTS AND NOTES FROM THE RECORDS.

The above engraving represents the PICKMAN HOUSE, as it appeared in 1832, then owned and occupied by the third Col. Benjamin Pickman, a grandson of the first Col. Benjamin Pickman, who built the same in 1750, who took so prominent a part in the founding of this church and society, and is frequently alluded to in this memoir.

On its site once stood a house built by Henry Bartholemew, soon after the settlement of the town, and which was purchased in 1680, by Timothy Lindall, a prominent merchant in his day — Mr. Lindall died in 1699 and gave it to his widow, who, about the time of her death in 1732, gave it to her daughter, Sarah Lindall. In 1749, Sarah Lindall (then Mrs. Morehead) gave the house and land to her nephew, Benjamin Pickman, who, in 1750, pulled it down and built the house above alluded to. The house stands on Essex street, opposite the head of St. Peter street, and is now owned by Mrs. Lemaster, who has erected stores on the front extending to the street.

COVENANT

ADOPTED AND SIGNED JULY 19, 1772.

"We, the subscribers, late members of the First Church of Christ in Salem, but regularly dismissed therefrom, humbly sensible of the frowns of God upon us, in this separation from our brethren with whom we are still desirous of living in all christian fellowship and charity, being desirous to form ourselves into a complete organic church, and to enjoy the institutions and ordinances of the Lord Jesus Christ and have them regularly administered to us,

Do now, in the first place, humbly and solemnly renew the dedication of ourselves and offspring to the great God, Father, Son and Holy Ghost, and we do hereby profess our firm belief of the Holy Scriptures contained in the Old and New Testaments, and taking them for our sole and sufficient rule of faith and practice, we do covenant and engage to and with each other, that we will walk together as a christian society, in the faith and order of the gospel, agreeable to the laudable practice of the congregational churches in New England, and we do hereby engage for ourselves (and as far as in our power, for all under our care) that we will live as becomes the true disciples of Jesus Christ, in all good carriage and behaviour, both towards God and towards man, hereby recognizing and renewing the substance of the first covenant entered into by our pious ancestors at their first founding a church in New England, in this town, Aug. 6, 1629, professing ourselves nevertheless, to be in charity with all men who love the Lord Jesus Christ in sincerity and truth.

And all this we engage faithfully to perform, not in our own strength, but by the assistance of the divine spirit which we are encouraged to hope for, relying upon the atonement purchased by the blood of the great mediator for the pardon of our manifold sins, and praying that the glorious Jesus, the great Head of the Church, would strengthen and enable us to keep this, our covenant, inviolate, and establish and settle us, and at last present us faultless before the presence of his glory with exceeding joy."

The following is the covenant referred to above as "the substance of the first covenant entered into by our pious ancestors at their first founding a church in New England, in this town, Aug. 6, 1629;" and which the subscribers to the covenant of the North Church, "recognized and renewed" and made a part of their own. It was not strictly the first covenant, as adopted Aug. 6, 1629: that was gone; but it was that covenant as "renewed" in 1636. For the age of this covenant, therefore, we cannot, with historical accuracy, go beyond the last-named date.

"We, whose names are here underwritten, members of the present church of Christ in Salem, having found by sad experience how dangerous it is to sit loose to the covenant we make with our God; and how apt we are to wander into by-paths, even to the losing of our first aims in entering into church fellowship: Do therefore, solemnly, in the presence of the Eternal God, both for our own comforts and those which shall or may be joined unto us, renew that church covenant we find this church bound unto at their first beginning, viz:— That we covenant with the Lord, and one with another; and do bind ourselves in the presence of God, to walk together in all his ways, according as he is pleased to reveal himself unto us in his blessed word of truth, and do more explicitly, in the name and fear of God, profess and protest to walk as followeth, through the power and grace of our Lord Jesus Christ.

1. First we avow the Lord to be our God, and ourselves his people in the truth and simplicity of our spirits.

2. We give ourselves to the Lord Jesus Christ and the word of his grace, for the teaching, ruling and sanctifying of us in matters of worship and conversation, resolving to cleave to Him alone, for life and glory; and oppose all contrary ways, constitutions and canons of men in his worship.

3. We promise to walk with our brethren and sisters in this congregation with all watchfulness and tenderness, avoiding all jealousies, suspicions, backbitings, censurings, provokings, secret risings of spirit

against them; but in all offences to follow the rule of the Lord Jesus, and to bear and forbear, give and forgive, as he hath taught us.

4. In public or private, we will willingly do nothing to the offence of the church, but will be willing to take advice for ourselves and ours, as occasion shall be presented.

5. We will not, in the congregation, be forward either to show our own gifts and parts in speaking or scrupling, or there discover the failing of our brethren or sisters, but attend an orderly call thereunto; knowing how much the Lord may be dishonored, and his gospel, in the profession of it, slighted by our distempers and weaknesses in public.

6. We bind ourselves to study the advancement of the gospel in all truth and peace, both in regard of those that are within or without, no way slighting our sister churches, but using their counsel as need shall be: nor laying a stumbling block before any, no not the Indians, whose good we desire to promote, and so to converse, as we may avoid the very appearance of evil.

7. We hereby promise to carry ourselves in all lawful obedience to those that are over us, in church or common weal, knowing how well pleasing it will be to the Lord, that they should have encouragement in their places by our not grieving their spirits through our irregularities.

8. We resolve to approve ourselves to the Lord in our particular callings, shunning idleness as the bane of any state, nor will we deal hardly, or oppressingly, with any, wherein we are the Lord's stewards: also,

9. Promising to our best ability, to teach our children and servants the knowledge of God and his will, that they may serve him also; and all this, not by any strength of our own, but by the Lord Jesus Christ, whose blood we desire may sprinkle this our covenant made in his name."

The following are the names of the persons who signed this covenant and were gathered into a church on the 19th of July.

John Nutting,	William Browne,	Sarah Curwen,
Benj. Pickman,	Samuel Holman,	Susannah Grafton,
Joshua Ward,	Benj. Pickman, Jr.	Mary Grafton,
Samuel West,		Priscilla Ropes,
E. A. Holyoke,	Love Pickman,	Sarah Gardner,
John Lankford,	Katharine Sargent,	Elizabeth Field,
James Gould,	Elizabeth Nutting,	Priscilla Field,

Mary Pickman,	Hannah Watts,	Mehitable Cook,
Mary Gill,	Ruth Holman,	Mary Cox,
Mary West,	Hannah Symonds,	Mary Grant,
Sarah Cook,	Elizabeth Symonds,	Bethiah Ruck,
Hannah Chapman,	Abigail West,	Mary Holman,
Hannah Gillingham,	Elizabeth Holman,	Mary Archer,
Elizabeth Lunt,	Elizabeth Archer,	Eunice Crowninshield,
Mary West,	Mary Blaney,	Mary Glover,
Sarah Foster,	Elizabeth Newhall,	Martha Morong,
Lydia Jane,	Jane Ropes,	Sarah Lankford.
Mehitable Ward,		

It was

Voted, On the day that the church was formed "That if any person of sober life and conversation incline to join us previous to the settlement of a minister, they may be admitted by manifesting their desire to the brethren, and obtaining their consent, and subscribing to the foregoing covenant."

Agreeably to this vote the following persons became members by signing the covenant within the time prescribed.

Samuel Curwen,	Lydia King,	Thomas Barnard, Jr.,
Abigail Curwen,	Elizabeth King,	Rebecca, servant of Mr.
Francis Cabot,	Lydia King, Jr.,	Ebenezer Ward,
James King,	Sarah Pickman,	Rebecca Bickford,
William Vans,	Mehitable Ward,	Martha Gavit,
Richard Ward,	Abial Bright,	Jacob Ashton,
David Mason,*	Sarah Curwen, Jr.,	Susanna Ashton,
Henry Rust,	Margaret Daniell,	Mary Symonds,
Eleazer Moses,	Sarah Pickering,	Jonathan Goodhue,
Jonathan Gavit,	Lois Barnard,†	Elizabeth Giles.
William Paine,	Lydia Chapman,	
Sarah Kimball,	Lydia Rust.	

The record of admissions to the church from the ordination of Mr. Barnard to the year 1836, when the society left their first meeting house, is here given. Mr. Barnard did not record the

---

* " Dismissed from Dr. Boyle's church, Boston."
† If Mrs. Barnard was received into the church in 1772, it must have been as Lois Gardner, as her marriage with Rev. Mr. Barnard did not take place till May 31st of the following year. Her name, however, is found among those who signed the covenant previous to the settlement of a minister.

dates of admission; some later hand has supplied various dates, some of them indefinite, beginning with the year 1790; they bear the marks of care, and may be taken, it is believed, as in the main. trustworthy.

Hannah Ward,
Francis Skerry,
Ann Johnston,
William Pickman,
Elizabeth Symonds,
Margaret Symonds,
Benjamin Symonds,
Martha Allentt,
William West,
Elizabeth Symonds,
Sarah Ward,
Elizabeth Tink,
Eunice Symonds,
Nathaniel Holman,
Hannah Holman,
Robert Alcock,
Elizabeth Alcock,
Abigail Bromfield,
Elizabeth Ravell,
Eunice Glover,
Mary King,
Samuel King,
Elizabeth Cook,
Betty Ingalls,
Isaac White,
Sarah White,
Cæsar—"a black man,"
Susannah Gerrish,
Dorothy Goodhue,
Sarah Hastie,
Hannah Lampriel,
Elizabeth Dodge,
Lydia Grafton,
Lydia Skerry,
Mary Ingersoll,
Hitty Williams,
Elizabeth Pickman,
Caleb Smith,
Sarah Palfray,
Mercy Smith,

Hopestill Hardy,
Lydia Gray,
Benjamin Watkins,
Warwick Palfray,
Ann Watkins,
Samuel Field,
Benjamin Goodhue, Jun.,
Rachel Forrester,
Mary Goodale,
Henry Gibbs,
Mercy Gibbs,
Samuel M'Intire,
Elizabeth M'Intire,
Judith King,
Sarah Dorton,
Habakkuk Bowditch,
Mary Bowditch,
Lois Phippen,
Mary Skerry,
Mary West,
Elizabeth Henderson,
Lydia Needham,
Nathaniel Symonds, Jun.
Jacob Sanderson,
Catherine Sanderson,
Elijah Sanderson,
Mary Sanderson,
Elizabeth Symonds,
Mary Austin,
Sarah Hales,
Elizabeth Dabney,
Elizabeth Gavett,
Jean Skerry,
Mercy Ashbe,
Eliza Benson,
Mary Andrew,
Eunice Sampson,
Mary Ashton, Jun.,
Abigail Downing,
Eliza M'Coomb,

Sarah Leonard,
Margaret Hiller,
Angier M'Intire,
Mary M'Intire,
Mercy Gibbs Frost,
Mary Brewer,
Margaret Holyoke,
Sally Knight,
Joseph Hiller,
Jonathan Herrick,
William Herrick,
Elizabeth Herrick,
Joseph M'Intire,
Mehitable Earvin,
Mary Andrew,
Sarah Phippen,
George Earvin,
Susannah Johnston,
Sarah Rust,
Sarah M'Intyre,
James Nichols,
Rebecca Pierce,
Sarah Lander,
Nabby Ward,
Eliza Carlton,
Warwick Palfray,
Sarah Gavett,
Jonathan Gavett, Jun.,
Ruth Holman, Jun.,
Lydia Rust,
Mehitable Andrew,
Margaret Ropes,
Hannah Frye,
Katharine Millet,
Anstiss Pickman.

1790.

Abigail Mason Dabney,
Abigail Northey,
Lydia Pope,

THE CHURCH.

1791 to 1795.
Samuel Holman, Jun.,
Eunice Holman,
Mary Bowditch,
Isaac Osgood,
Hannah Gardner,
Abigail Benson,
Eliza West,
Sarah Ward,
Elizabeth Symonds,
Hannah Hiller,
Dorcas C. Hiller,
Margaret Hiller,
Mary West,
Sarah Bacon,
Charles Cleveland,
Mercy Berry.

1795.
Edward Brown,
Mehitable Ward,
Mary Henderson,
Mary Foster,
Peggy Millet.

1796 to 1798.
Eliza Holman,
Eliza Peabody,
William Phippen,
Anna Phippen,
Rebecca T. Osgood,
Samuel Putnam,
Sarah Putnam.

1798.
Sally Archer,
Joseph Osgood, Jun.,
Polly Osgood,
Mary Pickman,
John Sabin,
Nathaniel Foster,
Lydia Nichols,
William Ward,
Nabby Perkins.

1799 to 1803.
Mehitable Carwick,
Elizabeth Gardner,
Mercy Walker,
Benjamin Pickman, Jun.
Hannah Clarke,
Hannah King,
Content Skerry,
Lucy Bright,
Sarah Emery,
Elizabeth Pickman,
Sarah Needham,
Sally Field,
Sarah Whittredge,
Nathaniel Knight,
Polly Goldthwait,
Abigail Very,
Peggy Sprague,
Susanna Ashton,
Mary Ashton,
Mary Andrews,
John Dabney,
Peggy Symonds,
Sukey Grafton,
Hannah Seccomb,
Benjamin Fisk,
Lydia Fisk,
Sarah Swett,
Martha Wheatland,
Mehitable Purbeck,
Sally Nichols.

1803 to 1807.
Daniel Clarke,
Mary Clarke,
John D. Treadwell,
Dorothy Treadwell,
Abigail Brewer,
Lydia R. Pierce,
Lydia Peele,
Sally Phippen,
Ichabod Nichols, 3d,
Frances Ashton,
Margaret Gerrish,

Hannah Cabot,
Mary Beckford,
Mary Allen,
Thomas C. Cushing,
Lois Balch,
Catharine Andrew,
Hannah Taylor,
Nancy Mackey,
Mehitable Cleveland,
Mary Farrington,
Betsey Butman.

1807 to 1809.
Ichabod Tucker,
Rachel Cushing,
Abigail Breed,
Rebecca M. Dow,
Polly Fuller,
Lydia Dodge,
Fanny Cabot,
Lucy Cabot,
Joseph Sprague,
Lydia Bryant,
Bartholomew Putnam,
Lucia Swett,
Polly Boutman,
John Fairfield, Jun.,
Martha Fairfield,
Benjamin R. Nichols,
Elizabeth Andrews.

1809.
Martha H. Tucker,
Sarah Marston,
Ruth Gray,
Eliza G. Dabney,
Frances Swett,
Sarah Grant,
Gideon Tucker.

1810 to 1813.
Oliver Parsons,
Rachel Forrester,
Benjamin Peirce,

THE CHURCH.

Hitty Osgood,
Sarah C. Bronsdon,
Sally Newhall,
Robert Procter,
Lydia Procter,
Dudley L. Pickman,
Catharine Pickman,
Joseph Peabody,
Elizabeth Peabody,
Robert F. Cloutman,
Mary Ann Cloutman,
Nancy Davis Gay,
E. Orne Tucker,
Susanna Tucker,
William Gibbs,
Mercy Gibbs,
Mary Shreve.

1813 to 1815.
Jonathan P. Saunders,
Mary Adams Saunders,
Abigail Buffinton,
Charlotte S. Forrester,
Rebecca Phippen,
Jonathan P. Dabney,
Mary Nichols,
Henry Peirce,
David Nichols.

1815.
John Emery Abbot,
Robert Emery,
Margaret G. Emery,
Rebecca Sutton,
Sarah Beckford,
Sarah Ashton,
Anna Ashton,
Leverett Saltonstall,
Mary Eliz. Saltonstall,
Thomas Cole,
Hannah Lucas Cole,
Abiel Chandler,
Elizabeth Endicott,
Anna Dodge,
Caroline Plummer.

L. Rawlins Pickman,
C. Gayton Pickman.

1816.
Abigail Frye,
Elizabeth Phillips,
Nancy F. Barstow,
Charlotte Saunders,
Lydia Sanderson,
Sarah Roberts,
Eliza Sanderson,
Thomas Pickman,
Sophia Pickman,
Nathaniel Peabody,
Elizabeth Peabody.

1817.
George Nichols,
Sarah H. Ropes,
Elizabeth Cole,
Hannah Putnam,
Louisa Putnam,
Elizabeth D. Pickman,
Maria Rea,
Sarah Holman,
Abigail Webber,
Mary Cook,
Abigail Spencer.

1819.
Francis Gerrish.

1820.
Martha Pickman,
John Brazer.

1821.
Mehitable M'Intire,
Amos Clark,
Pamela Clark,
Betsy W. Dodge,
Sarah Moses,
Martha Gale,
Elizabeth Cushing,
Elizabeth Hathorne,

Nancy Andrews,
Samuel Gerrish,
Rachel Barton,
Margaret O. Endicott,
Ruth Henderson,
Margaret Oliver,
Abby Oliver,
Anne W. Brazer,
Alice Punchard,
Frederick Howes,
Elizabeth Howes,
Lydia Suelling.

1822.
Eliza Amelia White,
Sally Bulson,
Martha Gavett,
Lydia Richardson,
Mehitable Neal,
Hannah Endicott,
Hannah L. Burchmore,
Nancy W. Bell.

1823.
Sarah Chandler,
Sally Chandler,
Elizabeth Burnham,
Sarah P. Nichols,
Elizabeth Kimball,
Mary T. Peabody,
Lydia R. Nichols,
Eliza H. Bott,
Sally G. Procter,
Lydia R. Treadwell,
Gideon Barstow,
Mary B. Osgood,
Elizabeth Churchill,
Jane Shillaber,
Catharine Kimball.

1824.
Ruth Driver,
Lydia Ward,
Rebecca Frye,
Lydia Cheever,

Archelaus Rea,
Susan Potter,
Mary Jane Page,
Martha Peabody,
Eliza. W. Brookhouse,
Andrew Bowers,
Catharine Hathorne,
Joseph Goss,
Harriet Endicott,
Eliza H. Mansfield,
Harriet Mansfield,
Elizabeth Frye,
Fanny Bowers,
Susannah Hathorne,
Sally Knight,
Mary Knight.

1825.
Benjamin Shillaber,
Joanna Payson,
Lydia Gavett,
Mary Beckford,
Hannah Symonds,
Mary J. Andrews,
Susan Buffum,
Lucy G. Ives,
Augustus Choate,
Elizabeth West,
Mary Jane Scobie,
Sarah Buffum,
Lydia Scobie,
E. A. Holyoke, Jun.,

1826.
Elizabeth West,
Abigail P. West,
Elijah Fuller,
Daniel Bray, Jun.,
Mary Bray,
Lucy C. Putnam,
Priscilla Archer,
Elizabeth Pearson,
Eliza Endicott,
Maria Osgood,
Sally Webb,

Susan H. King,
Eliza Felt,
Francis Ames Bowers,
Frances P. Bowers,
Ann M. B. Gale.

1827.
Charles Hoffman,
Anstiss D. Rogers,
Richard Wheatland,
Sophia Peabody,
Anne Savage,
Isabel Page,
Nancy Chamberlain,
Mary Goldthwaite,
Sarah Ormond,
Mary Crawford Wells,
Catherine Brown,
Eliza Chadwick Bridges,
Elizabeth Perkins.

1828.
Mary Wells,
Mercy Roche,
Allen Putnam, Jr.,
Sarah Osgood,
Lydia Maria Buxton,
Mary Anne Putnam.

1829.
Mary Page,
Harriet F. Peabody,
Clarissa Peabody,
Elizabeth Joplin,
David Cummins,
M. F. Cummins,
Lydia Whipple,
Martha T. Luscomb,
Amelia M. Payson,
Charles M. Endicott,
Sarah R. Endicott.

1830.
Caleb Foote,
Joseph Felt,

Sarah A Shillaber,
Sarah G. Putnam,
Margaret P. Dabney,
Mary L. Cloutman,
Susan W. Osgood.

1831.
Lydia L. Cloutman,
Elizabeth C. Cook,
E. H. Payson,
Margaret Savage.

1832.
Rebecca Farnham,
Susan L. Whittredge,
Mary Chandler,
Elizabeth Dodge,
Elizabeth Cummings,
Judith Dean,
Martha B. Jelly,
Lydia Owen,
Sarah Pearson.

1833.
Mary F. Nichols,
Martha B. Webster,
Frances G. Ashton,
Elizabeth Carlton,
Margaret Sprague,
Elizabeth Page,
Hannah Herrick.

1834.
Helen Ruee,
Elizabeth Redding,
Elizabeth Wheatland,
Sally Frye,
Charlotte Ingalls.

1835.
Harriet S. Dodge,
E. T. Brookhouse,
Sarah King,
Mary Ann B. Ward,
Laura W. Sprague,

THE CHURCH.   163

Hannah P. Frye,   Ann Bowden Freeman.   1836.
Ruth S. S. Bott,   Ichabod Nichols.   Sophia Jane Burnham,
Clarissa Balch,   Jane Lakeman.

OFFICERS OF THE CHURCH.

From quite an early period the New England churches were accustomed to have an order of officers, intermediate in authority and dignity, between the ministers and deacons, called Ruling Elders. They assisted the ministers in their pastoral duties, and were naturally their chief advisers among the laity. The North Church followed the custom of the Mother Church, and at its organization chose two Ruling Elders, the usual number. The last election of a member to this office was in 1826. The following persons were successively chosen Ruling Elders.

John Nutting,	chosen Aug. 20, 1772,	died May 20, 1790.
Joshua Ward,	" " " "	" Dec. 29, 1779.
Edward A. Holyoke,	" Jan. 12, 1873,	" Mch. 31, 1829.
Samuel Hohman,	" Nov. 10, 1793,	" Nov. 24, 1825.
Jacob Ashton,	" Feb. 7, 1826,	" Dec. 28, 1829.

The following persons were successively chosen to fill the office of Deacon in the church.

James Gould,	chosen Aug. 20, 1772,	dismissed Jan. 5, 1783.*
Samuel Hohman,	" " " "	died Nov. 24, 1825.†
Jacob Sanderson,	" Jan. 31, 1785,	" Feb. 12, 1810.
Elijah Sanderson,	" Dec. 22, 1814,	" Feb. 16, 1825.
Edward Brown,	" " " "	" June 10, 1844.
Thomas Cole,	" Sept. 1, 1825,	" June 24, 1852.
Edward A. Holyoke,	" Mch. 28, 1848,	" Dec. 19, 1855.‡
Daniel Bray,	" " " "	" Feb. 24, 1850.

In late years those who have acted as deacons have declined the office and title, but have consented temporarily to fulfil its duties. Edward H. Payson and Caleb Foote have thus served the church most acceptably for many years.

---

* At his own request.
† For thirty-two years Samuel Hohman held the offices, both, of Ruling Elder and Deacon.
‡ In Syracuse, New York.

William Browne was chosen the first "Scribe" or clerk of the church, Aug. 3, 1772, and performed the duties of the office till the settlement of Mr. Barnard.

Rev. Mr. Barnard acted as clerk during his ministry; and after his death, Ichabod Tucker, Esq., was chosen clerk, Oct. 31, 1814, and held the office till 1840 or later.

Charles M. Endicott was chosen clerk Oct. 1, 1842, and continued in the office till 1856 or later, there being no record of his resignation.

Henry M. Brooks was chosen clerk May 4, 1862, and still holds the office.

MINISTER'S LIBRARY.

The Rev. Mr. Abbot, shortly before his death, placed in the hands of his father the following memorandum:

"I wish to leave all the books which are marked in my Catalogue, to the North Society for the use of their Pastor for the time being. In this way I hope that when I shall speak to my beloved people no more, I may still, in a remote manner, be doing good to them and to their children."

The books thus given for the use of the minister numbered one hundred and sixty-eight volumes, many of them of high cost, and at the time standard works. Some of them have a less relative value now, having been superseded by later biblical studies and an ever-advancing learning.

The principle upon which the selection was made was evidently that the collection should contain for his successors' use the choicest books of his library. Subsequently, considerable additions were made to this library, principally by purchase, during the ministry of Dr. Brazer. For many years additions have nearly ceased.

THE SUNDAY SCHOOL.

The Sunday School was organized in June, 1828. It was the earliest formed of the Sunday Schools connected with the Unitarian churches of the town, though such schools were already common in churches of other denominations. It was not at first looked upon with favor by a large part of the society. Indeed the opposition to it was such that some would not allow their pews to be used by Sunday School classes. It began with thirty scholars. For three years its expenses (chiefly the cost of books) were borne by Mr. Leverett Saltonstall, the superintendent, Mr. Francis Choate, his assistant, and acting superintendent in the periods of his absence, and Rev. Dr. Brazer; Mr. Saltonstall contributed one hundred dollars, Mr. Choate more than fifty dollars, and Dr. Brazer a smaller sum. A subscription taken afterwards to reimburse these expenses amounted to seven dollars! So great was Mr. Saltonstall's interest, and so devoted his service, that during one of his summer recesses spent at Haverhill, he was accustomed to ride down to Salem in his gig, a distance of about twenty miles to attend the Sunday services of the church, and to discharge his duties as superintendent of the Sunday School. He continued to fill this office for eleven years, and brought the school to a high prosperity as to numbers, interest and usefulness. He may be said, in fact, to have been its founder, since the conclusion of the pastor, and such as he consulted before entering on the enterprise, was that, in view of the discouragements and prejudices which beset it, if Mr. Saltonstall would consent to become the superintendent, the experiment might be expected to succeed, otherwise not.

Singing was not introduced into its exercises till 1829.

The following gentlemen, so far as can now be ascertained, have been superintendents of the school.

1. Leverett Saltonstall, 1828 to 1838.
2. Francis Choate,* assistant superintendent from 1828 to 1838.
3. Thomas Barnard West, from Dec., 1838, to May, 1840.
4. Thomas Cole, from 1840 to 1842.
5. Edward A. Holyoke, from Oct. 1842 to 1844, and probably longer.
6. George Wheatland, from 1847 (?) to 1849. (?)
7. George B. Loring, from 1852 to 1854.
8. O. B. Frothingham,
9. Andrew B. Almon,
10. William F. Nichols,
11. Solomon Lincoln, Jr.
12. John K. Lakeman,
13. E. B. Willson.

EXTRACTS FROM THE RECORDS, AND NOTES.

1772, *Dec.* 14. "Publick Thanksgiving, December 3. Contributed £16—5—4. L. M. T."

1773, *Jan.* 11. *Voted*, "That the church recommend to Mr. Barnard to have a monthly lecture, if it is agreeable to the proprietors and they will attend."

1773, *Feb.* 26. *Voted*, unanimously, "That members be admitted to our communion for the future by signing personally, in presence of the minister or one of the elders, the covenant which the church first entered into, instead of having it propounded to them publickly."

1773, *May* 25. *Voted*, "That there should be public catechising in the meeting house."

1773, *May* 25. *Voted*, "That there should be a monthly lecture on the Wednesday preceding the sacrament to begin at three in the afternoon through the summer months, and at two through the winter."

1793, *Nov.* 10. The church voted unanimously that the minister might administer the ordinance of baptism in private houses on "application from adults, or from parents entitled to baptism according to the votes of this church, in behalf of their children," "not less than two brethren of the church," beside the minister, being present; the church "being of the opinion that neither the precepts of the gospel, nor the practice of the apostles are repugnant to such a mode of administration." Nevertheless this church "recommend when health will permit that the administration

---

* Mr. C. was associated with Mr. Saltonstall in the superintendency, during this time, and to him the school was indebted for many years of generous and devoted service.

of this ordinance be performed in the usual publick manner agreeable to the laudable practice of the churches in New England."

1807, *Sept.* 15. The usage having been, when the church sent its pastor and delegates abroad as its representatives in ordaining councils, or otherwise, that the expense was borne by the delegate, or delegates accompanying the pastor, the church voted that henceforth such expenses should be paid from the funds of the church.

1815, *Feb.* 3. *Voted,* "That the morning service in future begin with singing instead of the short prayer."

1815, *June* 2. *Voted,* "That the Covenant be now altered by striking out of the first section the words, Father, Son and Holy Ghost."

1818, *Dec.* 15. *Voted,* "That in future the Lord's Supper be celebrated in this church on the last sabbath in each month."

1824, *Jan.* 20. It was voted that half the income of the church, and half of the monthly contributions (after the cost of maintaining the communion table) should be committed to the pastor to be distributed among the poor of the church, and the other half reserved by the deacons for contingent expenses.

1824, *Dec.* 8. It is recorded that Dr. Edward A. Holyoke and Samuel Holman, "elders of the church" were "the only male members of the church living, who were members of the First Church in 1772, when, with others, they were dismissed from the First Church, and formed the North Church."

1830, *Jan.* 12. In closing the record of an invitation to send delegates to an ordination, the clerk, Ichabod Tucker, Esq., appends the following: "Memo. Why are not communications like the foregoing made to the society as well as to the church?"

1846, *Dec.* 26. A "committee of charity" was appointed to distribute the charities of the church ("as the office of deacon is now vacant"), and to officiate until such time as the church shall elect suitable persons to fill said office of deacons."

1847, *July* 4. "It was voted unanimously on motion of Mr. Frederic Howes, that the pastor be requested to offer to the society on communion Sundays the following invitation: All present who are desirous of a closer communion with Christ are invited to remain, and join with the church in celebrating the Lord's Supper."

1848, *Mch.* 28. A proposal to change the time of communion to the afternoon, and to have the observance less frequent, though presented and favored by the pastor, was not approved by a majority of the church.

MINISTERS,

MEETING HOUSES,

AND

BRIEF NOTICES

OF

Proprietors of the First House.

BY

HENRY WHEATLAND.

MINISTERS.

Thomas Barnard, D.D., ordained Jan. 13, 1773; died Oct. 1, 1814.

John Emery Abbot, ordained April 20, 1815; died Oct. 7, 1819.

John Brazer, D.D., ordained Nov. 14, 1820; died Feb. 26, 1846.

Octavius Brooks Frothingham, ordained March. 10, 1847; resigned April 9, 1855.

Charles Lowe, installed Sept. 27, 1855; resigned July 28, 1857.

Edmund Burke Willson, installed June 5, 1859.

REV. THOMAS BARNARD, Jr.

THOMAS BARNARD, JR., was born in Newbury, Feb. 5, 1748; graduated from Harvard College in 1766; studied theology with Dr. Williams of Bradford, afterwards professor in Harvard College. In 1794 he received the title of D.D., from the Universities of Edinburgh and Providence. His father, an uncle, a grandfather, and great-grandfather, had all been preachers. Francis Barnard, his first American ancestor, settled in Hadley. Francis had a son Thomas, settled in the ministry at Andover. The last named had a son John, who succeeded him in his parish. This John had two sons, one of whom, Edward, settled over a Society in Haverhill, and the other, Thomas, over a Society in Newbury, and afterwards over the First Church in Salem. Thomas, Jr., of the North Church was his son. The father, Thomas, Sr., was reported an Arminian, or, perhaps a Semi-Arian of Dr. Clarke's school. He left Newbury on account of opposition from the friends of Whitfield; studied and practised law after his dismission; but afterwards returned to the ministry and was settled at Salem, Sept. 18, 1755. He died Aug. 15, 1776. He was "a man of superior talents and acquirements, and of excellent character;" much beloved by his society here, and "highly esteemed by the public," says Felt. "His manner of preaching was grave, slow and distinct," says Dr. Eliot. He "had not sufficient animation in his delivery, but his sermons were rational and judicious, calculated for hearers of thoughtful minds." It was observed by men of good sense that his style was not the most perspicuous. Bishop

Butler was his favorite author. Rev. Thomas Barnard, Jr., was married to Lois, second daughter of Samuel and Esther (Orne) Gardner, May 31, 1773. He died suddenly, Oct. 1, 1814. His children were Thomas, baptized April 24, 1774; Sally, baptized Aug. 12, 1775, married Robert Emery and died Sept. 25, 1809.

William Pickman, Henry Gibbs, Jacob Ashton, Benjamin Goodhue, all of Salem, were college classmates of Thomas Barnard, Jr., and after his settlement were his parishioners.

The following is believed to be a list, nearly, if not quite complete, of the published sermons and addresses of Rev. Dr. Barnard.

Sermon at the ordination of Rev. Aaron Bancroft in Worcester, Feb. 1, 1786. 8vo. Worcester. 1786.

Sermon before the Ancient and Honorable Artillery company, June 1, 1789. 8vo. Boston. 1789.

Sermon before the Convention of Ministers, May 30, 1793. 8vo. Boston. 1793.

Discourse before the Massachusetts Humane Society, June 19, 1794. 8vo. Boston. 1794.

Thanksgiving Sermon, Feb. 19, 1795. 8vo. Salem. 1795.

Dudleian Lecture Sermon at Harvard College, Sept. 3, 1795. 8vo Boston. 1795.

Fast Day Sermon, March 31, 1796. 8vo. Salem. 1796.

Thanksgiving Sermon, Dec. 15, 1796. 8vo. Salem. 1796.

Sermon on the death of Washington, Dec. 29, 1799. 8vo. Salem. 1799.

Right Hand of Fellowship at the ordination of Rev. S. Dana in Marblehead, Oct. 7, 1801.

Charge at the ordination of Rev. H. May in Marblehead, June 23, 1803.

Sermon before the Salem Female Charitable Society, July 6, 1803. 8vo. Salem. 1803.

Charge at the installation of J. S. Popkin in Newbury, Sept. 19, 1804.

Discourse before the Society for propagating the Gospel among the Indians, Nov. 6, 1806. 8vo. Charlestown. 1806.

Sermon at the ordination of Rev. Ichabod Nichols in Portland, June 7, 1809. 8vo. Portland. 1809.

Sermon before the Bible Society of Salem and vicinity, April 20, 1814. 8vo. Salem. 1814.

Sermon on the death of Rev. Dr. Payson, January 11, 1801.

Yours Ever
J. E. Abbot

REV. JOHN EMERY ABBOT.

Rev. John Emery Abbot, born at Exeter, New Hampshire, Aug. 6, 1793, graduated at Bowdoin College in 1810, with reputation. After leaving college he commenced his preparation for the ministry partly at the University in Cambridge and partly under the direction of Rev. W. E. Channing of Boston. He was ordained Pastor of the North Church April 20th, 1815; died at Exeter, Oct. 7, 1819, unmarried, after a long illness.

His father, Benjamin Abbot, LL.D., was born at Andover, Mass., Sept. 17, 1762; graduated at Harvard College, 1788, died at Exeter, New Hampshire, Oct. 25, 1849; was for more than fifty years the distinguished head of Phillips (Exeter) Academy, a position which his peculiar qualifications enabled him to fill with great success — son of Capt. John and Abigail (Abbot) Abbot of Andover, Mass., who lived with his father, enterprising and industrious, and managed the ancestral farm well and profitably which had descended through a line of worthy ancestors, a grandson of Capt. John Abbot, a great-grandson of Deacon John Abbot, a great-great-grandson of John, and a great-great-great-grandson of George, the venerable progenitor and ancestor of a numerous progeny, who emigrated, as tradition reports, from Yorkshire, England, about 1640, and was among the first settlers of Andover.

His mother, Hannah Tracy Emery, was the only daughter of John and Margaret (Gookin) Emery, and died at Exeter, Dec. 6, 1793, aged 22, a granddaughter of Noah and Joanna (Perryman) Emery.

A volume of his sermons, with a memoir of his life by Rev. Henry Ware, Jr., was printed at Boston in 1829 — a fitting tribute to his memory. His ministry, though short, is remembered as one of the bright spots in the annals of this church and society.

REV. JOHN BRAZER, D.D.

Rev. John Brazer, D.D., was born in Worcester, Mass., Sept. 21, 1789. His father, Samuel Brazer, a baker in Charlestown, was burnt out when the British destroyed the town in 1775, and afterwards went to Worcester and established his bakery in that place.

He received a common school education in his native town. Influenced by the express wish of his parents he entered a store in Boston. But his tastes led him to widely different pursuits, and in 1810 he entered Harvard College, where he graduated in 1813 with the highest honors of his class. In 1815 he was appointed tutor in Greek, 1817 to 1820 he was Professor in Latin, ordained at Salem, Nov. 14, 1820, and labored there in the ministry until his death. He married April 19, 1821, Annie Warren Sever, daughter of William and Sarah (Warren) Sever of Worcester. She died at Salem, Jan. 30, 1843, aged 54.

In 1836 he delivered the Dudleian Lecture at Harvard, and received the honorary degree of D.D. In January, 1846, declining health induced him to try the effect of a change of climate; he went to Charleston, South Carolina, and died at the plantation of his true friend, Dr. Huger, on Cooper River, Feb. 26, 1846, and although in a land of strangers he received from them the kindest attention that a tender friendship, assisted by high medical skill, could give. Children:—

1st. Mary Chandler Brazer, born July 13, 1823; married John W. Draper and now resides in Cambridge.

2d. John Allen Brazer
3rd. William Sever Brazer* } born Sept. 9, 1826.

4th. Anne Warren Brazer, born June 10, 1829; married ―――― Ellis.

5th. Edward Winslow, born Nov. 17, 1831; d. June 8, 1854, at Dorchester.

---

* W. S. graduated Harvard College, in 1846; died at West Point, 17th Aug., 1849.

The following discourses and other publications of Dr. Brazer have been printed.

A Discourse before the Society for the Promotion of Christian Education in Harvard University, Aug. 28, 1825. 8vo. Boston. 1825.

Discourse at the interment of E. A. Holyoke, April 4, 1829. 8vo. Salem. 1829.

Sermon at the ordination of Rev. Jonathan Cole, in Kingston, Jan. 21, 1829. 8vo. Salem. 1829.

Power of Unitarianism over the Affections (Am. Unit. Association, Tracts, 1st. ser., No. 27). 1829.

Biographical Memoirs of Edward Augustus Holyoke (appended to a collection of his writings). 1830.

A Sermon on the value of the Public Services of our Religion (Liberal Preacher, N. S., vol. 1, No. 2). 1832.

The Efficacy of Prayer (in the Unitarian Advocate). 1832.

The Same. 12mo. Boston. 1832.

The Same, reprinted for the Am. Unitarian Association, Tracts, 1st ser., No. 88. 12mo. Boston. 1834.

A Discourse at the Installation of Rev. Andrew Bigelow, in Taunton, April 10, 1833. 8vo. Cambridge. 1833.

A Dudleian Lecture at Harvard College, May 13, 1835. 8vo. Cambridge. 1835.

Essay on the doctrine of Divine Influence on the Human Soul. 1835.

Address before the Seaman's Widow and Orphan Association, Dec. 25, 1835. 8vo. Salem. 1836.

Introduction to "A Good Life," by Thomas Wright. 16mo. Boston. 1836.

Sermon on the Anniversary of Ordination, Nov. 19, 1837. 8vo. Salem. 1837.

The Present Darkness of God's Providence. 8vo. Boston. 1841.

Notice of a "Collection of Hymns for the Christian Church and Home." by the Rev. James Flint (in the Monthly Miscellany). 1843.

Discourse Aug. 20, 1843, on the death of Benjamin Pickman. 8vo. Salem. 1843.

A Discourse on the life and character of the late Leverett Saltonstall. May 18, 1845. 8vo. Salem. 1845.

A volume of Sermons published after his death: with a memoir by his son W. S. B. 12mo. Boston. 1849.

Besides Dr. Brazer was a frequent contributor to the North American Review and the Christian Examiner, and it has been thought that some of these articles displayed more culture, learning, and ability than any of his separate publications.

REV. OCTAVIUS BROOKS FROTHINGHAM.

Rev. Octavius Brooks Frothingham, was born in Boston, Nov. 26, 1822. Prepared for college at the Latin School in Boston, and graduated at Harvard College, in the class of 1843. His father, was Rev. N. L. Frothingham, D.D., for many years the well known Pastor of the First Church in Boston, a poet and writer of great merit. Born at Boston, July 23, 1793; graduated at Harvard, 1811; died, April 3, 1870. His mother, Ann Gorham, was a daughter of Hon. Peter Chardon Brooks, one of the wealthiest of the sons of New England. Mr. Frothingham was ordained over the North Church, March 10, 1847, and continued in the ministry here till April 9, 1855, when he resigned his charge and accepted the pastorate of the First Unitarian Church in Jersey City, where he was installed Sept. 11, 1855. In 1860 he was installed over the New York (city) Third Unitarian Society. Married, March 23, 1847, in Boston, Caroline E. Curtis, daughter of Caleb Curtis, Esq., of Boston.

The following are the printed sermons, etc., by Mr. Frothingham.

"The New Commandment," a discourse June 4, 1854. 8vo. Salem. 1854.

"The Eternal Life," a discourse April 15, 1855. 8vo. Salem. 1855.

Discourse at the Installation of Rev. J. K. Karcher in Philadelphia, Oct. 5, 1859. 8vo. Philadelphia. 1859.

"Theodore Parker," a sermon in New York, June 10, 1860. 8vo. Boston. 1860.

"Seeds and Shells," a sermon in New York, Nov. 17, 1861. 8vo. New York. 1862.

Words spoken at the funeral of Robert F. Denyer, Oct. 19, 1862.

Words spoken at the funeral of John Hopper, July 31, 1864. 8vo. New York. 1864.

"A Plea for Frankness," a sermon in New York, May 6, 1866. 12mo. New York. 1866.

"Allegiance and Patronage," a sermon June 17, 1866. 12mo. New York. 1866.

"Leaving Home" and "Revelations," two sermons in New York, Dec. 9 and 16. 12mo. New York. 1866.

"Binding and Loosing," two sermons. 12mo. New York. 1867.

"Religion and Common Sense" and "The Spirit of the Times," sermons in New York, Dec. 30 and Jan. 13. 12mo. New York. 1867.

"The Worship of Tools," a sermon. 12mo. New York. 1868.

"Experience and Hope," a sermon. 12mo. New York. 1868.

"The Weightier Matters of the Law," a sermon. 12mo. New York. 1868.

"Reasonings about Faith," a sermon. 12mo. New York. 1868.

"The Issue with Superstition," a sermon Sept. 18, 1870, in Lyric Hall. 12mo. New York. 1870.

"The Radical Belief," a discourse in Lyric Hall, Oct. 23, 1870. 12mo. New York. 1870.

"Personal Independence," a sermon in Lyric Hall, Oct. 30, 1870. 12mo. New York. 1870.

"The Gospel of Character," a sermon in Lyric Hall. 12mo. New York. 1871.

"Prayer," a sermon in Lyric Hall, Jan. 29, 1871. 12mo. New York. 1871.

"The Immortalities of Man," a discourse in Lyric Hall, April 9, 1871. 12mo. New York. 1871.

Colonization, Anti-slavery Tract, No. 3.

"Believing Much and Believing Little," "No. 5. Tracts for the Times." 12mo. Albany. 1860.

Sermon before the Graduating Class, of the Forty-second Annual Visitation of the Divinity School of Harvard University. 8vo. Cambridge. 1868.

"The Unitarian Convention and the Times," a Palm Sunday Sermon.

"The Religion of Humanity." 1 vol. New York.

REV. CHARLES LOWE.

Rev. Charles Lowe, son of John and Ann (Simes) Lowe, was born at Portsmouth, New Hampshire, Nov. 18, 1828. In 1830 his parents removed to Exeter, New Hampshire, where they now reside. At Phillips Academy, Exeter, he qualified himself for admission to Harvard College, from which he graduated in the class of 1847. He pursued his professional studies one year with Rev. A. P. Peabody, then went to Germany and studied one year, and then spent a year in travelling in Europe, and he was appointed tutor in Greek and Latin at Harvard 1850-51, at the same time was connected with the Divinity school, at Cambridge, graduating from that school in 1851. He was ordained as colleague Pastor, with Rev. John Weiss of the Unitarian Church in New Bedford, July 28, 1852; resigned in 1854, on account of ill health.* Installed over the North Church Sept. 27, 1855, and resigned 28th July, 1857. On the 28th of May, 1859, installed over the Congregational Church (Unitarian) in Somerville, and after a successful ministry of nearly six years, was again compelled by the failure of his health to withdraw from the pastoral relation. He soon became, and for several years continued to be, the efficient and trusted secretary of the American Unitarian Association.

He married Sept. 16, 1857, Martha A. daughter of the late Justus and Hannah (Wood) Perry, of Keene, New Hampshire, and is now with his family in Europe.

---

* This cause has compelled him several times afterwards to withdraw for a time from his ministerial duties.

The following are some of the printed sermons and other publications, by Mr. Lowe.

"Death of President Lincoln," a sermon in Charleston, South Carolina, April 23, 1865. 12mo. Boston. 1865.

"The Condition and Prospects of the South," a discourse in Somerville, June 4, 1865. 8vo. Boston. 1865.

A Statement in regard to the Position and Policy of the American Unitarian Association. 12mo. Boston. 1868.

"Have we misrepresented Orthodoxy?" A reply to strictures in the Boston Recorder and elsewhere. 12mo. Boston. 1868.

A defence of the action of the American Unitarian Association. 12mo. Boston. 1870.

Mr. Lowe became editor of "Monthly Journal," beginning with the number for Sept., 1865, and continued to edit it till its suspension, at the end of 1869. He also edited four "Year Books," from 1868 to 1871. During the years of his connection with the Association, he of course wrote the Annual Reports; which, after 1869, were printed by themselves. There were also issued in pamphlet form, by the American Unitarian Association, the following — the first two having been previously published in the "Monthly Journal"— the third having been given at the Annual Meeting for that year — "A Statement of the Policy of the American Unitarian Association, July, 1868; "Have we misrepresented Orthodoxy?" Dec., 1868; "The Unitarian Position," June, 1870; "A Defence of the Action of the American Unitarian Association," Oct. 13, 1870.

REV. EDMUND B. WILLSON.

EDMUND B. WILLSON, son of Rev. Luther, and Sally (Bigelow) Willson, was born in Petersham, Aug. 15, 1820; entered Yale College in 1834; dismissed on account of sickness, Aug., 1835; studied for the ministry in the Cambridge Divinity School, graduating in 1843; received the degree of A.M. from Harvard College in 1853; ordained over the First Congregational Society in Grafton, Jan. 3, 1844; married Martha Anne, daughter of Stephen Buttrick of Framingham (granddaughter of Major John Buttrick of the "Concord Fight"), May 8, 1844; became pastor of the First Society in West Roxbury (the second church in Roxbury), July 18, 1852; installed minister of the North Society in Salem, June 5, 1859; commissioned chaplain of the twenty-fourth Regiment of Mass. Volunteers, Oct. 21, 1863; joined that regiment at St. Augustine, Florida, Dec. 17, 1863; resigned at Deep Bottom, Virginia, July 6, 1864.

His father, Rev. Luther Willson, son of Joseph and Sarah (Matthews) Willson, and grandson of Robert and Martha (Dunlap) Willson, was born in New Braintree, Apr. 26, 1783, graduated at Williams College in 1807; studied for the ministry; and having been three years and a half Principal of Leicester Academy, was settled in 1813, in Brooklyn, Conn., as colleague pastor with Rev. Josiah Whitney, D.D., over the First Congregational Society in that town. When settled he was a Trinitarian in belief. During the three or four years following he gave much examination to the doctrine of the Trinity, and having at length announced his conviction of the truth of the Unitarian doctrine of God, he was summoned by the Consociation of Windham county to answer to the charge of heresy. Denying the jurisdiction of that ecclesiastical court, he nevertheless proposed to state and defend his opinions before it. The consociation proceeded to try him, as it claimed that it had a right to do, and pronounced his deposition from his office. The majority of the society adhered to him, however, refused to acknowledge the authority of the consociation, and accepted his views; and when he resigned in Sept., 1817 (in the hope that under another minister the seceding members might return) he was soon succeeded by the late Rev. Samuel J. May of Syracuse. This was the origin of the First, and for many years the only, Unitarian Society in the State of Connecticut. It is believed to be still the only church of that faith in the state which maintains public worship. Mr. Willson was installed June 23, 1819, pastor of the First Parish in Petersham, Mass., of which he continued the minister for more than fifteen years. He died in Petersham, Nov. 20, 1864.

The following sermons and addresses of Mr. Willson have been published, besides occasional sermons and articles in magazines and newspapers.

1. Sermon containing historical notices of the First Congregational Church in Grafton, preached Dec. 27, 1846.
2. Address at consecration of Riverside cemetery, Grafton, April 29, 1851.
3. Sermon preached in West Roxbury, June 4, 1854, it being the Sunday after the return of Anthony Burns into slavery.
4. Address delivered in Petersham, July 4, 1854, in commemoration of the one hundredth anniversary of the incorporation of that town.
5. "In Memory of Christ:" A sermon preached in the North Church in Salem, March 4, 1860.
6. "Reasons for Thanksgiving:" A sermon preached on a National Thanksgiving day at the North Church, April 20, 1862.
7. "The Proclamation of Freedom:" A sermon preached in the North Church, Jan. 4, 1863.
8. "God a Father:" A sermon preached in the North Church, Feb. 2, 1868.

THE FIRST MEETING HOUSE,
1772-1836,
ON THE CORNER OF NORTH AND LYNDE STREETS.

[*See page* 20.]

The following papers are worthy of record, as illustrating some portions of the history of this Church and Parish.

DEED OF JOHN NUTTING TO JAMES ANDREW AND OTHERS.

Know all Men by these Presents, that I, John Nutting of Salem, in the county of Essex, in the Province of the Massachusetts Bay, Esq., in consideration of one hundred and ninety five pounds, six shillings and ten pence, lawfull money, paid me by James Andrew, housewright; Joseph Blaney, William Browne and Francis Cabot, Esq'rs; William Clough, mason; Samuel Curwen, Esq., Benjamin Daland, yeoman; Andrew Dalglish, merchant; Stephen Daniel, shipwright; Mary Eden, widow; John Felt, shoreman; Samuel Field, boat-builder; Nathaniel Foster, taylor; Robert Foster, blacksmith; Weld Gardner and Henry Gardner, merchants; Jona. Gavett, cabinet maker; Samuel Holman, hatter; Edward Augustus Holyoke, Esq., James King, shopkeeper; William Luscomb and William Luscomb, Jr., and Joseph McIntire, housewrights; David Mason, gentleman; Jonathan Mansfield, gentleman; John Millet, cooper; Eleazer Moses, sailmaker; Jeremiah Newhall, housewright; Benjamin Pickman and Benjamin Pickman, Jr., Esq's; Clark Gayton Pickman and William Pickman, merchants; Ebenezer Porter, housewright; Daniel Ropes, cordwainer; Samuel Symonds, Jr., shoreman; Joshua Ward, gentleman; Richard Ward, tanner; Miles Ward the third, glazier; Samuel West, gentleman; Samuel West, Jr., mariner; William West, merchant, and Benjamin West, mariner; all of Salem aforesaid, the receipt whereof I do hereby acknowledge, do hereby Give, Grant, sell and convey unto the said James Andrew, Joseph Blaney, Wm. Browne, Frs. Cabot, Wm. Clough, Samuel Curwen, Benj. Daland, Andrew Dalglish, Stephen Daniel, Mary Eden, Jno. Felt, Samuel Field, Nath'l Foster, Robert Foster, Weld Gardner, Henry Gardner, Jona. Gavett, Sam'l Holman, E. A. Holyoke, Jas. King, Wm. Luscomb, Wm. Luscomb, Jr., Joseph McIntire, Jona. Mansfield, David Mason, Jno. Millet, Eleazer Moses, Jer'h Newhall, Benj. Pickman, Benj. Pickman, Jr., C. G. Pickman, W. Pickman, Eb. Porter, Dan'l Ropes, Samuel Symonds, Jr., Joshua Ward, Rich'd. Ward, Miles Ward the third, Sam'l West, Sam'l West, Jr., William West and Benj. West, and their heirs, forty-two parts of a certain lot of land in Salem aforesaid, in forty-three equal parts to be divided, containing about twenty-four poles, and is bounded easterly on land of Abijah Northey and there measures seventy-five feet; southerly, partly on land belonging to the heirs of Geo. Daland, deceased, and partly on land of Elizabeth Henderson, and there measures eighty-one feet; westerly on an highway, and there measures seventy-nine feet; and northerly on an highway, and there measures eighty-eight feet, with the appurtenances. To have and to hold one forty-second part of the premises, to the said Jas. Andrew and his heirs, one other forty-second part to the said Joseph Blaney and his heirs, one other forty-second part to the said Wm. Browne and his heirs, one other forty-second part to the said Francis Cabot and his heirs, one other forty-second part to the said Wm. Clough and his heirs, one other forty-second part to the said Samuel Curwen and his heirs, one other forty-second part to the said Benjamin Daland and his heirs, one other forty-second part to the said Andrew Dalglish and his heirs, one other forty-second part to the said Daniel and his heirs, one other forty-second part to the said Mary Eden and her heirs, one other forty-second part to the said John Felt and his heirs, one other forty-second part to the said Sam'l Field and his heirs, one other forty-second part to the said Nath'l Foster and his heirs, one other forty-second part to the said Robert Foster and his heirs, one other forty-second part to the said Weld Gardner and his heirs, one other forty-second part to the said Henry Gardner and his heirs, one other forty-second part to the said Jona. Gavett and his heirs, one other forty-second part to the said Sam'l Holman and his heirs, one other forty-second part to the said E. A. Holyoke and his heirs, one other forty-second part to the said James King and his heirs, one other forty-second part to the said Wm. Luscomb and his heirs, one other forty-second part to the said Wm. Luscomb, Jr., and his heirs, one other forty-second part to the said Joseph McIntire and his heirs, one other forty-second part to the said Jonathan Mansfield and his heirs, one other forty-second part to the said David Mason and his heirs, one other forty-second part to the said John Millet and his heirs, one other forty-second part to the said Eleazer Moses and his heirs, one other forty-second part to the said Jer. Newhall and his heirs, one other forty-second part to the said B. Pickman and his heirs, one other forty-second part to the said B. Pickman, Jr., and his heirs, one other forty-second part to the said C. G. Pickman and his heirs, one other forty-second part to the said Wm. Pickman and his heirs, one other forty-second part to the said Eben Porter and his heirs, one other forty-second part to the said Daniel Ropes and his heirs, one other forty-second part to the said Samuel Symonds, Jr., and his heirs, one other forty-second part to the said Josh. Ward and his heirs, one other forty-second part to the said Richard Ward and his heirs, one other forty-second part to the said Miles Ward the third and his heirs, one other forty-second part to the said Samuel West and his heirs, one other forty-second part to the said Samuel West, Jr., and his heirs, one other forty-second part to the said William West and his heirs, one other forty second part to the said B. West and his heirs, and to their use and behoof respectively, forever; and I do covenant with the grantees aforenamed, their heirs and assigns, that I am lawfully seized in fee of the premises, that they are free of all incumbrances, that I have a good right to sell and convey the same to them, and that I will warrant and defend the same to the grantees aforenamed, their heirs and assigns, forever, against the lawful claims and demands of all persons.

In witness whereof I, the said John Nutting and Elizabeth my wife (in token of her consent hereto and in bar of her right of dower herein), have hereunto set our hands and seals this 14th day of Feb., Anno Domi, 1772, and in the twelfth year of his majesty's Reign.

Signed, sealed, and delivered, in presence of

Peter Frye.	Jno. Nutting and a seal.
Russell Wyer.	Eliz. Nutting and a seal.

The words "Jonathan Mansfield, gentleman," in the first page and "two," in the second page were interlined, before sealing.

ESSEX ss.
Salem, February 15, 1772.

Then John Nutting, Esq., and Eliza. Nutting, abovenamed, personally appeared and acknowledged the aforewritten instrument, to be their free Act and Deed.

Before Peter Frye, Justice of the Peace.

ESSEX ss.

Received on Record Sept. 2, 1772, recorded libro 130, folio 117, etc., and examined.

Attest,

John Higginson, Reg.

BOND OF JAMES ANDREW AND OTHERS TO JOHN NUTTING.

Know all men by these presents that We James Andrew Housewright Joseph Blaney William Browne & Francis Cabot Esqrs William Clough mason Samuel Curwen Esqr Benjamin Daland yeoman Andrew Dalglish merchant Stephen Daniel Shipwright Mary Eden Widow John Felt Shoreman Samuel Field Boat builder Nathaniel Foster Tailor Robert Foster Blacksmith Weld Gardner and Henry Gardner Merchants Jonathan Gavet Cabinet maker Samuel Holman Hatter Edward Augustus Holyoke Esqr James King Shop keeper William Luscomb & William Luscomb junr & Joseph McIntire Housewrights David Mason Gentleman Jonathan Mansfield Gentleman John Millet Cooper Eleazer Moses Sail maker Jeremiah Newhall Housewright Benjamin Pickman & Benjamin Pickman junr Esqrs Clark Gayton Pickman & William Pickman Merchants Ebenezer Porter Housewright Daniel Ropes Cordwainer Samuel Symonds junr Shoreman* Joshua Ward Gentleman Richard Ward Tanner Miles Ward the third Housewright† Samuel West Gentleman Samuel West junr Mariner William West Merchant and Benjamin West Mariner all of Salem in the County of Essex are held and stand firmly bound & obliged unto John Nutting of Salem aforesaid Esqr in the full and just sum of Three hundred and ninety one Pounds lawful money of the Province of the Massachusetts Bay to be paid unto the said John Nutting, his certain attorney, Executors, administrators, or assigns; To the which Payment well and truly to be made We bind ourselves our Heirs Executors and Administrators jointly & severally firmly by these Presents Sealed with our Seals. Dated this fourteenth Day of February Anno Domini one thousand seven hundred & seventy two and in the twelfth year of his Majesty's Reign.

The condition of this present Obligation is such, that if the abovenamed Obligors their Heirs Executors, or Administrators or any of them shall & do well & truly pay, or cause to be paid unto the above named John Nutting his Heirs Executors administrators or assigns the full sum of one hundred and ninety five Pounds six Shillings and ten Pence of like lawful

---

* Overwritten. † Overwritten "Glaziers."

money of the Province aforesaid with lawful Interest for the same on or before the fourteenth Day of February which will be in the year of our Lord one thousand seven hundred & seventy three without Fraud, Coven or further Delay then the foregoing obligation to be void and of none Effect; otherwise to abide and remain in full Force and Virtue.

Signed, Sealed & delivered
in presence of us
    Russell Wyer
    William Clark

James Andrew L. S.
Joseph Blaney L. S.
Willm Browne L. S.
Francis Cabot L. S.
William Clough L. S.
Saml Curwen L. S.
Benja Daland L. S.
Andw Dalglish L. S.
Stephen Daniell L. S.
meary eden L. S.
John Felt L. S.
Saml Field L. S.
Nathael Foster L. S.
Robert Foster L. S.
Weld Gardner L. S.
Henry Gardner L. S.
Jonathan Gavet L. S.
Saml Holman L. S.
E. A. Holyoke L. S.
James King L. S.

William Luscomb L. S.
William Luscomb jr L. S.
Joseph mackintire L. S.
David Mason L. S.
Jonathan mansfield L. S.
John Millet L. S.
Eleazer Moses L. S.
Jeremiah Newhall L. S.
Benj Pickman L. S.
Benja Pickman junr L. S.
C. G. Pickman L. S.
Wm Pickman L. S.
Ebener Porter L. S.
Daniel Ropes L. S.
Saml Symonds Jr L. S.
Joshua Ward L. S.
Richard Ward L. S.
M Ward tert L. S.
Saml West L. S.
Saml West Jnr L. S.
Willm West L. S.
Benj. West L. S.

14 Feby 1773 Recd 11-14-5 Interest upon the within Bond & fourteen Pounds fourteen shillings and eight pence of the Principal.

17 Feby 1774. Recd 5£ 16 in part of Interest by D. Ropes's note of Hand also 5£ 0-2 in full for Interest to the 13 Febry 1774 also 12-2 in part of Principal so that there is due of the Principal 180-0-0.

Salem 21 Febry 1775 Recd of Col. Pickman four Pounds and three pence half penny in part for Interest to the 14 Febry last.

Salem 24 Janry 1776 Recd 17-4-8 in full for Interest to the 14 of Febry next. Salem 14 Febry 1777 Recd Interest in full to this date.

Recd Interest to the 14 Febry 1778.

Recd Interest to 14 Febry 1779.

Recd: Interest in full to Febry 14th 1780.   J. Nutting.

Recd Interest in full to 14 Febry 1781.

Recd January 22d 1782 Ten pounds & sixteen Shillings Silver lawful money in full for the Interest of this Bond to the fourteenth day of February next—also recd one hundred & twenty Seven pounds and six Shillings Silver lawful money in part of the Principal and there is now due on this Bond Fifty two pounds & fourteen Shillings Silver lawful money. Recd Pr Jno. Nutting.

Salem May 7th 1784 Recd two years Interest for the above Sum.
Jno. Nutting.

Salem March 8th 1785.
Recd Interest for the above sum for one year.

Recd thirty Eight Pounds eighteen & six pence part of Principal of the above Bond.   p Jno. Nutting.

Remains Thirteen Pounds fifteen Shillings & Six pence Principal.

Recd of Mr. Rich Ward Treasurer Eleven Pounds 7-2 in a Note of Hand in full of the within Ballance this 6th Sept 1786.   Benj. Pickman.

DEED OF PEW 60 TO JOHN DABNEY.

Know all Men by these Presents, That we *Edward Augustus Holyoke Benjamin Pickman, Joseph Hiller and Jacob Ashton Esquires Samuel Holman Hatter Henry Rust merchant Miles Ward junr merchant Jacob Sanderson cabinetmaker and Abijah Northey shopkeeper* a Committee appointed by the Proprietors of the North Meeting-House in Salem to sell and convey the Pews in the same House, in Consideration of *Forty three Dollars and thirty three Cents* LAWFUL MONEY, paid us by *John Dabney of Salem in the County of Essex bookseller* the Receipt whereof we do hereby acknowledge, do hereby Give, Grant, Sell and Convey to the said *John Dabney his* Heirs and Assigns, a certain Pew *on the floor* of the same House, marked No. 60 with Appurtenances. To Have and to Hold the same to the said *John Dabney his* Heirs and Assigns; subject, nevertheless, to all legal Votes and Orders of the Proprietors of the Pews in the same House, made for the Settlement and Support of a Minister or Ministers, from Time to Time, as there shall be Occasion; and also for the necessary Repairs of the same House; AND FOR THE PAYMENT OF AN ANNUITY OF FIVE POUNDS SIX SHILLINGS AND EIGHT PENCE, LAWFUL MONEY, TO THE WIDOW ELIZABETH HENDERSON, FOR AND DURING HER NATURAL LIFE, and for incidental charges, but free of all other Incumbrances.

In Witness whereof we have hereunto set our Hands and Seals, the *Thirtyeth* Day of *March* A. D. 1796.

Signed, sealed and delivered in presence of us Wm West Richard Ward	E. A. Holyoke [L. S.] Benja Pickman [L. S.] Jos Hiller [L. S.] Jacob Ashton [L. S.] Sam'l Holman [L. S.] Henry Rust [L. S.] Miles Ward jnr [L. S.] Jacob Sanderson [L. S.] Abijah Northey [L. S.] **Proprietors Committee.**

Essex, ss.   April 2d, 1796.   Then *Edward Augustus Holyoke, Benjamin Pickman Joseph Hiller Jacob Ashton Samuel Holman Henry Rust Miles Ward Junr Jacob Sanderson and Abijah Northey* abovenamed personally appeared and severally acknowledged the above written Instrument to be their Deed.

    Before *RICHARD WARD,*

            Justice of the peace.

Proprietors' Meeting May 27, 1836.

The following votes were adopted :—

The said corporation will accept the conveyance of said New Meeting house and land, upon the following conditions, viz :—

1st. That the old meeting house, land and appurtenances, the bell, organ and clock, shall be sold for the most the same will bring.

2d. That the proceeds of said sale, shall be appropriated and applied as follows, viz :—in the first place, to the full payment and discharge of all the debts due from said corporation, and that the surplus shall be apportioned and divided among all the owners of pews, not held by the corporation, upon the following appraisement, that is to say, upon the original valuation of said pews, as the same is and long has been used for the assessment of the annual tax.

3rd. The Proprietors will occupy said New Meeting House as their place of worship.

4th. That a committee of five be appointed to make sale of the property for the most it will bring, and to take all proper measures to carry the vote into effect; and the following named gentlemen were chosen for that purpose with authority to give a deed of the land. John G. King, Wm. H. Foster, Nathaniel Saltonstall, George Peabody and Emery Johnson.

Voted, That the same committee be authorized to execute an agreement with the subscribers to the new house in relation to the reservation of the proceeds of the sale of pews in said house for reimbursing them for the expense of building the same.

The old Meeting House was in accordance with the above votes, sold at public auction on Monday June 27, 1836, with its appendages. T. P. Pingree, Esq., bought the house for $2,325, G. Tucker, Esq., bought for the New Church the organ at $600, and the bell at $28\frac{1}{2}$ cents per lb. (about $300). The clock and drapery sold for about $100 more. The net proceeds of the sale were divided in accordance with the above votes.

THE SECOND MEETING HOUSE.

1830-1873.

THE first Meeting house was often opened for public services. On Friday, July 4, 1834, its use was granted to "the Apprentices of Salem" for the delivery of an eulogy on Lafayette by Rev. Dr. James Flint. Soon after the audience had assembled, a defect in the flooring was detected, though not of sufficient importance to interrupt the exercises. On the following day an examination of the building was made, and the results communicated to the proprietors at a meeting held on Monday the 9th inst.; thereupon a committee, Col. B. Pickman, chairman, was appointed to take into consideration the condition of the house, and to report at a future meeting.

The first meeting of this committee was held in the house of the chairman, the same house (see page 154) in which the members of the church assembled for organization in 1772, then owned and occupied by the grandfather of the owner, the first Col. Benjamin Pickman.

At a proprietors' meeting on Monday, July 21, 1834, the recommendations of the committee were adopted, that it is expedient to erect a new Meeting House by a subscription in shares, upon the basis that the subscribers are to be indemnified for the expense, from the proceeds of the sale of the pews in the said house, and the appointment of a committee to ascertain whether a suitable lot of land for a Meeting House can be procured at a satisfactory price, and also to procure subscribers for shares and to report at an adjournment.

At a meeting, Thursday, July 31, 1834, in accordance with the recommendation of the committee it was

Voted, That the said subscribers, with such others as may hereafter sign the subscription paper, may purchase land and erect a Meeting House thereon, and may hold the pews in the same and sell and dispose of the same at such times, and in such manner as they may think expedient to indemnify themselves for the cost and expense they may incur in the premises.

At a meeting of the subscribers, Sept. 3, 1834, it was stated that the sum subscribed for the new church was twenty-five thousand dollars. A building committee was appointed, comprising Gideon Tucker, George Peabody, John W. Rogers, John C. Lee, George Wheatland, P. I. Farnham, Allen Putnam.

The committee was authorized to purchase such parcel or parcels of land as may be deemed necessary, and to take a deed or deeds thereof in their names for the use and benefit of said association, and to make contracts for the erection of a new Meeting House of such materials, and in such general form and manner as may be agreed upon by a vote of the subscribers. At a meeting Sept. 6, 1834, the committee reported that they had purchased land on Essex street of Mr. Savage, Dr. Treadwell and Mr. Oliver, about one hundred and twelve feet on said street, and recommend the erection of the church with rough granite of the Gothic order, which they think can be done for the sum of nineteen thousand dollars ($19,000) exclusive of the cost of the land; the front end to be either of Quincy or Gloucester stone, with butts, beds and builds. A drawing of the front of the church was exhibited and the dimensions given.

During the autumn and winter the foundation was laid.

Laying of the Corner-stone.

Saturday, May 16, 1835, the Corner-stone was laid with appropriate religious services. The devotional exercises were performed by the Rev. Dr. Flint. Previously to the ceremony of laying the Corner-stone the audience was addressed by the Pastor of the Church, Rev. John Brazer, as follows:—

"We are called together my Christian brethren and friends, on an occasion of deep and solemn interest. It is to lay the Corner-stone of a new edifice, which is to be consecrated to the purposes of public religious instruction and of social worship.

We would commence the service by invoking the blessing of Almighty God upon it, without whose aid all human labors are ineffectual, and all efforts are vain.

We lay this Corner-stone, as those who duly estimate and value the public institutions of Christianity; who believe them to be appointed and approved of God, and essential to the maintenance of good government, public peace, and social order; and who regard them as an inestimable means of instruction, improvement and satisfaction to the undying soul.

We lay this Corner-stone, as the children, subjects and worshippers of the one and only true God; as the disciples of Jesus Christ, His Son (our Lord and Saviour); and as those who rely on the blessed influence of God's Holy Spirit, in rendering effectual upon our hearts all the means of religious improvement.

We lay this Corner-stone, as the friends, assertors and defenders, of the great and leading principles of Protestant Christianity; namely, the sufficiency of the Scriptures as the Rule of Life, and Charter of immortal hopes; and of the invaluable and inalienable right of private judgment.

We lay this Corner-stone, in a spirit of Christian Love towards all our Christian Brethren, of every sect and name. And while, in the language of the Saviour, we believe it to be "life eternal to know the only true God, and Jesus Christ whom he hath sent;" and while we prize our distinctive principles as Christians above all earthly good, yet we cheerfully accord to all others the rights and privileges of thinking and acting, which we claim in our own behalf. And our constant prayer for them, as for ourselves, is — that they, as well as we, may ever keep the mind open to further light, and fuller developments of Divine Faith.

We lay this Corner-stone in the earnest hope that here may rise a temple, where we, and our children, and children's children, in a long succession of generations, may meet to unite in holy services; where the whole "truth, as it is in Jesus," shall be "spoken in love;" and be received into "honest and good hearts;" where the principles of free, but humble and sober inquiry shall ever be maintained; where every secret and every presumptuous sin shall be faithfully rebuked; where the attention of the thoughtless shall be arrested, the wanderer recalled, the guilty reclaimed, and all shall be guarded and strengthened against the temptations of life; where pious sentiments shall be excited, pure affections nurtured, good resolutions formed, good purposes established, and good principles confirmed; where prayers and hymns of praise shall rise from devout, grateful and contrite hearts, and ascend to the Father of our Spirits; where the Saviour's love, which was stronger than death, shall be gratefully commemorated, and all the sacred rites of his religion be duly honored and observed; where all the consoling and sustaining influences of the Everlasting Gospel shall be fully realized, and tenderly felt; and where all persons, of every age and condition, in a continually growing holiness, and ever increasing likeness to God, shall become, through his grace in Christ Jesus, prepared for that "Temple not made with hands," eternal in the heavens.

We close this part of the service as we began. And devoutly and renewedly imploring the favor of the Most High God upon this undertaking, commend it, reverentially and fervently, to His fostering and protecting care.

A copper box was then deposited under the Corner-stone, by Deacon Edward Brown. It contained the following articles.

A silver plate, having engraved upon it the date of erection, the name of the pastor of the North Society, the Committee for building the church, the Carpenter, Masons, and Architect; a roll of parchment, containing a copy of the Rev. John Brazer's address at the laying of the Corner-stone;

parchment, containing a list of the subscribers to the erection of the new church; parchment, containing the names of all the Pastors of the North Society, the dates of their ordinations and deaths; a copy of the Polyglot Bible, English Version: the American Almanac and Repository of Useful Knowledge, for 1835; Farmer's Almanac, 1835, by Thomas Spofford; Old Farmer's Almanac, 1835, by Robert B. Thomas; a Catalogue of the Members of the North Church, in Salem, with an Historical Sketch of the Church; a Discourse on the Efficacy of Prayer, by Rev. John Brazer; a Discourse at the Interment of Dr. Holyoke, by Rev. John Brazer; a Discourse at the Ordination of the Rev. A. Bigelow, by Rev. John Brazer; an article on the Power of Unitarianism over the Affections, by Rev. John Brazer, and a Tract, Some Uses of Affliction, by Rev. John Brazer. Salem Observer, Saturday, May 9, 1835; Essex Register, Monday, May 11, 1835; Essex Register, Thursday, May 14, 1835; Lighthouse, Monday, May 11, 1835; Salem Gazette, Tuesday, May 12, 1835; Salem Gazette, Friday, May 15, 1835; Commercial Advertiser, Wednesday, May 13, 1835; Salem Mercury, Wednesday, May 13, 1835; Landmark, Wednesday, May 13, 1835.

DEDICATION.

The House was dedicated on Wednesday, June 22, 1836, in the forenoon.

The introductory prayer was by Rev. Mr. Bartlett, of Marblehead, prayer of dedication by Rev. Mr. Upham, and a dedication hymn by a member of the society (Jones Very).

> We seek the truth which Jesus brought;
> His path of light we long to tread;
> Here be his holy doctrines taught,
> And here, their purest influence shed.
>
> May faith and hope, and love abound;
> Our sins and errors be forgiven;
> And we, in thy great day, be found
> Children of God, and heirs of heaven.
>
> To pour in music's solemn strain
> The heart's deep tide of grateful love;
> And kindle in thine earthly fane
> A spirit for his home above,
>
> Thou bad'st him on thine altar lay
> The holy thought, the pure desire,
> That light within a brighter ray
> Than sun-beam's glance, or vestal fire.

'Twill burn, when heaven's high altar-flame
  On yon blue height hath ceased to glow;
And o'er dark earth's dissolving frame
  The sun-light of the spirit throw.

Father! within thy courts we bow,
  To ask thy blessing, seek thy grace;
O smile upon thy children now!
  Look down on this, thy hallowed place.

And when its trembling walls shall feel
  Time's heavy hand upon them rest;
Thy nearer presence, Lord! reveal,
  And make thy children wholly blest.

The sermon by the Pastor, was marked by the just and vigorous thought, and the nervous and appropriate language, which uniformly characterized Mr. Brazer's public performances. The text, was from I Corinthians, chap. iii. verse 16. "Know ye not that ye are the temples of God." The concluding prayer was by Rev. Mr. Thayer of Beverly, and the benediction by the Pastor.

SUBSCRIBERS TO THE NEW BUILDING.

List of names of the subscribers, to build a stone church. 248 shares. Amount $24,800.

Catherine Andrew,	$800	Caleb Foote,	$100
John P. Andrews,	100	James D. Gillis,	200
Nancy Andrews,	300	Nancy D. Gay,	300
James N. Archer,	100	Chas. Hoffman,	200
Thos. P. Bancroft,	200	F. Howes and Miss Burley,	900
Gideon Barstow,	500	Oliver Hubbard,	400
Timo. Brooks,	100	William Ives,	100
Geo. C. Chase,	100	Emery Johnson,	300
James W. Chever,	150	E. K. Lakeman,	300
Amos Choate,	400	Asa Lamson, Jr.,	100
Francis Choate,	200	John C. Lee,	1,000
Thomas Cole,	100	Daniel Lord,	100
Samuel Cook,	150	Nath. J. Lord,	100
David Cummins,	600	John H. Nichols,	100
Aaron Endicott,	100	Nath. W. Osgood,	100
Nathan Endicott,	400	Rebecca Osgood,	200
P. I. Farnham,	600		
			$9,400

Brought forward,	$9,400	Arch. Rea,	$300
Edw. H. Payson,	100	John W. Rogers,	700
Francis Peabody,	500	N. L. Rogers,	400
George Peabody,	500	Leverett Saltonstall,	600
Joseph Peabody,	3,500	Nath. Saltonstall,	500
Joseph W. Peabody,	400	Eben Shillaber,	100
Nath. Peabody,	100	Jesse Smith, Jr.,	100
Benj. Pickman,	2,000	Benj. W. Stone,	200
D. L. Pickman,	1,800	Chas. Treadwell,	200
L. Rawlins Pickman,	300	Gideon Tucker,	400
Wm. Pickman,	1,200	Ichabod Tucker,	500
P. P. Pinel,	200	Stephen Webb,	100
Allen Putnam,	300	Geo. Wheatland,	400
			$24,800

Sale of Pews, etc.

At a Meeting of the subscribers to the New Church, June 11, 1836,

Voted, The Trustees (Gideon Tucker, John W. Rogers and John C. Lee,) be authorized to convey the Meeting House and land to the North Society on the above named conditions.

Voted, That the power to sell the pews be vested in the Trustees.

Voted, That the Trustees be authorized to purchase the organ and bell together with any article of furniture in the old church, they shall deem expedient.

In the afternoon of the day of the dedication, fifty-one of the pews were sold at public auction for upwards of $4,000 more than their appraisement. The whole amount of sales was about $20,000. The highest sum for a choice was $370.

Cost of the New House.

Memorandum of cost of North Stone Church.

The Building,		$22,494 33
Land,		6,758 98
Organ,	$706 50	
Bell,	342 25	
Furniture,	909 21	
Fence, Stone Posts, Paving, etc.,	1,157 34	
Yard, Trees, etc.,	140 75	
		3,256 05
		$32,509 36

VESTRY.

In accordance with the desire of the pastor, a considerable sum having been obtained by a subscription, the proprietors, at the annual meeting, April 26, 1853, granted an appropriation in aid of the erection of a wooden building, on land north of the church, to accommodate the Sunday School, and for other purposes. The building was erected during the summer of 1853, and when ready for occupancy, the rooms, previously used, in the basement of the church, were vacated, not being considered suitable.

PROPRIETORS AND OCCUPANTS OF PEWS IN THE FIRST MEETING HOUSE.

The following names were obtained from an examination of lists of the proprietors or occupants of pews, in the years 1772–1802–1820–1829 and 1836, which have come into our possession. A very large portion of the heads of families that were wont to worship in the first house are included in this enumeration, although many who were connected with the society for short periods, during the intervals between the above named dates, are unavoidably omitted.

1. ABBOT, GEORGE, son of George and Hannah (Lovejoy) Abbot, b. at Andover, Feb. 9, 1748; d. at Salem, Oct. 5, 1784; m. Feb. 22, 1772, Priscilla, dau. of Dr. Joseph and Eliza (Boardman) Manning of Ipswich; she d. at Salem, March, 1804. A trader. He was one of the volunteers of the Rhode Island Expedition, in 1778.

2. ANDREW, JAMES, son of William Andrew, b. in Salem village, North Danvers; bapt. June 25, 1732; m. Mary Glover of Salem in 1758, who d., July, 1821, aged 83; d. in Salem, New Hampshire, Jan., 1820. A housewright.

3. ANDREWS, JOSEPH, son of James and Mary (Glover) Andrews, b. at Salem, July 1, 1773; d. Aug. 13, 1824; m. May 14, 1797, Mary Bell of Portsmouth, New Hampshire. Merchant.

4. ANDREWS, JOHN HANCOCK, son of James and Mary (Glover) Andrews, b. at Salem, July 8, 1776; d. Aug. 5, 1832; m. Nancy, dau. of Samuel and Rebecca Page of Danvers, who d. Aug. 19, 1852, aged 70. Merchant.

5. ANDREW, JOHN, son of John and Elizabeth (Watson) Andrew, b. at Salem, July 9, 1774; d. July 7, 1829; m. Sept. 30, 1804, Catherine, dau. of Simon and Rachel (Hathorne) Forrester (b. March. 7, 1780; d. July 14, 1845). Merchant in Salem. For several years he had resided in Russia, a commission merchant.

6. ANDREWS, FERDINAND, son of Ephraim and Lucy (Lane) Andrews of Hingham, b. May 20, 1802; m. April 7, 1825, Elizabeth, dau. of John and Betsey (Putnam) Derby of Salem (b. July 16, 1804). A printer, formerly conducted the "Salem Gazette," also, the "Landmark" at Salem. Resided since in Boston, Lancaster and Washington, D. C.

7. ANDREWS, NEHEMIAH, b. Feb., 1753; d. Feb. 16, 1800; m. Aug. 7, 1772, Catherine Seamore (b. Jan., 1749; d. March 23, 1802). Master mariner.

8. ANDREWS, DANIEL, son of Nehemiah and Catherine (Seamore) Andrews, b. Sept. 25, 1779; d. Dec. 20, 1820; m. Sept. 20, 1807, Esther Holt (b. Dec. 9, 1781, for many years after the death of her husband a school teacher, in the eastern section of the city). A master mariner.

9. ANDREWS, NEHEMIAH, son of Nehemiah and Catherine (Seamore) Andrews, b. Dec. 9, 1781; d. Nov., 1820, aged 40. Master mariner.

10. ARCHER, SAMUEL, son of Samuel and Dorothy (Ropes) Archer, b. April 1, 1712; d. Oct. 19, 1825; m. Aug. 31, 1762, Mary Woodwell; 2d, May 13, 1815, Mary Buffton; he was a hardware dealer and had his shop on the north side of Old Paved street, near 252 Essex street.

11. ARCHER, JOHN, carpenter; d. Dec. 27, 1829 (aged 71).

12. ARCHER, JAMES, m. June 27, 1790, Priscilla, dau. of Daniel and Priscilla (Lambert) Ropes (b. Jan. 4, 1765; d. Apr. 24, 1843); he died Nov., 1802, aged 40.

13. ARCHER, JAMES NORRIS, son of James and Priscilla (Ropes) Archer, bapt. July 26, 1801; d. at Salem, May 7, 1852, aged 51; m., 1st, Sarah, dau. of Jacob Lee; 2d, Charlotte Baker. Auctioneer and commission merchant.

14. ASHTON, JACOB, son of Jacob and Mary (Ropes) Ashton, b. Sept. 5, 1744; gr. Harv. Coll. 1766; d. Dec. 28, 1829; m. May 16, 1771, Susanna, dau. of Richard and Hannah (Hubbard) Lee (b. Apr. 15, 1747; d. Apr. 21, 1817). A merchant; for many years President of Salem Marine Insurance Company.

15. BALCH, BENJAMIN, son of William and Rebecca (Bailey) Balch, and grandson of Rev. William Balch, who settled over the Church and Society of East Bradford as their first minister, in 1728; b. in East Bradford, Nov. 9, 1774, came to Salem, July 13, 1796; m. Dec. 4, 1800, Lois, dau. of William Phippen. (No. 207). d. June 6, 1860. A watchmaker.

16. BACON, JACOB (Dr.) d. July, 1816, aged 65. His wife Sarah, d. Apr. 17, 1785, aged 41. m. Sept. 16, 1790, Sarah Adams.

17. BANCROFT, THOMAS POYNTON, son of Thomas and Elizabeth (Ives) Bancroft, b. at Salem, Dec. 20, 1798; d. at New Orleans, March 16, 1852; m. Dec. 9, 1822, Hannah, dau. of Samuel (No. 228.) and Sarah (Gool) Putnam (b. June 21, 1799; d. Aug. 4, 1872). Merchant in Salem and Boston.

18. BARNARD, EDWARD, son of Rev. Edward and Sarah (Cary) Barnard, of Haverhill, b. at Haverhill, Sept. 28, 1755; gr. Harv. Coll. 1774; d. Dec. 13, 1822; m. in 1780, Judith, dau. of Benjamin and Elizabeth Herbert of Salem; she d. July 31, 1845, aged 90. An apothecary.

19. BARNARD, EDWARD, son of Edward and Judith (Herbert) Barnard, b. at Salem, and d. Dec. 12, 1859, aged 77; m. May 4, 1808, Elizabeth Martin; 2d, Julia Ryan. Master mariner.

20. BARSTOW, GIDEON, son of Gideon and Anna (Mead) Barstow, b. at Mattapoiset, Sept. 7, 1783; d. in St. Augustine, Fla., where he had gone for his health, March 26, 1852; m. Nancy, dau. of Simon and Rachel (Hathorne) Forrester, who now resides in Boston. He was first a practising physician, afterwards a merchant in Salem; member of both branches of Massachusetts Legislature, Representative to Congress, 1821–3.

21. BARTOLL, SAMUEL, ——— ——— Revolutionary Pensioner, an ornamental painter, etc., d. Jan. 24, 1835, aged 70. Hannah, widow, d. March 9, 1836, aged 78.

22. BARTON, CALEB, son of Joseph and Mary (Wescott) Barton, b. June 2, 1775; d. at Salem, Sept. 5, 1820; m. Rachel Thompson of Chester, N. H. (d. at Salem, March 20, 1822, aged 45). An innholder, kept Salem Hotel, he was commander of the Essex Hussars.

23. BARTON, JABEZ W. son of Caleb and Rachel (Thompson) Barton, b. in Chester, Vt., Sept. 20, 1802; m. Rebecca F. Rogers of Billerica. Innholder, succeeded his father in the Salem Hotel; afterwards moved to Boston and had charge of several of the leading hotels.

24. BLANEY, JOSEPH, son of Joseph and Elizabeth Blaney, b at Marblehead, Feb. 12, 1730; gr. Harv. Coll. 1751; m. May 19, 1757, Abigail, dau. of Samuel and Catherine (Winthrop) Browne of Salem (b. April 27, 1735; d. Dec. 22, 1776). After his marriage he removed to Salem. A merchant, and for many years one of the Selectmen; d. at Salem, June, 1786.

25. BOTT, JAMES, a native of Tudbury, England, came to this country before the Revolution and settled in Salem. A chaise and harness maker, shop north side of Essex near Beckford street; m., 1st, Dolly Newhall of Lynnfield; 2d, Ruth Hathorne of Salem; 3rd, Phebe Newhall, of Lynnfield. He died Dec. 30, 1829.

26. BRAY, DANIEL, son of Daniel and Mary (Ingalls) Bray, m. Mary Hodgdon, who d. Oct. 9, 1852, aged 71; he d. Feb. 24, 1850, aged 72. A master mariner.

27. BRIGGS, CORNELIUS, son of William and Mary (Copeland) Briggs, b. at Scituate Mass. Aug. 2, 1776, came to Salem in 1793; m. Oct. 28, 1807, Nancy, dau. of Samuel and Desire (Foster) Tucker; she d. May 15, 1862, aged 78; he d. Sept. 12, 1838, at Salem. A shipwright.

28. BRIGGS, ELIJAH, son of William and Mary (Copeland) Briggs, b. in Scituate, Mass., July 17, 1762; m. Aug. 6, 1789, Hannah, dau. of James and Prudence (Proctor) Buffington of Salem (b. Jan. 30, 1767; d. May 29, 1847); he d. in Salem, Aug. 24, 1838. A shipwright.

29. BRIGGS, LEMUEL, son of William and Mary (Copeland) Briggs, b. in Scituate, March 25, 1765; d. at Salem, Sept. 25, 1844, aged 79; m. May 26, 1793, widow Elizabeth Wyman (b. Jan. 12, 1767; d. Oct. 1806); m., 2d, Dec. 31, 1807, Phebe, dau. of John and Phebe (Tidd) Wright, (b. July 20, 1764; d. Aug. 24, 1844), aged 80. A ship carpenter.

30. BRIGHT, JONATHAN, ―― upholsterer; d. June 1817, aged 49.

31. BROOKHOUSE, ROBERT, son of Robert and Elizabeth (Reeves) Brookhouse, b. Dec. 8, 1779; m., 1st, Martha Farley; m., 2d, Eliza W. Grafton; m., 3rd, Mary Follansbee; d. June 10, 1866. Merchant.

32. BROOKS, TIMOTHY, son of Timothy and Abigail Brooks, m. Feb., 1809, Mary King Mason; d. March 2, 1862, aged 75. A grocer.

33. BROWN, ABRAHAM, a brother of Thomas. (No. 36.)

34. BROWN, BARTHOLOMEW, JR. son of Bartholomew and Sarah (Rea) Brown; bapt. Jan'y 27, 1750, at the Salem village (Danvers); m. Mehitable Flint; d. in Salem, Nov. 10, 1805. Housewright.

35. BROWN, EDWARD, son of Thomas and Elizabeth Brown, b. at Wenham, April 8, 1756; m. Catherine ―― ―― (b. 1760; d. Feb. 10, 1831), aged 71 years. A carpenter. He d. June 10, 1844, aged 88.

36. BROWN, THOMAS, m. July 2, 1769, Margaret Skerry. A carpenter. d. July 1793, aged 46.

37. BROWNE, WILLIAM, son of Samuel and Catherine (Winthrop) Browne, gr. Harv. Coll. 1755; m. in 1774, Ruth, dau. of Gov. Wanton of Rhode Island. A judge of the Supreme Court, a colonel of the Essex Regiment, left in 1775; a refugee. Governor of Bermuda in 1782; d. in London, England, Feb. 13, 1802, aged 65.

38. BRYANT, TIMOTHY, son of Timothy and Rebecca Bryant, b. at Cambridge; m. Sept. 10, 1786, Lydia Brookhouse, who d. Dec. 7, 1844, aged 76. Master mariner, he d. at Salem, Apr. 3, 1838.

39. BUFFINGTON, JAMES, son of James and Prudence (Proctor) Buffington, m. Abigail Osborn March 31, 1798; d. at Newmarket, N. H., on a visit, April 28, 1838, aged 67. A master mariner.

40. BUFFUM, JAMES R., a bookseller for many years in Salem; m. Susan Mansfield; d. Feb. 12, 1863, aged 68 years.

41. BURCHMORE, ZACHARIAH, son of Zachariah and Mary (Leach) Burchmore, m. Sarah Daniels, Jan. 8, 1770; d. May 15, 1807, aged 64. Master mariner and merchant, widely known, and greatly respected.

42. BURCHMORE, HANNAH L., dau. of Zachariah and Sarah (Daniels) Burchmore, d. Aug. 8, 1843, aged 57. Unmarried.

43. BURNHAM, JOHN, son of John and Elizabeth (McIntire) Burnham, b. Nov. 19, 1800; m. Jan. 17, 1826, Sophia Jane Felton of Lynnfield; d. ―― ――. A master mariner.

44. CABOT, FRANCIS, son of John and Anna (Orne) Cabot, married,

June 20, 1745, Mary Fitch, of Portsmouth, N. H., she d. June 15, 1756; m. 2d, Mrs. Elizabeth Gardner, who d. June 14, 1785, aged 68. He d. April 13, 1786. An eminent merchant in Salem.

45. CABOT, WILLIAM, son of Francis and Mary (Fitch) Cabot, bapt. May 3, 1752; d. unmarried at Cambridgeport, Mass., Oct. 22, 1828, aged 76.

46. CARNES, JONATHAN, son of John and Hannah Carnes, bapt. May 29, 1757; d. Dec. 10, 1827. Master mariner, one of the earliest navigators from Salem to the East Indies; m. April 26, 1784, Rebecca, dau. of Wm. (No. 280) and Mary (Clark) Vans, who d. Nov. 9, 1846, aged 83.

47. CHADWICK, GILBERT, b. at Boxford, Oct. 2, 1748; d. at Salem, Nov. 10, 1829, aged 82. Butcher in Salem.

48. CHADWICK, JOHN, son of Gilbert (No. 47) and Elizabeth (Kimball) Chadwick, d. May 11, 1868, aged 77 years; m. June 10, 1824, Elizabeth W. dau. of Israel and Elizabeth (Waite) Williams, who d. Oct. 15, 1870, aged 72 years. For many years cashier of Exchange Bank.

49. CHANDLER, JOHN, b. March 25, 1752; d. March 4, 1821; m. Sarah Dodge, (b. July 16, 1753; d. Sept. 11, 1835). An officer of the Revolution. Housewright.

50. CHANDLER, JOSEPH DODGE, son of John and Sarah (Dodge) Chandler, b. at Salem, March 14, 1789; m. Mary Mc'Donald, June 12, 1827; d. May 17, 1861. Druggist and Grocer.

51. CHAPMAN, BENJAMIN, son of Isaac and Hannah (Dean) Chapman, bapt. April 8, 1739; m. 1st, Sarah Buffington; 2d, Sarah Henderson; d. about 1783. A mariner.

52. CHAPMAN, GEORGE, son of Isaac and Hannah (Dean) Chapman, bapt. July 26, 1741; m. Nov. 1, 1762, Lydia, dau. of Edmund and Lydia (Hardy) Henfield (b. Dec. 28, 1745; d. March 8, 1830). In early life actively engaged in maritime pursuits. In 1798 appointed first keeper of lights on Baker's Island and continued 17 years. Died March 20, 1824, aged 84.

53. CHASE, GEORGE C., son of Henry and Betsey (Abbot) Chase, b. at Salem, May 2, 1803; m. Mary, dau. of Daniel Bray, Jr. (No. 26). Agent Forest River Lead Company in Salem.

54. CHOATE, AMOS, son of Stephen Choate of Ipswich, m., 1st, Lucy dau. of Aaron and Lucy (Baker) Smith of Ipswich; she died Jan. 12, 1833, aged 52; 2d, Mehitable, dau. of Jonathan and Mehitable (Eden) Neal of Salem, who d. Oct. 20, 1856, aged 73. Merchant; for many years Register of Deeds of Essex; d. at Salem, Aug. 7, 1844, aged 69.

55. CHURCHILL, BENJAMIN KING, son of Joseph and Ann (Northey) Churchill, b. in Kennebunk, Me., July 13, 1774; d. at Hamlet, R. I., April 24, 1858, aged 83; m. 1st, Clarissa Eaton; 2d, March 3, 1822, Eliza, dau. of Samuel Holman (No. 134) and widow of Henry L. Norris; lived in Salem many years. A master mariner.

56. CLEVELAND, CHARLES, son of Aaron and Abiah (Hyde) Cleveland, b. June 21, 1772; m. Mehitable, dau. of John Treadwell (No. 271). Merchant in Salem, afterwards, many years the venerable city missionary of Boston; d. in Boston, June 5, 1872.

57. CLOUGH, WILLIAM, a mason; m. widow Margery Mansfield.

58. CLOUTMAN, JOSEPH, son of Benjamin and Elizabeth (Frye) Cloutman, b. Dec. 31, 1796; m. Oct. 12, 1821, Lydia L., dau. of William Richardson. Trader, afterwards town and city clerk, from 1853 to 1863; he d. March 16, 1872.

59. CLOUTMAN, ROBERT F., brother of the preceding, m. June 23, 1811, Mary Ann Fenno, who d. May, 1813. aged 23; he d. at Charleston, S. C., Feb. 2, 1821, aged 35. Hardware dealer.

60. COLE, THOMAS, son of Jonathan and Hannah (Palfrey) Cole, b. in Boston, Dec. 24, 1779; gr. Harv. Coll. 1798; m. 1st, Hannah L. Cogswell of Ipswich; m. 2d, Nancy D. Gay of Salem; came to Salem in 1808, and was, many years, a successful teacher; d. June 24, 1852.

61. CONVERSE, JOSHUA, yeoman and victualler; his widow Mary, d. Jan. 1822, aged 81.

62. COOK, JONATHAN, son of Jonathan Cook, bapt. June 16, 1751; d. 1803. A shoresman.

63. COOK, SAMUEL, son of Samuel and Abigail Cook, bapt. Sept. 18, 1737; d. Dec. 1813, aged 80. Mariner.

64. COOK, SAMUEL, son of Stephen and Elizabeth (Newhall) Cook, m. Nov. 9, 1800, Sarah, dau. of James and Sarah (Brown) Chever; d. Dec. 10, 1861, aged 92. Master mariner, merchant.

65. CREAMER, BENJAMIN, son of Dr. Edward and Eunice (Daland) Creamer, b. at Boothbay, Me., May 11, 1794; m. May 1, 1821, Ann M. dau. of Capt. James and Mary (Doyle) Brace. Merchant; d. May 21, 1854.

66. CUMMINS, DAVID, son of David and Mehitable (Cave) Cummins, b. at Topsfield, Aug. 14, 1785; read law with S. Putnam (No. 228) began to practise in Salem in 1809; removed after many years to Springfield, thence to Dorchester, where he d. March 30, 1855; judge of C. C. P. from 1828 to death; m. 1st, Sally, dau. of Daniel Porter of Topsfield; 2d, Catherine, and 3rd, Maria Franklin, daus. of Dr. Thomas Kittredge of Andover.

67. CURWEN, SAMUEL, son of Rev. George and Mehitable (Parkman) Curwen, b. Dec. 17, 1715; gr. Harv. Coll. 1735; m. May, 1750, Abigail, dau. of Hon. Daniel Russell of Charlestown. Judge of admiralty, merchant, refugee from May 12, 1775, to Sept., 1784; d. at Salem, April, 1802.

68. CUSHING, MRS. SARAH, dau. of Richard and Mehitable (Curwen) Ward, b. Aug. 1, 1769; m. James Cushing of Sanbornton, N. H., Dec. 1, 1793 (b. March 9, 1765; d. Sept. 7, 1796, at Alexandria. Merchant). She d. at New Brighton, Staten Island, N. Y., June 9, 1862.

69. CUSHING, ISAAC, son of Dea. Isaac and Mary (Jones) Cushing of Hingham, b. in that town, Aug. 16, 1779; m. at Hingham, May 25, 1815, Elizabeth Shute, dau. of Dr. Daniel and Betsey (Cushing) Shute of Hingham (b. Oct. 9, 1791; d. at Fitchburg, April 28, 1852). They resided in Salem about ten years. He was a bookbinder, afterwards removed to Fitchburg where he d. Feb. 7, 1836, aged 56.

70. CUSHING, THOMAS C., son of Benjamin and Ruth (Croade) Cushing of Hingham, m. 1st, Sarah Dean of Salem; 2d, Rachel Andrew of Hing-

ham; d. Sept. 28, 1824, aged 60; came to Salem and established a paper with John Dabney (No. 71) under the title of Salem Mercury; 1st number issued Oct. 14, 1786; the name was changed in 1790, to that of Salem Gazette; also a bookseller, firm of Cushing and Appleton.

71. DABNEY, JOHN, son of Charles and Elizabeth (Gardner) Dabney, b. at Boston, July 31, 1752; m. Abigail, dau. of Jonathan and Margaret (Mason) Peele (b. Nov. 1, 1767; d. Sept. 17, 1834). Printer, bookseller, and for more than twenty years postmaster of Salem; d. Oct. 11, 1819.

72. DALAND, TUCKER, son of John and Betsey (Tucker) Daland, m. 1st, Eliza, dau. of Thomas Whittredge (No. 303); 2d, Eliza, dau. of James Silver; d. May 31, 1858, aged 63 years. Merchant in Salem.

73. DALGLEISCH, ANDREW, a merchant; a refugee in the Revolution.

74. DANIELS, DAVID, son of Asa and Bathsheba (Fairbanks) Daniels, b. at Medway, Nov. 25, 1757; gr. Harv. Coll. 1776; m. Betsey, dau. of Robert and Elizabeth (Proctor) Shillaber of Danvers. Studied divinity, preached a short time, but relinquished the profession on account of his health, afterwards engaged in trade; d. at Danvers, Dec. 16, 1827.

75. DANIELS, STEPHEN, son of Stephen and Margaret Daniels, d. March 1803, aged 88. Shipwright.

76. DAVIDSON, MOSES, b. in Newburyport; m. Martha Ann Marsh of Amesbury. Carriage painter, resides at 20 Albion street, Salem.

77. DEAN, GEORGE, son of John and Rebecca (Bowers) Dean, b. Nov. 2, 1777; m. Judith, dau. of Enos Briggs; d. March 12, 1831. A trader, colonel of Salem Regiment of Infantry.

78. DEWING, JOSIAH, d. April, 1787. A victualler.

79. DODGE, BETSEY W., dau. of Samuel and Sally (Pedrick) Waite, m. John Dodge, son of Joshua and Elizabeth (Crowninshield) Dodge, a merchant, and captain of the Salem Cadets, who d. June, 1820, aged 36; d. June 25, 1829, aged 42.

79a. DRIVER, STEPHEN, son of Stephen and Sara Driver, m Ruth Metcalf, who d. Aug. 22, 1837, aged 67; d. March 24, 1850, aged 78. Cordwainer.

80. DUTCH, DANIEL, b. at Ipswich; m. 1st, Sarah Dodge; 2d, Mrs. Lucy Staniford; d. Oct. 15, 1851, aged 86. For many years a deputy sheriff.

81. EDEN, MARY, dau. of John and Mary (Dean) West, bapt. March 12, 1727; m. 1st, Aug. 9, 1745, John Beadle; 2d, July 11, 1751, Capt. Thomas Eden, who d. July 1, 1768, aged 45; she d. Aug., 1789.

82. ENDICOTT, AARON, son of Joseph and Sarah (Hathorne) Endicott, b. at Danvers, Sept. 12, 1779; m. Hannah Osgood of Salem; d. August 6, 1853, at Salem. Master mariner.

83. ENDICOTT, CHARLES MOSES, son of Moses and Anna (Towne) Endicott, b. at Danvers Dec. 6, 1793; received a mercantile education, supercargo in the East India trade, President of the East India Marine Society, Cashier of Salem Bank; m. Sarah R. dau. of Samuel and Sarah (Purbeck) Blythe; d. at Northampton, Dec. 15, 1863.

84. ENDICOTT, NATHAN, son of Moses and Anna (Towne) Endicott, b. at Danvers, Sept. 19, 1790; captain and supercargo, principally in the Russian trade; President of the Oriental Insurance Co.; m. Margaret O. Hicks of Boston; d. August 30, 1857.

85. ENDICOTT, SAMUEL, son of John and Martha (Putnam) Endicott, b. in Danvers, June 1763; m. Elizabeth, dau. of William Putnam of Sterling; d. May 1, 1828. Master mariner and merchant.

86. ENDICOTT, TIMOTHY, son of John and Martha (Putnam) Endicott, b. July 27, 1785; m. Harriet Martin of Sterling; d. at Sterling.

87. EUSTIS, JOSHUA, b. June 15, 1758; m., Lydia, dau. of William and Mary (Waters) Shillaber of Danvers; d. July 22, 1822. A trader in Salem.

88. FABENS, BENJAMIN, son of William (No. 89) and Rebecca (Gray) Fabens, b. Sept. 9, 1785; m. 1st, Hannah Stone; 2d, Mary Tay; d. May 24, 1850. A merchant.

89. FABENS, WILLIAM, son of James and Sarah (Henderson) Fabens. m. Rebecca Gray, who d. Nov. 11, 1837, aged 75; d. April 10, 1828. Merchant.

90. FABENS, WILLIAM, son of William (No. 89) and Rebecca (Gray) Fabens, b. Dec. 1, 1782; m. Sarah Brown; d. Jan. 2, 1834. Master mariner and merchant.

91. FARLESS, THOMAS, son of Thomas and Sally (Cook) Farless, b. June 11, 1787; m. Eliza Conant; d. August 21, 1864. Rigger.

92. FARNHAM, PUTNAM I., son of James and Rebecca (Ingalls) Farnham, b. in North Andover, Mass., March 10, 1788; m. Rebecca Ingalls of Merrimack, N. H.; came to Salem in 1813 and for many years was a prominent merchant; removed to Roxbury in October 1848, where he d. Nov. 25, 1852.

93. FELT, JOHN, son of Jonathan and Hannah (Silsbee) Felt; m. 1st, Deborah Skerry; m. 2d, widow Catherine Turner; d. in 1785. Shoresman.

93a. FELT, JOHN, son of John (No. 93) and Deborah (Skerry) Felt. b. Sept. 16, 1754; m. July 13, 1780, Mary Porter (b. Jan. 25, 1762; d. Dec. 27, 1817); d. Sept. 12, 1796. A master mariner.

94. FELT, JOSEPH.

95. FELT, JOSEPH, JR., son of John (No. 93) and Catherine Felt. m. Dec. 29, 1795, Sarah, dau. of Elisha and Sarah Bradish, who d. Jan. 20, 1845, aged 77; d. May 30, 1852, aged 75. Farmer.

96. FELT, EPHRAIM, son of John (No. 93a) and Mary (Porter) Felt. b. Feb. 16, 1795; m. Eliza, dau. of George Ropes; d. Dec. 7, 1872.

97. FIELD, SAMUEL, son of Samuel and Elizabeth (Dean) Field, bapt. April 30, 1732; m. Priscilla Ingalls of Marblehead; d. Nov. 3, 1786, aged 54. A boatbuilder and merchant.

98. FIELD, STEPHEN, m. Sally Hovey; d. Jan. 15, 1844, aged 72. A master mariner.

99. FORRESTER, SIMON, son of Thomas and Elinor (Haley) Forrester, b. May 10, 1748; came to Salem from Ireland April 17, 1765; m. Rachel Hathorne; d. July 4, 1817. A successful and wealthy merchant.

100. FORRESTER, JOHN, son of Simon (No. 99) and Rachel (Hathorne) Forrester, b. Oct. 3, 1781; gr. Harv. Coll. 1801; m. Charlotte, dau. of Elisha and Mehitable (Pedricke) Story of Marblehead; d. July 25, 1837. Merchant.

101. FOSTER, JOHN, son of Robert Foster, (No. 102) b. 1770; m. Mary, dau. of Z. Burchmore (No. 41); d. April 1821. Master mariner.

102. FOSTER, ROBERT, son of Caleb and Abigail (Gould) Foster, b. in Salem, March 11, 1742; m. 1st, Mary Procter; 2d, Mrs. Sarah Putnam; 3d, Mrs. Lucy Woodman; d. Aug. 12, 1814. First Master of Essex Lodge of F. and A. Masons. Blacksmith.

103. FOSTER, NATHANIEL, son of Nathaniel and Sarah (Daland) Foster, bapt. Nov. 7, 1742; m. Elizabeth, dau. of Nathaniel Yell; d. April 29, 1773, aged 32.

104. FOSTER, WILLIAM H., son of John (No. 101) and Mary (Burchmore) Foster. Cashier of Asiatic National Bank, Salem.

105. FROST, JOHN, son of John and Lucy (Lowe) Frost, b. at Danvers, Dec. 22, 1786; m. 1st, Lucy Frye, dau. of Daniel (No. 106); d. Sept. 27, 1824, aged 37; 2d, Hannah Buffington, dau. of James (No. 39). A master mariner and merchant.

106. FRYE, DANIEL, son of William Frye, b. in Andover 1757; m. Prudence, widow of James Buffington. For many years kept a tavern in Salem; d. Nov. 1813.

107. FRYE, NATHAN, son of William, b. in Andover Jan. 10, 1755; m. Hannah Nutting; d. Jan. 10, 1810. A distiller in Salem.

107a. FRYE, JOSEPH S., son of William and Sarah (Marshall) Frye, b. at Danvers, Jan. 10, 1802; m. May 8, 1825, Hannah, dau. of John and Huldah Parsons of Gilmanton, N. H. (b. Jan. 23, 1805). Superintends a bark grinding mill, Goodhue street, Salem.

108. FULLER, ELIJAH, son of Rev. Daniel and Hannah (Bowers) Fuller, b. in Gloucester, 1778; m. 1st, Mary Phippen, dau. of William (No. 207); 2d, Harriet Symonds; d. Sept. 22, 1852. Tinplate worker. His father for fifty years was the beloved pastor of the church in West or 2d Parish, Gloucester.

109. GARDNER, HENRY, son of Samuel and Esther (Orne) Gardner, b. Oct. 17, 1747, gr. Harv. Coll. 1765; m. Sarah, dau. of John Turner. For many years a merchant in Salem; retired afterwards to Malden where he died Nov. 8, 1817.

110. GARDNER, WELD, son of Samuel and Esther (Orne) Gardner, b. Dec. 3, 1745; d. Nov. 6, 1801. Merchant.

111. GAVETT, JONATHAN, son of Joseph and Mary (Williams) Gavett, b. July 3, 1731; m. 1st, Sarah Whittemore; 2d, Mary Symonds; d. in 1806. Cabinet maker and turner.

112. GAVETT, WILLIAM, son of Jonathan (No. 111) and Sarah (Whittemore) Gavett, b. Jan. 2, 1767; m. Oct. 27, 1799, Martha, dau. of Peter and Martha (Grover) Richardson of Woburn; (b. July 15, 1776; d. Nov. 9, 1823); d. Jan. 8, 1856. A turner; for many years sexton of the church.

113. GERRISH, JAMES S., teacher of the East School from April 25, 1818, to March 15, 1822, resigned and soon opened a private school for boys; m. Dorcas Barrett of Concord; d. at Salem, Aug. 5, 1835, aged 42.

114. GERRISH, SAMUEL, son of Benjamin and Margaret (Cabot) Gerrish, b. at Salem, March 16, 1749; m. 1st, Sarah Williams of Marblehead; 2d, Elizabeth Chipman; d. Sept. 2, 1844, aged 95 years and 6 months; having passed most of his long life in his home No. 85 Federal street.

115. GIBBS, HENRY, son of Henry and Katharine (Willard) Gibbs, b. at Salem, May 7, 1749; gr. Harv. Coll., 1766. Having taught school in several places, he afterwards entered into mercantile business at Salem; m. Mercy, dau. of Benjamin and Rebecca (Minot) Prescott (b. Feb. 5, 1755; d. May 19, 1809); d. June 29, 1794.

116. GIBBS, WILLIAM, son of Henry (No. 115) and Mercy (Prescott) Gibbs, b. at Salem, Feb. 17, 1785; resided at Salem, Concord and Lexington; m. Mercy, dau. of Peter and Mary (Prescott) Barrett of Concord, (b. Sept. 13, 1783; d. Feb. 7, 1837); d. in Lexington, Dec. 23, 1853; distinguished for his genealogical and historical researches.

117. GLOVER, JONATHAN, son of Joseph and Mary (Cook) Glover, bapt. Oct. 25, 1741; m. Nov. 29, 1764, Mary Newhall, dau. of Samuel Newhall of Lynnfield. Mariner and fisherman.

118. GLOVER, SAMUEL, son of Joseph and Mary (Cook) Glover, bapt. Nov. 13, 1743; m. Eunice West, June 15, 1771, who d. Dec., 1788, aged 47; d. ———. A fisherman and mariner.

119. GOODALE, NATHAN, son of Joshua and Experience (Judd) Goodale, b. Dec. 14, 1740; gr. Harv. Coll., 1759; m. Mary, dau. of Mitchell and Mary (Cabot) Sewall; d. at Newton, Aug. 9, 1806. Merchant at Salem for several years, 1st clerk of the District Court of Mass.

120. GOODHUE, BENJAMIN, son of Benjamin and Martha (Hardy) Goodhue, b. at Salem, Sept. 20, 1748; gr. Harv. Coll., 1766; m. 1st, Frances Ritchie of Philadelphia; m. 2d, Anna Willard of Lancaster; d. July 28, 1814. Merchant at Salem, Representative and Senator U. S. Congress.

121. GOODHUE, JONATHAN, son of Benjamin and Martha (Hardy) Goodhue, b. at Salem, Dec. 31, 1744; gr. Harv. Coll., 1764; m. Dorothy Ashton, sister of Jacob Ashton (No. 14); d. April 19, 1778. Merchant in Salem.

122. GOODHUE, WILLIAM.

123. GOULD, JAMES, son of James and Margarite Gould, bapt. July 3, 1736; m. Mehitable Townsend of Lynn; d. July, 1810, aged 74. Deacon of the church. Block maker.

124. GOULD, ROBERT W., son of James W. and Mary (Watts) Gould, b. at Salem, Jan. 9, 1784; m. Jan. 12, 1812, Sarah Osgood; d. April 21, 1873. Master mariner; several years an officer in the Custom House.

125. GRAFTON, SUSANNAH, dau. of Joseph and Mary Grafton, d. Oct., 1794, aged 73. Unmarried.

126. GRAY, SAMUEL, son of Samuel and Mary (Moses) Gray, b. June 7, 1765; m. Ruth, dau. of Daniel and Priscilla (Lambert) Ropes (b. Dec. 20, 1768; d. March 5, 1844); d. Oct. 11, 1850. Boot and shoe manufacturer.

127. GWINN, THADDEUS, son of Thomas Gwinn, b. in Nantucket; came to Salem in early life, where he resided until his decease which occurred May 9, 1829, aged 66; m. 1st, Mercy Beadle; 2d, widow Mary Brown, a dau. of Daniel Ropes (No. 236). A ropemaker.

128. HASTIE, JAMES, came from Scotland to Salem, a trader; m. Sarah, youngest dau. of Gabriel and Elizabeth (Reeves) Holman (bapt. March 10, 1754; d. April 2, 1781); in 1783 he was a resident of Newport, R. I.

129. HENDERSON, BENJAMIN, son of Benjamin Henderson; b. Dec. 3, 1761; m. Mary, dau. of Daniel and Mary (Ingalls) Bray and sister of Daniel Bray (No. 26); d. June 28, 1836. A soldier in the Revolutionary Army, afterwards a master mariner.

130. HENDERSON, JOSEPH, son of Benjamin (No. 129) and Mary (Bray) Henderson, b. Oct. 29, 1793; m. 1st, Mary Glazier; 2d, Elizabeth Adams; d. Feb. 23, 1856. Painter.

131. HERRICK, BARNABAS, son of Daniel and Sarah (Raymond) Herrick of Beverly, b. Oct. 28, 1738; m. Lydia Murray of Salem; d. at Salem in 1832, aged 94.

132. HILLER, JOSEPH, son of Joseph and Hannah (Welsh) Hiller, b. in Boston, March 24, 1748; m. Margaret Cleveland; d. in Lancaster, Mass., Feb. 9, 1814. A major in U. S. Army during the Revolution; naval officer of the Port of Salem, under the State Government, and collector for the same through the whole of the administrations of Washington and Adams.

133. HOFFMAN, CHARLES. Merchant, resides in 26 Chestnut street.

134. HOLMAN, SAMUEL, son of Gabriel and Elizabeth (Reeves) Holman, bapt. Aug. 24, 1737; m. Ruth, dau. of William and Eunice (Bowditch) Hunt; d. Nov. 24, 1825, aged 89. Hatter; he had been deacon of the church fifty-two years.

135. HOLMAN, SAMUEL, son of Samuel and Ruth (Hunt) Holman, b. Oct. 10, 1764; m. Elizabeth King; d. Oct. 24, 1854, aged 90. Hatter; for many years one of the assessors of Salem.

136. HOLMAN, SAMUEL, b. Dec. 21, 1792; m. Lydia, dau. of George and Hannah (Phippen) Hodges; d. at Andover on a visit, May 29, 1845. Merchant.

137. HOLYOKE, EDWARD AUGUSTUS, son of Rev. Edward and Margaret (Appleton) Holyoke, b. Aug. 1, 1728; gr. Harv. Coll., 1746; commenced practice of medicine in Salem in 1749; m. June 1, 1755, Judith, dau. of B. Pickman (No. 209); she d. Nov. 19, 1756; m. 2d, Nov 22, 1759, Mary, dau. of Nath'l Vial of Boston (b. Dec. 19. 1737; d. April 15, 1802). He d. March 31, 1829. A distinguished practitioner of medicine, first President of Mass. Med. Society, also President of Am. Acad. of Arts and Sciences, a prominent member of the various scientific and literary institutions of this city during a long and useful life.

138. HOLYOKE, EDWARD AUGUSTUS, son of William and Judith (Holyoke) Turner, a grandson of E. A. Holyoke (No. 137); b. in Boston, July 12, 1796; gr. Harv. Coll., 1817. At the close of his studies in 1821

or 22, dropped the name of Turner; m. Maria Osgood; d. at Syracuse, N. Y., Dec. 19, 1855, to which place he removed several years previous, from Salem, where he had been a practitioner of medicine.

139. HOWES, FREDERICK, son of Anthony and Bethia Howes, b. at Dennis in 1782; m. Elizabeth, dau. of William Burley, of Beverly; commenced the practice of law in Salem, residing however for some time in Danvers, and representing the town in the Legislature; returned to Salem and was for several years President of Salem Marine Insurance Company; d. Nov. 12, 1855.

140. HUBBARD, OLIVER, son of John Hubbard, b. at Hamilton, Aug. 3, 1770; educated by the late Rev. Dr. M. Cutler; commenced the practice of medicine in Portland; came to Salem in March, 1811, and continued a successful practitioner until his decease, which occurred Aug. 27, 1849; unmarried.

141. INGERSOLL, JONATHAN, son of Nathaniel, d. at Windsor, Vt., July 9, 1840, aged 89; a native of Salem and from early boyhood followed the seas for a period of thirty years; he retired upon a farm in Danvers where he lived for twenty years, thence removed to a beautiful farm on the Connecticut river; he m. 1st, Mary Hodges; 2d, Mary Pool; 3d, Sarah, widow of Samuel Blythe, and dau. of Aaron Purbeck (b. Feb., 1759, d. March, 1812).

142. IVES, WILLIAM, son of William and Mary (Bradshaw) Ives. Printer, and for nearly fifty years one of the editors and proprietors of the Salem Observer.

143. JACOBS, DANIEL, son of John Jacobs, bapt. Nov. 5, 1711; m. Sarah Dudley of Boston, June 17, 1735; d. Oct., 1809, in his 99th year, having lived to this advanced age on his farm in Danvers near the Salem boundary line in North Fields; in early life a shoemaker, afterwards a farmer.

144. JANES, JOSEPH, ―― ―― m. Oct. 9, 1737, Lydia, dau. of George and Bethia (Peters) Deland (bapt. April 14, 1717; d. March, 1793).

144a. JANES, JOSEPH, son of Joseph and Lydia (Deland) Janes, bapt. Aug. 28, 1737; d. Sept. 1789; m. March 26, 1764, Mary Collins.

145. JOHNSON, EMERY, son of Eli and Miriam (Burbank) Johnson, b. in Weston, Mass., Aug. 24, 1790; m. March, 1824, Sarah, dau. of Daniel Saunders of Salem; d. at Salem, Jan. 19, 1845. Master mariner and merchant.

146. JOHNSON, JOHN.

147. JOHNSON, SAMUEL, son of Joshua and Martha (Spofford) Johnson, b. at Andover, Dec. 18, 1790; gr. Harv. Coll., 1811; m. 1st, Anna Dodge; 2d, Lucy P. Robinson. A practitioner of medicine; resides in No. 4 Chestnut street.

148. KIMBALL, NATHAN, son of James and Mary (Lovering) Kimball, b. at Wenham, Aug. 20, 1741; removed to Salem, where he d. May 10, 1808; m. Sarah dau. of James Friend, of Wenham (b. 1740; d. May 10, 1808). A shoemaker.

149. KIMBALL, JAMES, son of Nathan (No. 148), b. Dec. 7, 1777; m. Nov. 29, 1807, Catherine, dau. of William and Mary (Richardson) Russell (b. in Cambridge, March 4, 1784; d. in Salem, Feb. 15, 1861); d. Oct., 1822.

150. KING, JAMES, son of James King, b. in Salem, May 10, 1752; d. June 3, 1831; m. 1st, Judith Norris; 2d, Elizabeth Grant. A trader.

151. KING, JOHN GLEN, son of James King (No. 150), b. March 19, 1787; gr. Harv. Coll., 1807; m. Nov. 10, 1815, Susan H., dau. of Frederick and A. H. Gilman, of Gloucester; d. July 26, 1857. Counsellor at law; first president of City Council of Salem. He was the youngest of that corps of scholars who gave the type and character to the Essex Bar, in the generation that has recently passed away.

152. KNIGHT, NATHANIEL, son of Nathaniel and Sarah (Mascoll) Knight, b. at Salem, May 11, 1764; m. Oct. 26, 1784, Sarah, dau. of Ebenezer and Mehitable (Buttolph) Ward, who d. April 26, 1846, aged 85; d. Feb. 19, 1845. Master mariner from the port of Salem; and many years wharfinger of Derby wharf.

153. LAKEMAN, EBEN KNOWLTON, son of Richard and Lucy (Knowlton) Lakeman, b. at Ipswich, Dec. 10, 1799; came to Salem in his boyhood, where he resided until his decease which occurred May 27, 1857; m. June 20, 1826, Jane, dau. of Benjamin (No. 250) and Jane Shillaber. Watchmaker.

154. LAMSON, ASA, son of Asa and Deborah (Cox) Lamson of Beverly, m. Rebecca, dau. of Knott Martin Vickery of Beverly; d. April 14, 1870, aged 77.

155. LANG, EDWARD SYMMES, son of Edward and Rachel (Ward) Lang, b. Jan. 21, 1770; m. June 5, 1796, Hannah, dau. of Joseph (No. 132) and Margaret (Cleveland) Hiller (b. Sept. 6, 1771; d. April, 1823); m. 2d, Rebecca Brimmer of Beverly; d. Feb. 12, 1833. Apothecary, on the eastern corner of Essex and Liberty Streets.

156. LEACH, ROBERT, m. Nov. 29, 1770, Abigail Luscomb; d. Nov. 25, 1825, aged 78. Shoreman, afterwards merchant.

157. LEE, JOHN CLARKE, son of Nathaniel Cabot and Mary Ann (Cabot) Lee, b. April 9, 1804; gr. Harv. Coll., 1823; m. July 29, 1826, Harriet Paine, dau. of Joseph Warren and Harriet (Paine) Rose; resides in No. 14 Chestnut street.

158. LORD, DANIEL, son of Daniel and Sarah (Holland) Lord, b. at Ipswich, March 26, 1788. Worker in marble, Market wharf, Salem.

159. LORD, JOSEPH H., brother of No. 158. b. at Ipswich, Nov. 2, 1794; m. Judith, dau. of Ellis and Abigail (Herbert) Mansfield; d. at Worcester, Jan. 6, 1867. Resident of Salem many years. A trader.

160. LORD, JAMES, son of Daniel and Hannah (Safford) Lord, b. at Ipswich, Jan. 9, 1799; m. Dec., 1822, Sarah, dau. of Ebenezer (No. 165a) and Sarah (Buffington) Mann (b. Oct. 18, 1798); he d. Nov. 11, 1871, in Salem. Tanner.

161. LUSCOMB, WILLIAM, probably son of William and Jane Luscomb, bapt. Apr. 5, 1724; m. Sarah Henderson. Housewright.

162. LUSCOMB, WILLIAM, son of William and Sarah (Henderson) Luscomb, m. Jan. 20, 1773, Susanna Cook; d. April 10, 1827, aged 80. Painter.

163. MCINTIRE, JOSEPH, son of John and Mehitable McIntire, bapt. Feb. 26, 1726-7; m. Sarah Ruck, March 19, 1746-7; d. in 1776. A housewright.

164. MCINTIRE, JOSEPH, son of Joseph (No. 163) and Sarah (Ruck) McIntire; m. Jan., 1773, Ann Bowden of Boston, who d. Sept. 1813; d. June 1825, aged 77. A housewright.

164a. MCINTIRE, JOSEPH, son of Joseph (No. 164) and Ann (Bowden) McIntire, bapt. Feb., 1779; d. Sept. 21, 1852. Unmarried; a carver.

165. MCINTIRE, SAMUEL, son of Joseph (No. 163) and Sarah (Ruck) McIntire, bapt. Jan. 16, 1757; m. Oct. 31, 1778, Elizabeth, dau. of Samuel (No. 97) and Priscilla (Ingalls) Field; d. Feb., 1811. The skilful and noted carver and architect of Salem.

165a. MANN, EBENEZER, son of Ebenezer Mann, b. at Pembroke, Aug. 6, 1758; came to Salem in 1783, and commenced building vessels; in 1800 he engaged in the grocery business; m. Dec. 30, 1791, Sarah, dau. of James and Prudence (Proctor) Bullington, a sister of James (No. 39), (b. Sept. 27, 1772; d. May 17, 1851); he d. in Salem, March 19, 1836.

166. MANSFIELD, JONATHAN, came from Lynn and settled in Salem. A trader; d. March, 1791, aged 74.

167. MARSTON, WILLIAM, a grocer, in a building which stood in the centre of Washington street, removed when Eastern Railroad Tunnel was built in 1839; d. May 1848, aged 67.

168. MASON, DAVID, son of David and Susanna Mason, b. in Boston, March 19, 1726; d. in Boston, Sept. 17, 1794. He was a meritorious officer in the Revolution; resided in Salem several years previous to the commencement of hostilities.

169. MERRITT, DAVID, son of David and Elizabeth (Badcock) Merritt, b. at Ticehurst, Sussex Co., England, April 20, 1775; m. July 30, 1804, Anne, dau. of William and Anne Ashby of Battle, Sussex; arrived in this country, Oct. 18, 1804; settled at Utica, N. Y., thence at Sackett Harbor, N. Y. and Marblehead; came to Salem in Oct., 1824. Trader till the year 1827; then established a wagon express between Boston and Salem and elsewhere, after the opening of the Eastern Railroad by rail; d. July 28, 1862.

170. MILLET, JOHN, son of Andrew and Ruth Millet, bapt. Oct 23, 1737; m. 1761, Mary Roberts, who d. Aug., 1788, aged 48; d. Oct., 1793. A cooper.

171. MORGAN, THEODORE, son of Lucas and Tryphena (Smith) Morgan, b. at West Springfield, Mass., Nov. 19, 1778; m. Sept. 20, 1806, Abigail, dau. of Thomas Manning; d. at Salem, Dec. 10, 1845. A watchmaker.

172. MOSES, ELEAZER, son of Eleazer and Mary Moses; bapt. Jan. 19, 1734; m. Mary, dau. of Peter Henderson; d. Feb., 1786. Sailmaker.

173. NEEDHAM, BENJAMIN.

174. NEWHALL, ISAAC, son of Joel and Lucy (Mansfield) Newhall, b. in

Lynn, Aug. 24, 1782. A trader in Salem several years; author of a work, published in 1831, entitled, "Letters on Junius". He was twice married. His first wife was Sarah Lewis, who d. May, 1821; he returned to Lynn and spent his latter days at the old homestead, and there d. July 6, 1858.

175. NEWHALL, JEREMIAH, son of Jeremiah and Sarah (Bates) Newhall, b. in Lynn, Dec. 25, 1737; m. 1761, Elizabeth Grant. Housewright.

176. NEWHALL, JOEL, son of Joel and Lucy (Mansfield) Newhall, b. in Lynn, Oct. 12, 1779. A trader in Salem with his brother Isaac (No. 174), afterwards kept a dry goods store in Marblehead; he returned to the old homestead in Lynn, and d. there Oct. 8, 1839.

177. NICHOLS, ICHABOD, son of David and Hannah (Gaskell) Nichols, b. in Salem, Apr. 20, 1749; resided in Portsmouth, N. H., several years of his early life. Merchant in Salem; m. Lydia, dau. of Benjamin and Ruth (Hardy) Ropes (b. Dec. 4, 1754; d. Feb. 25, 1835); he d. at Salem, July 2, 1839.

178. NICHOLS, BENJAMIN ROPES, son of Ichabod (No. 177) and Lydia (Ropes) Nichols, b. at Portsmouth, May 18, 1786; gr. Harv. Coll., 1804. Counsellor at Law, in Salem, many years; and from 1824, until his decease, in Boston, which occurred April 30, 1848; m. Mary, dau. of Timothy and Rebecca (White) Pickering.

179. NICHOLS, GEORGE, son of Ichabod (No. 177) and Lydia (Ropes) Nichols, b. at Salem, July 4, 1778; m. 1st, Sally; 2d, Lydia Peirce, dau. of Jerathmael and Sarah (Ropes) Peirce; d. Oct. 19, 1865. Merchant in Salem.

180. NICHOLS, SAMUEL, son of Stephen and Abigail (Moulton) Nichols, b. Dec. 6, 1800; m. Dec. 17, 1826, Mary M. Flint; d. Oct. 17, 1854. A tanner in Salem.

181. NICHOLS, WILLIAM FRYE, son of Ichabod and Cassandra (Frye) Nichols, b. Apr. 4, 1801; m. June 8, 1830, Abigail, dau. of James (No. 39) Buffington. A tanner in Salem.

182. NORTHEY, ABIJAH, son of Abijah and Abigail (Wood) Northey, m. 1st, April 18, 1795, Sally G. King; 2d, Lydia, dau. of Gabriel and Lydia (Mansfield) Holman (b. Dec. 9, 1777; ———— ————); d. Oct. 25, 1853, aged 79¾ years. Master mariner and merchant.

183. NUTTING, JOHN, b. in Cambridge, Jan. 7, 1694; gr. Harv. Coll., 1712; came to Salem in 1718, and kept the school for many years; collector of the port at different times; register of deeds, etc.; m. Feb. 12, 1719-20, Ruth Gardner, she d. Nov. 12, 1736; m. 2d, Elizabeth, dau. of Benjamin and Abigail (Lindall) Pickman (b. Jan. 22, 1714; d. June 10, 1785); d. May 20, 1790, aged 96; the oldest graduate for several years on the College catalogue.

184. OLIVER, WILLIAM W., son of Hubbard and Rebecca (Wallis) Oliver, d. Dec. 29, 1869, aged 91. Many years deputy collector of the customs at the port of Salem.

185. OSBORN, WILLIAM.

185a. ORMAN, SARAH, dau. of Joseph and Sarah (Ruck) Orman, d. at Salem, Sept. 21, 1843, aged 79. Unmarried.

186. OSGOOD, JOSEPH, son of Joseph and Margaret Osgood of Andover, m. June 14, 1770, Lucretia, dau. of Miles and Hannah (Derby) Ward (b. Aug. 28, 1748; d. Sept., 1809); d. June, 1812, aged 65. A physician in Danvers and Salem.

187. OSGOOD, JOSEPH, son of Dr. Joseph Osgood (No. 186); m. Oct. 23, 1796, Mary, dau. of Ebenezer and Hannah (Hunt) Beckford (b. Sept. 23, 1774; d. March, 1822, aged 47); d. in England in 1806. Supercargo of ship George Washington.

188. OSGOOD, ISAAC, son of Peter and Sarah (Johnson) Osgood, b. at North Andover, July 15, 1756; m. 1st, Sally Pickman, Oct. 12, 1790, who d. Aug. 10, 1791, aged 20; 2d, Rebecca T. Pickman, Dec. 8, 1794, who d. Aug. 29, 1801, aged 29; daughters of C. G. Pickman (No. 213); m. 3d, Mary T., dau. of Benjamin Pickman (No. 210), June 28, 1803, who d. Sept. 7, 1856, aged 90. Resident of Salem and Andover; an underwriter, clerk of the courts of Essex; d. at Andover, Sept. 30, 1847.

189. OSGOOD, JOHN, son of John and Susanna (Williams) Osgood of Salem, bapt. Sept. 18, 1757; m. Rebecca, dau. of William and Ann (Wellman) Messervy, Oct. 1782; he d. Dec. 2, 1826, aged 69. Master mariner and merchant.

190. OSGOOD, NATHANIEL WARD, son of Joseph Osgood, Jr. (No. 187), m. June 26, 1822, Mary B. Archer; d. March 21, 1863, aged 65. Tanner.

191. PAGE, JEREMIAH, son of Samuel and Rebecca (Putnam) Page, b. in Danvers, June 2, 1796; m. Mary Pindar of Danvers; d. at Salem, Nov. 1, 1867. Master mariner, and president of Salem Marine Insurance Company.

192. PAGE, RUTH, dau. of Samuel Holman (No. 134), b. June 15, 1761; d. Sept. 28, 1833; m. John Page, the second son of Samuel and Elizabeth Page of Medford (b. in Medford, Nov. 20, 1754; d. in Salem, Dec. 1, 1838) who was connected in the ship chandlery business for upwards of forty years in Salem under the firm of Page and Ropes. He was a revolutionary veteran.

193. PAGE, SAMUEL, son of Samuel and Lois (Lee) Page, b. Nov 14, 1777; m. Dec. 2, 1810, Jane, dau. of Henry (No. 238) and Lydia (Janes) Rust, she d. Dec. 25, 1843, aged 60; d. Feb. 1, 1834. Master mariner.

194. PALFRAY, THOMAS, son of Thomas and Martha (Crowninshield) Palfray, b. ——— 1793; m. Dec. 18, 1821, Hannah Dale; d. ——— at sea. Master mariner.

195. PARSONS, OLIVER, b. in Gloucester; m. Apr. 15, 1816, Betsey Ives; d. at Worcester, Aug. 25, 1845, aged 60. Blacksmith.

196. PAYSON, EDWARD H., son of Lemuel and Joanna (Newhall) Payson, m. Amelia Mellus. Cashier of First National Bank, Salem.

197. PEABODY, NATHANIEL, son of Isaac and Mary (Potter) Peabody, b. March 30, 1774; gr. Dart. Coll., 1800; m. Nov. 2, 1802, Elizabeth Palmer; d. in Boston, Jan. 1, 1855. For many years a dentist in Salem.

198. PEABODY, JOSEPH, son of Francis and Margaret (Knight) Peabody, b. in Middleton, Dec. 12, 1757; m. 1st, Aug. 28, 1791, Catharine; 2d, Oct. 24, 1795, Elizabeth, daughters of Rev. Elias Smith of Middleton; d. Jan. 5, 1844. An eminent merchant at Salem and extensively known throughout the commercial world.

199. PEABODY, FRANCIS, son of Joseph (No. 198) and Elizabeth (Smith) Peabody, b. Dec. 7, 1801; m. July 7, 1823, Martha, dau. of Samuel (No. 85) and Elizabeth (Putnam) Endicott; d. at Salem, Oct. 31, 1867. A merchant and manufacturer.

200. PEABODY, JOSEPH AUGUSTUS, son of Joseph (198) and Elizabeth (Smith) Peabody, b. Aug. 7, 1796; gr. Harv. Coll. 1816; m. Louisa, dau. of Samuel (No. 228) and Sarah (Gool) Putnam, Sept. 3, 1821; d. June 18, 1828. A merchant at Salem.

201. PEABODY, JOSEPH W., son of Asa and Anna (Gould) Peabody, b. in Middleton, May 18, 1787; m. Harriet French of Milford, N. H.; d. Sept. 16, 1842. Merchant.

202. PEABODY, SAMUEL, son of Bimsley and Ruth (Marston) Peabody of Middleton and Boxford, b. Jan. 7, 1759; m. Sept. 21, 1782, Abigail Trask; d. Jan. 26, 1839. A grocer in Salem.

203. PEIRCE, BENJAMIN, son of Jerathmael and Sarah (Ropes) Peirce, b. Sept. 30, 1778; gr. Harv. Coll. 1801; m. his cousin Lydia R., dau. of Ichabod (No. 177) and Lydia (Ropes) Nichols (b. Jan. 3, 1781; d. at Cambridge, Oct. 22, 1868). Merchant for many years at Salem; in 1826 was appointed Librarian at Harvard College Library and d. in Cambridge, July 26, 1831.

204. PEIRCE, NATHAN, son of Nathan and Sarah Peirce, b. at Newbury, June 17, 1749; d. at Salem, May 22, 1812; his wife Rebecca, widow of John Hill, dau. of Mr. Allen, b. 1742; d. July 18, 1815. In early life a tobacconist; afterwards a successful merchant.

205. PHILLIPS, STEPHEN, son of Stephen and Elizabeth (Elkins) Phillips, b. in Marblehead, Nov. 13, 1761. In early life was a shipmaster; in 1800 moved to Salem and engaged in commercial pursuits; m. 1st, Dorcas dau. of Dudley and Dorcas (March) Woodbridge, she d. June, 1802, aged 29; m. 2d, Eliza, dau. of Nathan Peirce (No. 204); he d. at Salem, Oct. 19, 1838.

206. PHIPPEN, THOMAS, son of Thomas and Margaret (Driver) Phippen, b. Dec. 25, 1750; m. Dec. 27, 1774, Rebecca Wellman (b. Oct. 3, 1755); d. Dec. 22, 1839. A mariner.

207. PHIPPEN, WILLIAM, brother of (No. 206) and son of Thomas and Margaret (Driver) Phippen, b. Feb. 27, 1752; m. Nov. 22, 1777, Lois Hitchings of Lynn, and had among other children, Lois, wife of B. Balch (No. 15) and Mary, wife of E. Fuller (No. 108); m. 2d, widow Anna Ring; d. in 1796. A trader.

208. PICKERING, JOHN, son of William and Eunice (Pickering) Pickering, b. Jan. 2, 1738; m. Hannah Ingersoll, sister of Jonathan (No. 141); removed to Richmond, N. H., where he d. Oct. 27, 1823; his wife Hannah, d. Jan. 5, 1795, aged 55.

209. Pickman, Benjamin, son of Benjamin and Abigail (Lindall) Pickman, b. Jan. 28, 1707; m. Oct., 1731, Love Rawlins, who d. June 9, 1786, aged 77; he d. Aug. 20, 1773. Merchant, judge of Common Pleas Court, etc.

210. Pickman, Benjamin, son of Benjamin (No. 209) and Love Rawlins Pickman, b. Nov. 7, 1740; gr. Harv. Coll., 1759; m. Apr. 22, 1762, Mary Toppan, who d. in 1817; he d. May 12, 1819. Merchant.

211. Pickman, Benjamin, son of Benjamin (210) and Mary Toppan Pickman, b. Sept. 30, 1763; gr. Harv. Coll., 1784; m. Oct. 20, 1789, Anstiss, dau. of E. Hasket Derby (b. Oct. 6, 1769; d. June 1, 1833); d. Aug. 16, 1843. Merchant, Representative and Senator in Massachusetts Legislature; member of the Constitutional Convention, Massachusetts, 1820, and of the Executive Council of Massachusetts; and Representative in United States Congress 1809-11.

212. Pickman, Clarke Gayton, son of Benjamin (No. 209) and Love (Rawlins) Pickman, b. July 30, 1746; m. Sarah, dau. of Timothy and Rebecca (Taylor) Orne (b. June 5, 1752; d. Sept., 1812); d. Nov. 29, 1781. Merchant.

213. Pickman, William, son of Benjamin (No. 209) and Love (Rawlins) Pickman, b. March 12, 1748; gr. Harv. Coll., 1766; m. Elizabeth, dau. of Rev. Dudley and Mary (Pickering) Leavitt (b. Sept. 16, 1759; d. Oct. 13, 1782); he d. Nov. 5, 1815. Merchant and naval officer of the Port of Salem.

214. Pickman, William, son of Benjamin (No. 210) and Mary Toppan Pickman, b. June 25, 1774; d. May 1, 1857. In early life a merchant in Boston; lived many years in Salem; retired from the active duties of life.

215. Pickman, Dudley Leavitt, son of William (No. 213) and Elizabeth (Leavitt) Pickman, bapt. May, 1779; m. Sept. 6, 1810, Catherine, dau. of Thomas and Elizabeth (Elkins) Saunders (bapt. Aug. 29, 1784; d. May 18, 1823); d. Nov. 4, 1846. Merchant.

216. Pickman, Thomas, son of Benjamin (No. 210) and Mary Toppan Pickman, b. May 10, 1773; gr. Harv. Coll., 1791; m. 1st, Mary, dau. of Capt. Jonathan Haraden, she d. Sept., 1806, aged 31; m. 2d, Sophia, dau. of Joseph P. and Catherine H. Palmer (b. in Boston; d. in Salem, Dec. 22, 1862, aged 76); d. Jan. 2, 1817. A physician in Salem.

217. Pinel, Philip Payn, b. in Growville, Isle of Jersey, July 9, 1782; m. Jan. 5, 1812, Susan, dau. of Benjamin and Hannah (Shillaber) Peters; d. in Salem, Nov. 21, 1864. A master mariner.

218. Pitman, Benjamin, son of Michael and Sarah (Carwick) Pitman, b. Dec. 24, 1792; m. July 26, 1825, Catherine, dau. of Jacob (No. 244) Sanderson, and widow of Henry Carwick; resides in Andover street. Book-keeper, many years, in Asiatic Bank, Salem.

219. Pope, Ebenezer, son of Eben and Sarah (Pope) Pope, b. in Danvers, July 7, 1759; m. Aug., 1779, Mehitable, dau. of Capt. Samuel and Mehitable (Williams) Carroll, she d. in 1784; m. 2d, Jan. 31, 1790, Lydia,

widow of James Hayes of Salem, and dau. of William Darling of Cambridge, she d. Feb. 16, 1816, aged 62; he d. Feb. 14, 1821. A baker in Salem.

220. PORTER, EBENEZER, came from Wenham to Salem. Housewright; m. Nov. 10, 1771, Mary, dau. of John and Sarah (Titcomb) Ropes.

221. POTTER, JESSE, son of William and Elizabeth (Safford) Potter, b. at Ipswich Hamlet (Hamilton), Dec. 27, 1782; m. Nov. 5, 1819, Susan, dau. of Samuel and Mary (Stevens) Punchard (b. Jan. 10, 1790; d. Jan. 10, 1844); d. at sea, Aug. 28, 1829. A master mariner.

222. PROCTOR, ROBERT, son of Robert and Hannah (Goodhue) Proctor, b. at Salem, Dec. 23, 1760; m. Nov. 28, 1808, Lydia Kilburn (d. Feb. 18, 1857, aged 76); d. Dec. 4, 1841. A trader and farmer.

223. PROCTOR, WILLIAM, son of William and Elizabeth (Masury) Proctor, b. at Salem; m. Sarah, dau. of Joseph and Sarah (Peirce) Holman (b. July 28, 1792; ——— ———). Merchant; in 1827 removed to Brooklyn, N. Y.

224. PURBECK, WILLIAM.

225. PUTNAM, ALLEN, son of Thomas and Mary (Fitz) Putnam, b. Dec. 12, 1794; m. Eliza, dau. of Samuel and Rebecca (Putnam) Page, a sister of Jeremiah (No. 191); she d. July 15, 1864, aged 70; he d. Sept. 5, 1868. Master mariner; President of East India Marine Society, and at the time of his death one of the assessors of Salem.

226. PUTNAM, BARTHOLOMEW, son of Bartholomew and Ruth (Gardner) Putnam, b. at Salem, Feb. 2, 1737; d. Apr. 17, 1815; m. May 13, 1760, Sarah, dau. of Gamaliel Hodges (b. July 31, 1740; d. Oct. 17, 1830). Surveyor of the port.

227. PUTNAM, NATHANIEL, son of Nathaniel and Mary (Ober) Putnam, b. in Danvers, March 2, 1774; m 1st, Polly Warner; 2d, Hannah, dau. of Simon and Mehitable (Dutch) Pendar; 3d, Betsey Waters. Removed to New York city about 1830, and d. in that place June 10, 1849; when a resident of Danvers, a trader; in New York a commission merchant.

228. PUTNAM, SAMUEL, son of Gideon and Hannah Putnam, b. in Danvers, Apr. 13, 1768; gr. Harv. Coll., 1787; m. Oct. 28, 1795, Sarah, dau. of John and Lois (Pickering) Gool. For many years a prominent lawyer and politician in Salem. Justice in Supreme Court of Mass.; removed to Boston in 1833; d. at Somerville, July 3, 1853.

229. REA, ARCHELAUS, son of Archelaus and Mary (Cook) Rea, b. Feb. 12, 1778; m. Nov. 17, 1805, Elizabeth, dau. of Jonathan Mason, Jr., 2d, Apr. 17, 1814, Maria March Woodbridge. Master mariner and agent of Salem Iron Factory Company; about 1840, he moved to Roxbury where he d. Aug. 18, 1864, aged 76.

230. REA, SAMUEL, son of Archelaus and Mary (Cook) Rea, b. Feb. 3, 1782; m. Sept. 3, 1807, Sarah, dau. of James and Eunice (Carlton) Barr, (b. July 3, 1782; d. Nov. 17, 1862); he d. Sept. 30, 1842. Master mariner and merchant.

231. ROBERTS, WILLIAM, son of William and Rebecca (Goldthwaite)

Roberts, b. in South Parish of Danvers (Peabody), Sept. 3, 1783; m. June 21, 1805, Sally, dau. of Elijah (No. 243) and Mary Saunderson; d. at Salem, March 30, 1872. Mason.

232. ROGERS, NATHANIEL, son of Rev. Nathaniel and Mary (Burnham) (Staniford) Rogers, b. at Ipswich, March 11, 1762; gr. Harv. Coll., 1782; m. Abigail, dau. of Col. Abraham Dodge of Ipswich; d. at Saco, Me., in 1799. He removed to Salem about 1788, and both he and his wife were eminently successful as teachers.

233. ROGERS, NATHANIEL LEVERETT, son of Nathaniel (No. 232) and Abigail (Dodge) Rogers, b. at Ipswich, Aug. 6, 1785; m. Oct. 24, 1813, Harriet, dau. of Aaron and Elizabeth (Call) Waite; d. July 31, 1858. Merchant; President of East India Marine Society, and held other offices of trust and honor.

234. ROGERS, JOHN WHITTINGHAM, son of Nathaniel (No. 232) and Abigail (Dodge) Rogers, b. at Ipswich, Nov. 10, 1787; came to Salem in early childhood; received a mercantile education. Merchant in Salem and Boston; m. Anstiss, dau. of Benjamin (No. 211) and Anstiss (Derby) Pickman; d. in Boston, Dec. 9, 1872.

235. ROPES, JANE, dau. of Mr. Bartlett of Exeter, N. H., m. John Ropes of Salem, a son of John and Dorothea (Bartlett) Ropes (b. July 27, 1709; d., 1764; a trader); she survived him until the summer of 1784.

236. ROPES, DANIEL, son of Joseph and Elizabeth Ropes, b. June 13, 1737; m. Nov. 19, 1761, Priscilla, dau. of Samuel and Mary (Williams) Lambert (b. Feb. 25, 1738; d. Sept. 22, 1808); he d. Oct. 8, 1821. A cordwainer.

237. ROSS, JOSEPH.

238. RUST, HENRY, came from Gloucester to Salem when a young man, and was successful in his business operations, b. Aug. 23, 1737; d. Sept. 28, 1812; m. Dec. 25, 1759, Lydia Janes (b. May 12, 1740; d. Aug. 23, 1808); m. 2d, Abigail (Benson) Foster, who d. Jan. 1823, aged 78.

239. RUST, JACOB PARSONS, son of Henry (No. 238) and Lydia (Janes) Rust, b. Aug. 15, 1774; m. Mary Adams of Boston, who d. Oct. 1817, aged 44; he d. at Boston, Jan. 5, 1828, aged 54. Merchant at Salem and Boston.

240. SAFFORD, ABRAHAM, son of —— ——, b. in Ipswich, March 20, 1735; m. Martha, dau. of Rev. John Dennis; d. in Bath, N. H., Jan. 5, 1829. In early life was engaged in the French and Indian war; on the 19th of April 1775 was lieutenant of the Salem Company and in command of the same, the captain being sick.

241. SALTONSTALL, LEVERETT, son of Nathaniel and Anna (White) Saltonstall, b. at Haverhill, June 13, 1783; gr. Harv. Coll., 1802; m. March 7, 1811, Mary Elizabeth, dau. of Thomas and Elizabeth (Elkins) Sanders who d. Jan. 11, 1858, aged 70; d. May 8, 1845. Lawyer in Salem; Speaker of Mass. House of Representatives; President of Mass. Senate; Representative U. S. Cong.; first Mayor of the city of Salem.

242. SALTONSTALL, NATHANIEL, son of Nathaniel and Anna (White) Saltonstall, b. at Haverhill, Oct. 1, 1784; m. Nov. 20, 1820, Caroline,

youngest dau. of Thomas and Elizabeth (Elkins) Sanders; d. at New Market, N. H., Oct. 19, 1838, during a visit, in the performance of his duties as treasurer of the manufacturing corporation in that place. Merchant at Baltimore and Salem.

243. SANDERSON, ELIJAH, son of Jonathan and Mary (Bemis) Sanderson, b. at Waltham, Oct. 10, 1751; m. Mary Mulliken, of Lexington, who d. at Salem, Oct. 23, 1843, aged 86; d. at Salem, Feb. 15, 1825. Cabinet maker; for many years deacon of the church.

244. SANDERSON, JACOB, son of Jonathan and Mary (Bemis) Sanderson, b. at Waltham, Oct. 21, 1757; m. June 26, 1781, Catherine Harrington of Watertown (b. Aug. 26, 1755; d. Dec., 1811); d. at Salem, Feb. 12, 1810. Cabinet maker.

245. SANDERSON, JOHN, son of Elijah (No. 243) and Mary (Mulliken) Sanderson, b. at Salem, Jan. 21, 1797; m. Dec. 7, 1824, Abigail Haskell; d. Oct. 26, 1858. Cabinet maker.

246. SANDERS, CHARLES, eldest son of Thomas and Elizabeth (Elkins) Sanders, b. in Salem; gr. Harv. Coll. 1802; m. Charlotte, dau. of Ichabod (No. 177) and Lydia (Ropes) Nichols (b. at Portsmouth, Nov. 26, 1788; d. at Cambridge, March 29, 1872); he d. at Cambridge, April 7, 1864, aged 80. Merchant in Salem; steward of Harv. Coll. 1827–30; resided principally at Salem and Cambridge, occasionally at Boxford and other places.

247. SAUNDERS, JONATHAN PEELE, son of Daniel and Sarah (Peele) Saunders, bapt. July 10, 1785; m. Dec. 26, 1811, Mary, dau. of Moses and Sarah Adams, (b. in Beverly; d. in Salem, May 5, 1871, aged 80); he d. Feb. 22, 1844, aged 58. A surveyor, and many years town clerk.

248. SCOBIE, JOHN, came from Scotland to Salem; m. Lydia, dau. of Jonathan Mason and widow of Benjamin Mally; d. July, 1853, aged 59. A trader.

249. SECCOMB, EBENEZER, son of Joseph and Ruth (Brooks) Seccomb, b. at Kingston, N. H., June 19, 1778; m. Nov. 27, 1802, Hannah Williams, who d. Nov. 17, 1810, aged 30; m. 2d, Mary, dau. of William and Mehitable (Osgood) Marston, who d. April, 1824, aged 40; he d. June 21, 1835. A merchant in Salem.

250. SHILLABER, BENJAMIN, son of William and Mary (Waters) Shillaber, b. June 27, 1758, at Danvers; m. Nov. 19, 1784, Sarah Proctor, who d. July 21, 1794, aged 38; m. 2d, Sept. 15, 1795, Jane, dau. of John and Abigail (Hawkes) Ropes, and widow of John Titcombe; (b. Jan. 7, 1769; d. April 19, 1842). He d. Aug. 16, 1823. Master mariner.

250a. SHILLABER, BENJAMIN, son of Benjamin (No. 250), b. June 20, 1788; m. 1st, Sarah, dau. of Col John Hathorne; she d. Aug. 1824, aged 31; 2d, Sarah Austin; d. Dec. 31, 1840. Master mariner.

251. SHILLABER, EBENEZER, son of Samuel and Susanna (Reeves) Shillaber, m. 1st, Deborah, dau. of Samuel and Mary (Putnam) Endicott, (bapt. March 17, 1767; d. Nov., 1801); m. 2d, Hannah Jones, of Beverly, who survived him; he d. Dec., 1807, aged 43. Master mariner.

252. SHILLABER, SALLY, dau. of Benjamin Shillaber (No. 250), b. April 27, 1792. Resides in Salem.

253. SHREVE, BENJAMIN, b. Dec. 6, 1780; m. July 8, 1804, Mary, dau. of Benjamin Goodhue (No. 120), (b. Oct. 15, 1781; d. June 30, 1839); d. March 8, 1839. Master mariner, and merchant in Salem. Treasurer of Salem Savings Bank.

254. SIBLEY, LITTLEFIELD, son of Samuel and Merebah (Bartlett) Sibley, b. May, 1739; m. Sarah Lambert; d. at sea in 1780. Master mariner and commanded the Letter of Marque schooner Nancy.

255. SKERRY, EPHRAIM, son of Francis and Hannah Skerry, bapt. Feb. 1, 1746; d. Jan., 1821.

256. SKERRY, FRANCIS, son of Ephraim and Margaret (Silsbee) Skerry, bapt. March 15, 1719; m. Nov. 11, 1741, Anna Symonds; d. 1790. Yeoman.

257. SKERRY, SAMUEL, son of Samuel and Lydia (Cheever) Skerry, b. Jan. 18, 1772; m. Sept. 9, 1798, Content, dau. of Ebenezer (No. 282) and Mehitable (Buttolph) Ward (b. Sept. 2, 1773; d. May 6, 1854); d. at Salem, Oct. 23, 1808; a master mariner; a few years previous to his death had retired to a farm in Brookfield.

258. SMITH, JESSE, son of Aaron and Lucy (Baker) Smith; b. at Ipswich, Dec. 12, 1789; came to Salem when young and learned the watch maker's trade, and was engaged in this business during his life; m. Priscilla Treadwell; d. July 4, 1866.

259. SMITH, EBENEZER, b. at Ipswich, Sept. 24, 1767; m. Sally Griffen, March 22, 1789, who d. July 1, 1824, aged 59; he d. June 5, 1825, aged 57. A baker in Salem.

260. SPRAGUE, JOSEPH, son of Major Joseph Sprague, gr. Harv. Coll., 1792; m. Feb. 6, 1801, Margaret, dau. of Dr. Joseph (No. 186) and Lucy (Ward) Osgood; d. June, 1833. Merchant.

261. STEVENS, TIMOTHY, J., son of Peter and Nabby (Johnson) Stevens; b. in North Andover, Aug. 30, 1788; m. Almira H., dau. of Edmund and Hittie (Curtis) Herrick (b. Dec. 12, 1791; resides in Salem). He died at Salem, Sept. 1, 1864. A shoe manufacturer.

262. STICKNEY, JUDITH, dau. of Col. Peter and Love (Pickman) Frye; b. in Salem; m. William Stickney, a master mariner, son of William and Mary (Sawyer) Stickney of Rowley, who d. on board of his ship at Martha's Vineyard, June, 1788; she d. in Boxford, July 15, 1837, aged 76.

263. STONE, ROBERT, son of Robert and Austiss (Babbidge) Stone, b. March 16, 1776; m. June 5, 1808, Rebecca, dau. of John (No. 189) and Rebecca (Messervy) Osgood; d. Sept. 21, 1860. A merchant.

264. STORY, JOSEPH, son of Dr. Elisha and Mehitable (Pedrick) Story, b. in Marblehead, Sept. 18, 1779; gr. Harv. Coll., 1798; m. Dec. 9, 1804, Mary Lynde, dau. of Rev. Thomas F. and Sarah (Pynchon) Oliver; she d. June 22, 1805; m. 2d, Aug. 27, 1808, Sarah Waldo, dau. of Hon. W. Wetmore; he removed to Salem in 1801, a lawyer of distinction, Speaker of Massachusetts House of Representatives; Representative U. S. Congress, 1808, 9; from 1811 until his decease, Judge U. S. Supreme Court;

in 1830 removed to Cambridge, having received the appointment of Dane professor of law in Harvard University; d. Sept. 10, 1845.

264a. STRAW, ISAIAH, son of Jacob and Betsey (Burbank) Straw, b. in Hopkinton, N. H., Feb. 8, 1797; m. Rhoda Merrill; came to Salem, March, 1818. Tanner.

265. SYMONDS, EPHRAIM, son of Benjamin and Margaret (Skerry) Symonds. m. March 20, 1770, Elizabeth Downing.

266. SYMONDS, JONATHAN, son of Benjamin and Hannah (Bullen) Symonds, bapt. Sept. 19, 1742; m. Jan. 8, 1767, Mary Ramsdell, who d. Dec., 1814, aged 72.

266a. SYMONDS, JOSEPH, son of William (No. 268) and Eunice (Gardner) Symonds, b. March 14, 1783; m. Catherine, dau. of Edward (No. 35) and Catherine (Felt) Brown; d. Feb. 25, 1840. Shoemaker.

267. SYMONDS, SAMUEL, son of Samuel and Mary (Hooper) Symonds, bapt. Jan. 31, 1741; m. Aug. 10, 1760, Mary, dau. of Samuel and Abigail Cook and sister of Samuel (No. 63); d. before 1797.

268. SYMONDS, Mrs. ELIZABETH.

268a. SYMONDS, JOHN, son of Benjamin and Margaret (Skerry) Symonds, m. July 22, 1786, Susanna Webb.

268b. SYMONDS, THOMAS, son of Samuel and Mary (Hooper) Symonds, m. April 10, 1769, Mary Chapman, dau. of Isaac and Hannah (Dean) and sister of Benjamin and George (Nos. 51, 52). (bapt. Dec. 28, 1746; d. March 19, 1832, aged 85).

268c. SYMONDS, WILLIAM, son of Nathaniel and Jane (Phips) Symonds, b. Jan. 8, 1749-50; m. Nov. 15, 1772, Eunice, dau. of Joseph and Mehitable (Pope) Gardner; d. Sept. 8, 1830, aged 77; he d. July 25, 1830.

269. TREADWELL, CHARLES, son of Nathaniel and Eliza (White) Treadwell, b. in Ipswich, March 18, 1789, and d. in that town, Feb. 28, 1855; m. May 2, 1819, Lydia R., dau. of Benjamin and Jane Shillaber (b. June 27, 1796; d. Nov. 9, 1842). Master mariner; lieut. of private armed ship Alfred, in the war of 1812; president of Essex Insurance Company of Salem.

270. TREADWELL, EPHRAIM, son of Elisha and Lydia (Crocker) Treadwell, b. in Ipswich, Sept. 24, 1789. Trader; moved from Salem to New York.

271. TREADWELL, JOHN, son of John and Hannah (Boardman) Treadwell, b. in Ipswich, Sept. 20, 1738; gr. Harv. Coll., 1758. Minister of the First Congregational Church in Lynn, 1763-1782; taught the Grammar School in Ipswich, 1783-1785; removed to Salem, where he resided until his death, which occurred Jan. 5, 1811; was State Senator; Judge of Court of Common Pleas; and m. 1st, Mehitable, dau. of Dr. Richard Dexter of Topsfield; 2d, Dorothy, widow of Jonathan Goodhue (No. 121) and dau. of Jacob and Mary (Ropes) Ashton; 3d, Miss Austin of Charlestown; she survived him and d. Aug., 1816, aged 63.

272. TREADWELL, JOHN DEXTER, son of John (No. 271) and Mehitable (Dexter) Treadwell, b. in Lynn, May 29, 1768; gr. Harv. Coll., 1788;

studied medicine with Dr. E. A. Holyoke (No. 137); practised the profession the first two or three years in Marblehead, afterwards in Salem, with considerable celebrity until his decease, which took place June 6, 1833; m. Dorothy, dau. of Jonathan (No. 124) and Dorothy (Ashton) Goodhue, who was b. Feb., 1777; d. Jan. 29, 1858.

273. TRULL, HERBERT.

274. TUCKER, EDWARD, son of Andrew and Blanche (Skinner) Tucker, m. Elizabeth Foster; 2d, widow Hannah Stone, who survived him many years; d. 1803, aged about 50. A blacksmith.

275. TUCKER, GIDEON, son of John and Lydia (Jacobs) Tucker, b. March 7, 1778; m. June 21, 1804, Martha Hardy, dau. of Benjamin (No. 120) and Frances (Ritchie) Goodhue (b. April 20, 1787; d. April 23, 1848); d. Feb. 18, 1861. Merchant in Salem, president of Exchange Bank.

276. TUCKER, ICHABOD, son of Benjamin and Martha (Davis) Tucker, b. at Leicester, Mass., April 17, 1765; gr. Harv. Coll., 1791; m. Sept. 16, 1798, Maria, dau. of Dr. Joseph and Mary (Leavitt) Orne (b. Nov. 13, 1775; d. Dec. 14, 1806); m. 2d, Oct. 13, 1811, Esther Orne, widow of Joseph Cabot and dau. of Dr. William and Lois (Orne) Paine of Salem and Worcester (b. Aug. 29, 1774; d. Jan. 29, 1854). He commenced the practice of the law in Haverhill, afterwards removed to Salem, clerk of the courts for Essex upwards of thirty years; d. at Salem, Oct. 22, 1846.

277. TURNER, CHRISTOPHER, son of Nathaniel and Lucinda (Turner) Turner; b. at Pembroke in 1767, where he learned the trade of shipwright; came to Salem a young man and worked at his trade; m. June 9, 1791, Sally Osborne; d. at the Charlestown Navy Yard, Dec. 23, 1812.

278. TURNER, LUCY, dau. of Christopher (No. 277) and Sally (Osborne) Turner, d. unmarried, July 16, 1843, aged 52.

279. TURNER, SALLY, sister of the above, d. unmarried, July 16, 1847, aged 52.

280. VANS, WILLIAM, came from Boston to Salem; merchant and auctioneer; m. Oct. 8, 1761, Mary, dau. of John and Ann (Furnese) Clark, (b. June 24, 1735; d. May 19, 1770); he d. May 23, 1797, aged 67.

281. WARD, ANDREW, son of John and Hannah (Higginson) Ward, b. Oct. 6, 1742; m. Sarah, dau. of Edmund and Lydia (Hardy) Henfield (b. May 14, 1750; d. Dec., 1817); d. Jan. 1816.

282. WARD, EBENEZER, JR., son of Ebenezer and Rachel (Pickman) Ward, b. May 26, 1738; m. Mehitable Buttolph; d. Oct. 26, 1773.

283. WARD, GEORGE ATKINSON, son of Samuel Curwen and Jane (Ropes) Ward, b. at Salem, March 29, 1793; m. Oct. 5, 1816, Mehitable, dau. of James and Sarah (Ward) Cushing (No. 68), (b. Feb. 28, 1795; d. Oct. 4, 1862); d. at Salem, Sept. 22, 1864. Merchant at Salem and New York.

284. WARD, JOSHUA, son of Miles and Sarah (Massey) Ward, b. 1699; m. 1st, Sarah, dau. of Richard Trevett of Marblehead; 2d, Lydia (Burrill) Hawkes; 3d, Ruth Woodward; d. Dec. 29, 1779. One of the ruling elders of the church.

285. WARD, MILES, 3d, son of Ebenezer and Rachel (Pickman) Ward,

brother of No. 282, b. July 12, 1744; m. May 20, 1772, Hannah, dau. of Rev. John and Rebecca (Hale) Chipman of Beverly, who d. April 22, 1829, aged 86; d. Oct. 22, 1796. A glazier.

286. WARD, RICHARD, son of Joshua (No. 284) and Sarah (Trevett) Ward, b. April 5, 1741; m. Nov. 8, 1764, Mehitable, dau. of George and Sarah (Pickman) Curwen; d. Nov. 4, 1824. A tanner.

287. WARD, WILLIAM, son of William and Ruth (Putnam) Ward, b. Dec. 28, 1761; m. Martha, dau. of Robert and Hannah (Goodhue) Proctor, who d. Jan. 16, 1788, aged 25; m. 2d, Joanna, dau. of John Chipman of Marblehead (b. July 1, 1761; d. Dec. 10, 1831); d. at Medford, May 9, 1827, to which place he had removed several years previous. Master mariner, and merchant in Salem.

288. WATKINS, BENJAMIN, trader, d. Jan. 26, 1828, aged 75.

289. WATTS, HANNAH, dau. of George and Bethiah (Peters) Deland, bapt. Aug. 27, 1737; m. May 22, 1755, Robert Watts, a native of the Isle of Wight and a skipper of a fishing vessel, lost at sea about the year 1767; she d. Jan., 1817, aged 80.

290. WEBB, BENJAMIN, son of Benjamin and Hannah (Bray) Webb, bapt. July 1, 1787; m. May 5, 1810, Sarah, dau. of John and Mary (Porter) Felt (b. July 24, 1790; d. at Worcester, Oct., 1849); d. Sept. 30, 1840, aged 57. An apothecary.

291. WEBB, STEPHEN, son of Benjamin and Hannah (Bray) Webb, bapt. Sept. 20, 1801; m. Oct. 5, 1831, Martha T., dau. of William and Mehitable (Mansfield) Luscomb; d. May 2, 1869, aged 67 years 8 months. Cashier of Mercantile Bank, Salem, and in the Internal Revenue office.

292. WENDELL, ABRAHAM, son of Thomas and Abigail Wendell, came from Marblehead to Salem; m. Martha L. Ballister, who d. at Lynn, Nov. 19, 1852, aged 81; d. at Ipswich, Oct. 4, 1850, aged 76. A wheelwright.

293. WEST, BENJAMIN, son of John and Margaret (Ward) West, b. Jan. 7, 1738-9; m. Aug. 9, 1762, Abigail Phippen (b. Feb. 6, 1742-3; d. Dec. 26, 1797); d. March 22, 1809. Master mariner; for many years master of the Salem Marine Society.

294. WEST, DANIEL, probably son of Daniel and Elizabeth West, bapt. April 3, 1748.

295. WEST, EDWARD, son of William (No. 299) and Mary (Beckford) West, bapt. Aug. 31, 1760; m. May 9, 1790, Elizabeth, dau. of Daniel and Esther (Gardner) Mackay. When a resident of Salem, a master mariner and merchant; afterwards removed to Andover, where he d. March 20, 1843.

296. WEST, SAMUEL, son of Samuel and Mary (Poor) West, m. 1st, Mary Gale; 2d, ——— ———; 3d, widow Mary Ingalls of Marblehead; d. Sept., 1776. Saddler.

297. WEST, SAMUEL, son of Samuel (No. 296) and Mary (Gale) West, bapt. June 20, 1722; m. Oct. 8, 1747, Mary Massey, who d. Jan., 1801, aged 81; d. April, 1774. Mariner.

298. WEST, THOMAS, son of Benjamin (No. 293) and Abigail (Phippen)

West, b. May 4, 1777; m. Elizabeth Moseley, who d. Feb. 25, 1864, aged 80; d. Jan. 24, 1849. Master mariner, and many years an officer in the Salem Custom House.

299. WEST, WILLIAM, son of Samuel (No. 296) and Mary (Gale) West, bapt. May 12, 1728; m. Nov. 25, 1750, Mary Beckford, who d. Sept., 1813, aged 85; d. Aug. 3, 1803, aged 75. Merchant.

300. WHEATLAND, GEORGE, son of Richard (No. 301) and Martha (Goodhue) Wheatland, b. Nov. 10, 1804; gr. Harv. Coll., 1824; m. Feb. 6, 1833, Hannah Bemis, dau. of John and Hannah (Bemis) Richardson of Newton (b. Dec. 23, 1811; d. at Salem, March 15, 1840). Counsellor at law in Salem.

301. WHEATLAND, RICHARD, son of Peter and Bridget (Foxcroft) Wheatland, b. at Wareham, England, Oct. 20, 1762; came to Salem in 1783; m. 1st, Margaret, dau. of John and Isabella (Brown) Silver; 2d, Martha, dau. of Stephen and Martha (Prescott) Goodhue (b. Feb. 2, 1770; d. Aug. 13, 1826); d. March 18, 1830. Master mariner and merchant.

302. WHEATLAND, RICHARD, son of Peter and Sarah (Forsey) Wheatland, a nephew of Richard (No. 301), b. at Wareham, England, Oct. 26, 1786; came to Salem in 1800, m. Oct. 3, 1822, Elizabeth, dau. of Elijah (No. 28) and Hannah (Buffington) Briggs (b. at Scituate, March 12, 1796; d. at Salem, Oct. 15, 1866); he d Feb. 5, 1867. Master mariner.

303. WHITTREDGE, THOMAS, son of Thomas and Sarah (Osborn) Whittredge, b. at Danvers in 1776; m. Sarah Trask, who d. Aug. 16, 1845, aged 78; d. at Salem, Sept. 15, 1829. Master mariner and merchant.

304. WHITTREDGE, THOMAS COOK, son of Thomas (No. 303) and Sarah (Trask) Whittredge, b. May 28, 1799; gr. Harv. Coll., 1818; m. May 7, 1827, Susan L., dau. of John and Susan Mead, who d. April 10, 1859, aged 56; d. Jan. 26, 1854. Master mariner and merchant.

ERRATUM.

The left hand column of the Centennial Hymn on page 7 should be inserted after the left hand column on page 6.

West, b. May 4, 1777; m. Elizabeth Moseley, who d. Feb. 25, 1864, aged 80; d. Jan. 24, 1849. Master mariner, and many years an officer in the Salem Custom House.

299. WEST, WILLIAM, son of Samuel (No. 296) and Mary (Gale) West, bapt. May 12, 1728; m. Nov. 25, 1750, Mary Beckford, who d. Sept., 1813, aged 85; d. Aug. 3, 1803, aged 75. Merchant.

300. WHEATLAND, GEORGE, son of Richard (No. 301) and Martha (Goodhue) Wheatland, b. Nov. 10, 1804; gr. Harv. Coll., 1824; m. Feb. 6, 1833, Hannah Bemis, dau. of John and Hannah (Bemis) Richardson of Newton (b. Dec. 23, 1811; d. at Salem, March 15, 1840). Counsellor at

www.ingramcontent.com/pod-product-compliance
Lightning Source LLC
Chambersburg PA
CBHW022007220426
43663CB00007B/993